ANALYZING JUSTICIA

A FROLIC IN PSYCHIATRY OF LAW

BRAD LANCASTER

Library of Congress Cataloguing in Publication Data:
Lancaster, Brad.
Analyzing Justicia: A Frolic in Psychiatry of Law
Includes epitomes of core texts
Includes bibliography

ISBN 978-0-9986435-3-3

Published by:
    Saint George's Hill Press
    17503 10th Avenue N.E.
    Shoreline, Washington 98155

First Printing: 2020

This book is printed in Times New Roman font.

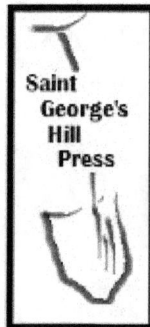

Printed in the United States of America.

For the members of Witless Protection Program,
Who read (mostly) excellent books together,
Who laugh, interrupt, listen, yammer,
Who eat cinnamon bread (yum),
Who share joy and pain
On Saturday morns;
Who help and test,
Who blabber,
Who open
Hearts.

᪐

"There is, unfortunately, no coherent understanding of justice in the modern world."

> John W. De Gruchy
> *Reconciliation: Restoring Justice*
> 2002

"Justice, which is the end of law, is the ideal compromise between the activities of each and the activities of all in a crowded world. The law seeks to harmonize these activities and to adjust the relations of every man with his fellows so as to accord with the moral sense of the community. When the community is at one in its ideas of justice, this is possible. When the community is divided and diversified, and groups and classes and interests, understanding each other none too well, have conflicting ideas of justice, the task is extremely difficult. It is impossible that legal and ethical ideas should be in entire accord in such a society"[1]

> Roscoe Pound
> 1906

---

[1] Pound, "The Causes of Popular Dissatisfaction with the Administration of Justice," *American Bar Association Report*, Part I, 395-417, 1906.

TABLE OF CONTENTS

TRAIN TO MIYAJIMA

Oh, Miyajima.
Your gate so tall,
Floating in azure sea.
Your shrines, your mounts.
Island of gods, miracles,
Of quiet forests, silken paths,
Of Buddhas eschewing evils.
We long for you.

We read no Kanji signs,
Fathom no Hiragana or Katakana.
A train we board, south from Hiroshima,
We see the lovely island,
In the distance, below us.
Yet we climb, the train climbs,
Ever farther from Miyajima,
The sacred beauty spot.

ONE NEVER ARRIVES AT THE ISLAND OF GODS ABOARD A TRAIN BOUND ELSEWHERE.

We protest, we long.
We inquire, we despair.
One never strides the heartfelt island
From this train headed elsewhere.
Shall we suffer this conveyance
Bound nowhere desired?
Or repent, backtrack, to discover
The train to Miyajima.

宮島

CHAPTER 1
ANALYZING JUSTICIA

Concepts of justice proliferate. Justicia, seated in her toga, fitted with blindfold, and armed with scales and sword, suffers multiple personalities. Justicia, the marble statue, promises impartiality (hence, the blindfold), deliberated equity (hence, the scales) and onrushing vengeance (hence, the sword), all packaged in a sturdy, sane-looking woman. But Justicia is an immigrant with a history. She found a first incarnation in Maat, the Egyptian female deity representing truth, balance, order, law, and morality. On her scales, Maat weighed a decedent's soul against the feather of Maat. Souls unfreighted by evil failed to tip the scales, and won eternity. If laden, Ammit the god-lioness devoured defective souls, who exit the Hall of Two Truths mid-bowel, to become toxic compost in Duat, the Egyptian underworld. Later, Justicia found limestone existence in Isis of Egypt, as well as Themis and Dike of Greece, before Roman legions captured her. Justicia's tenure in the Eternal City worked narcissistic vindication of aristocratic privilege, seasoned with contempt for slaves and common-ers. The Brits taught Justicia some morals and religion, but fractured her sanity. America gave English Justicia a visa, ill-aware of her ranting demons. So, who is Justicia, really? Can one catch a glimpse of a sane Justicia amid the improbable the-atrics of courts and lawyers?

I have spied Justicia wandering Puget Sound courthouses, disoriented.

Two decades ago, I stood before a King County district court judge (who has proved, as the years have passed, to be a very fine human being). My client stood accused of violating his ex-spouse's order for protection. The ex-wife offered to put her teenage daughter (from a previous relationship) on the stand to confirm the ex-wife's tale. The judge unexpectedly accepted the ex-wife's proposal, commencing an impromptu trial of the matter on the spot, over both parties' objections. The judge took the daughter's testimony, as well as my cli-ent's and his ex-spouse's, doing some of the cross-examination himself. The judge adopted as fact all the allegations of the wife and daughter, de-spite my client's receipt showing that he was, at the time of the reported incident, ordering coffee with his credit card at a Starbucks twenty miles from the ex-spouse's location. The judge sol-emnly ordered no consequences for my client's now-adjudicated violation. Everyone, except me, stormed out. I shot my jurist quizzical eyebrows. The judge said to me, "I don't feel like I have done my job unless everyone slams the door on their

> **WHAT**
> **IS**
> **JUSTICE?**

way out." One might call this the "universal unhappiness" theory of justice. Justicia dispenses disappointment. Denying parties what they want; that is justice.

Around 1,000 B.C., Solomon became king of Israel. Solomon was the son of King David, who captured the throne by coup, and Bathsheba, David's plural wife, whom David wed after he ogled her naked, relished the view, and commanded her husband Uriah to a suicide mission. Solomon executed his half-brother and rightful heir to the throne, Adonijah. In Jerusalem, two housemate prostitutes bore. One infant died when its mother, unaware, rolled upon her baby during sleep. The bereaved mother exchanged her dead baby for her roommate's infant. The two came before Solomon, who, hearing their tales juxtaposed, drew a sword and offered each half of the living newborn. One mother approved the plan, but the other withdrew from the contest. Solomon awarded the child to the reticent mother. Solomon tricked the fraudulent harlot into betraying her deceit. Justicia set a cunning trap. I worked long ago prosecuting misdemeanors in King County. Some juries proved Solomonic, wrangling truth from behind an interposed shrubbery of lies. Justice lay, for those panels, in distilling truth from the putrid nectar of lying lips. Ferreting beclouded facts; that is justice.

In courthouse hallways, opposing counsel and I sometimes settle cases. Frequently, we split the baby, using Solomon's language, now distorted from the king's sense and devoid of his wisdom. I offer to split the difference between respective positions; counsel nods and rushes off. Justicia waxes pragmatic. Favoring finality over facts; that is justice.

Perhaps, given her fluctuating personalities, Justicia requires some psychiatric intervention. This little book invites eminent analysts to diagnose Justicia's troubled psyche: Rawls, Nozick, Jesus, Confucius, Locke, Moses, Marx, the Amish of Nickel Mines elementary, and a monkey. Others join the fray at the margins.

Imagine Justicia prone on a psychiatric divan. Her sword, scales, and blindfold lie a-jumble on the coffee table. Justicia pours her troubled, stony heart into the ear of scribbling philosophical shrinks. Each extracts his pathologic nutcracker, smiling ever so faintly.

CHAPTER 2
CAPUCHIN

LADY JUSTICE, JUSTICIA, GOES TO HER FIRST PSYCHIATRIC APPOINTMENT. *When Justicia enters her psychiatrist's office, there sits a skinny monkey in a nicely-styled black business suit. An equally skinny necktie, also black, snakes down his tiny starched white shirt. The monkey removes his mini-fedora, and nestles it on a cherry end table to his right, where a half-eaten banana waits further attention, and small black box rests. The capuchin's tail strokes his left ear.*

CAPUCHIN: Have a seat, Justicia. Name's Capuchin. Lost your toga?

JUSTICIA: Oh, the toga? I'm off today. My analysis appointment is a sick day for justice in America. Jeans and sweatshirt for me. The whole Lady Justice gig. Yuck. Everyone's always kibitzing. If I were not made of marble, it would wear me down. . . . Capuchin, you say? Nice to meet you, Capuchin. I must say I am surprised to see a monkey working as a psychiatrist.

CAPUCHIN: Market's been tough. Got downsized when the organ grinding business fell off. Tried the tracks, riding as a greyhound jockey. Did a few movies in Hollywood. Entirely too wacky for me. Grad school worked. Besides, this is fiction, Justicia. Don't make too much of a psychiatric monkey.

Justicia smiles comfortably and settles onto Capuchin's divan. Capuchin sips his itty-bitty latte.

CAPUCHIN: Tell me why you have come to see me, Justicia.

JUSTICIA: I am a bit confused, mostly about myself. I have one thought; it seems good to me. I hear another concept; then that idea seems preferable. I am constantly waffling. I cannot stay any course.

CAPUCHIN: Tell me more about this indecision, Justicia.

JUSTICIA: I might have post-traumatic stress disorder, you know. You see, every time a judge fails to grasp details, or a lawyer lies, and every time the law contradicts common sense, I get blamed. The ranters get out their sticks and chase me, screaming, "Commie anarchist!" or "One Percenter!" or "The Sky Is Falling!" Seems no matter what I do, someone scolds. I am not sure I can take this battering any more. It's just too much.

CAPUCHIN: I see. You sound distressed. Is there more?

JUSTICIA: I can't address a hundred cultures. Can one theory encompass maritime trade and pet law? How is divorce like predatory lending? How do transgender morality and Islamic Shariah mesh? I am asked to do so much with so little.... I am just a country girl from Egypt. You know, some days I feel a twinge of tenderness. Then, wham, just like that, I slash and gore with my sword of retribution. I am plainly unhinged. Do you have any insights, Capuchin?

Capuchin strokes his chin hairs, and squints a bit. Capuchin puffs his mahogany burl pipe, aping Freud. A shiny black box sits next to Capuchin on the coffee table. It pops open. There is nothing inside. The box closes as mysteriously as it had opened. (What is that about?)

CAPUCHIN: Perhaps we should try to simplify things a bit. Let me recount some research. Sarah Brosnan, from Georgia State University, paired up some of my people and offered them cucumber slices in exchange for little rocks. If either capuchin partner traded with a researcher, both got cucumber. Capuchin pairs were situated in cages where they could see the exchanges of other pairs. Researchers began upgrading some of the trades. A trader's partner would get a grape instead of cucumber, while the trader got cucumber. Or a trader in the next cage would get a grape, while the observer continued to get cucumber. The capuchins objected. When nonidentical rewards were proffered, the capuchins stopped trading altogether. They refused to eat their treats. Some flung rewards back at researchers. Inequity offended the capuchin sense of justice. At root, the human sense of justice emerges from deeply rooted brain structures that humans share with complex animal life generally.

JUSTICIA: So, it should be simple. Look to the primitive brain and there lies the gold nugget of justice?

CAPUCHIN: Not likely. Humans build cultures. In cultures, social groups cope with specific problems and answer unanswerable questions. Every group embellishes the root sense of fairness uniquely, with rules and thoughts specific to themselves. The rudiment of justice is not, however, mere local invention. Justice has murky neurological foundations in cooperative survival and empathy and social mirroring.

> **JUSTICE IS:**
>
> A DEEP
> MAMMALIAN
> FEELING.

JUSTICIA: Okay. So, that's not nothing. Humans may share some fundamental emotions about justice.

CAPUCHIN: And capuchins share them also. Our time seems to be up.

JUSTICIA: You are little, but I just love you. Would you like to get some dinner?

CAPUCHIN: No, thank you, Justicia. Your affection for me is just transference. Besides, I am given to capuchin ladies. Stone women never really rock me.

JUSTICIA: I see. Next week, I'll have a different shrink?

Capuchin nods. Justicia drags her confused self out the door. Her lower lip trembles, in a stony sort of way.

CHAPTER 3
RAWLS

LADY JUSTICE, JUSTICIA, GOES TO HER SECOND PSYCHIATRIC APPOINTMENT. *When Justicia enters, a tweedy professorial-type, suffering severe comb-over, perches on a chair. He sports eyeglasses with dated domed lenses. A black-lacquer wooden box with a hinged lid sits next to the academic. Justicia hesitates.*

RAWLS: Sit, Justicia. I seldom bite. My name is John Rawls. I used to teach political philosophy at Harvard. I wrote *Justice as Fairness*. Then I died. By means I do not entirely grasp, I am resurrected today as your psychiatrist. You appear a solid, eminently sane lady.

JUSTICIA: That mask is pure courthouse game-face. All my friends find me deeply confused. And lonely.

RAWLS: How so, Justicia? In what way are you jumbled?

JUSTICIA: I have been so hashed over, tweaked, ignored, and regurgitated, I never know what's up. Lawyers and courts relegate me to the rules of civil procedure and precedent, there to molder. Anarchists invoke me when they bomb children. Politicians pound their fists about me when getting their friends sweet deals. Most ignore my heart. My heart is stony, but not cold.

RAWLS: Tell me about your heart, Justicia.

JUSTICIA: That is my problem, Dr. Rawls. I cannot articulate my fractured heart. The Mediterranean toga, sword, scales, blindfold, sitting around court-houses all day. Where is my heart in all that? My deepest self has something to do with children, sick people, the ignored. Yet, every day I slash. My sword of retribution skewers criminals and wrong-doers. The gore I make feels right—but also wrong. I am torn. I sometimes peek past my blindfold. I gag. Often, I crush poor people who have nicked rich people's sense of entitlement. Most days, I suffer intense self-loathing.

Justicia cries, wetting a lachrymal trail down limestone cheeks. Rawls waits silently, offering a Kleenex.

RAWLS: I spent most of my life thinking about you, Justicia. I am one of your admirers.

The black box on the coffee table pops open. A six-inch tall human stands up from his miniature La-Z-Boy within. "No, John. You are not Justicia's champion. You want Justicia to coerce every person into unchosen uniformity under a government-mandated leftist morality. For you, good behavior lacks consequences; all citizens are theoretically identical, especially regarding property. Your advice is just thoughtful neo-communism, a closeted knock-off of Marx. No offense, John. You know I am your buddy." *The mini-man winks. Dr. Rawls beams at the vocal little creature, and asks him to sit again. Rawls closes the box top.*

RAWLS: That was Robert Nozick. Robert inhabits the black box of conscience wherever I go. He was harsh in critique but dear as a colleague. Well-intentioned critics become a man's conscience. I am grateful for Robert, though he is a dreadfully misguided libertarian.

JUSTICIA: Tell me how you think I should sort myself out, Dr. Rawls.

RAWLS: As you wish. The big problem in conceiving justice is self-interested rhetoric. That is your problem, Justicia. Every person argues for what serves him, and calls it justice. That confuses you. One must, in fabricating a just society, duck into an intentionally amnesiac mindset. One forgets one's situation and gifts, one's self and personality, one's culture and its history, classes and prejudices among persons—quite literally, everything vanishes behind a veil of ignorance. From this "original position," one joins with other amnesiacs to fabricate rules for society that will apply to all. In the coming realm, one never knows whether she will be a queen or a pauper. Two principles moderate all original position deliberations. First, individual freedoms must be as expansive as is compatible with the equivalent liberties of others. And, second, opportunities (and the skills necessary to capitalize on opportunities) must be open to all. Social and economic inequalities can be tolerated only to the extent that they benefit disadvantaged persons. That's it, I think.

JUSTICE IS:

MICROMANAGING
SOCIETAL
MALFORMATIONS.

JUSTICIA: What about little Nozick? Would you have me drag people kicking and screaming to a just society they do not want and for which they will be required to pay?

RAWLS: Robert is right. One cannot countenance a just system that prioritizes community well-being and simultaneously does full justice to individual autonomy. One must choose an emphasis and make compromises. I focus on the community and the plight of those getting demolished by society's malformations. Nozick tolerates politically-induced suffering in favor of insulating individual liberties from communal erosion or obliteration.

JUSTICIA: How should I work out my mental troubles, in your view, Dr. Rawls?

RAWLS: A psychiatrist draws maps. The patient chooses her destination.

JUSTICIA: Shirker. And you think my heart is made of stone.

Justicia squeezes Rawls's hand and flutters her eyelashes at the professor.

RAWLS: I have affection for you, but love lies elsewhere. I've a nice wife, four children. Gotta go.

Justicia pouts.

Rawls, John. *Justice as Fairness, A Restatement.* Cambridge, Massachusetts: The Belnap Press of Harvard University Press, 2001.

John Rawls (1921-2002) was an American moral and political philosopher. One of Rawls's young brothers died after contracting diphtheria from Rawls. The following year, Rawls suffered pneumonia; another brother caught the ailment and also died. After serving as a private in the Pacific theater of World War II, Rawls returned home to study moral philosophy. Rawls received his Ph.D. in 1950, and taught at Harvard University most of his career. Rawls stuttered, and abhorred public roles. Rawls died from a series of strokes.

Preface.[2] By this restatement of his career-long exchanges with colleagues, Rawls hopes, near the end of his life, to correct errors that marred his earlier work, *A Theory of Justice*, and to unify his arguments from both the earlier book and essays into a coherent and concise statement of Rawls's position. Rawls describes the nature of the changes he has made to his previous argument.

Part 1: Fundamental Ideas

§1: Four Roles of Political Philosophy. Political philosophy can: 1) help settle divisive political disputes by finding philosophical commonalities among disputants, 2) orient citizens to their political institutions by guiding their thinking about those structures, 3) justify political

---

[2] A word about epitomes. In my view, the best books are colloquia. Those excellent tomes bring together the thought of diverse others, often the best minds history offers, to hone some topic. An "epitome" summarizes a written work. Such a brief version of a book could also be called an abstract or abridgement. I epitomize the works of others because, first, those works are excellent, and, second, because you need to read them (but probably never will).

As I epitomize other people's work, I attempt to focus on the author's core argument, to the neglect of digressions, examples, illustrations, tables, worksheets, and other useful, but voluminous, explanatory tools. Generally, my epitomes capture twenty to forty pages of original material per epitomized page. Habitually, Greeks and Roman authors epitomized the works of colleagues, often for the purpose of arguing intelligently against their core points. Epicurus epitomized his own work. He argues that, for those unable to examine his longer works, capturing an outline of thoughts is better than nothing. Epicurus, *Letter to Herodotus* in *The Essential Epicurus*, 19. Kant also self-epitomized. See *Prolegomena to any Future Metaphysics*, 9 (Introduction). More recently, Peter Block self-epitomizes his work, *Community*. I have epitomized my most expansive work, *Cull: Choosing Well*, at page 431 of the first volume of that two-volume effort.

One may ask, *Why condense pivotal books to a few pages? Should one not just read the originals?* Summaries distort what they condense; these epitomes are no exception. But epitomizing forces one to decide an author's meaning. Reframing an author's thoughts aids recollection. Given the time constraints of higher education and life's many demands, few read thousands of pages of ethics. These time-starved many, nevertheless, suffer an unrecognized need for the counsel and offense these unread texts impart. The wisdom (and idiocy) closeted in these texts informs the global deliberation of human weal. Epitomes provide a texture, if not the entire fabric, of core books and essays. Some ethical classics are, frankly, opaque and ponderous (though worth the effort to cull). Epitomes offer guidance in comprehension. As opportunity emerges, read originals, at least those which pique interest.

I attempt, when epitomizing, to state the author's argument plainly. I do not interpret or apologize, except to the extent required for understanding itself. I attempt to approach each author's work with diligence, sympathy, and openness. I am certain I have failed in this effort regularly. Where an author's terminology hides his argument, I abandon or simplify that terminology. I infrequently annotate epitomes. Where I have done so, my interpolations are contained in brackets.

structures to somewhat alienated citizens within those structures, reconciling them to their circumstance; citizens never constitute a community, but rather exist as pluralistic society which all enter involuntarily, which facts delimits their liberty; society, when just, offers a fair system in which to cooperate over transgenerational time, and 4) afford citizens the "realistically utopian" hope that their democratic political system may prove decent and reasonably just, under circumstances that include pluralism and the live possibility of deep societal change.

§2: **Society as a Fair System of Cooperation**. 2.1. One looks to political culture and founding documents for initial tentative ideas about political justice. Some are fundamental. Most fundamental is the idea that justice means society offers a "fair system of social cooperation" over transgenerational periods. This is Rawls's first fundamental idea. Two associated ideas cling to this fundament: first, citizens are free and equal, and, second, citizens share a view of the "well-ordered society," which boils down to general agreement about the demands of justice. Such a society is never wedded to a particular political or religious point of view, and believes no party within society may deny another basic political rights. 2.2. Societal cooperation: a) is governed by public rules citizens accept, b) is fair and reciprocal as between citizens, and c) supports each citizen's "rational advantage" (which is for that person the "good"). Rational and reasonable differ in meaning. Reasonable citizens honor fair terms of cooperation, even when rationality tells them that periodic defection would benefit them individually. 2.3. Political justice allocates the burdens and benefits of fair social cooperation. The core question of political philosophy is: What conception of justice coordinates fair terms of cooperation among free and equal citizens trans-generationally in a manner that is reasonable, rational, and normal? This is the big question Rawls seeks to answer.

§3. **The Idea of a Well-Ordered Society.** 3.1. In well-ordered societies: 1) citizens accept, and know others accept, the same political conception of justice (as though they had contracted to that effect), 2) citizens accept that the existing system conforms to their sense of justice, and 3) citizens understand and apply their shared principles of justice. 3.2. "Well-ordered society" is Rawls's second fundamental idea. No "well-ordered society" exists. Ideas of justice that offer something less to citizens are defective. In pluralism, many "comprehensive doctrines" of justice (moral, theological, ideological) may agree that one political view of justice suffices for diverse citizens. This is the liberal political ideal.

§4. **The Idea of the Basic Structure**. 4.1. Societal features (economy, property, family, constitution), working together, constitute a society's "basic structure." This is Rawls's third fundamental idea. The basic structure may be just or unjust, forming a backdrop of actual justice or injustice. 4.2. Rawls's theory focuses primarily upon basic structures. What is fair in basic structure may not be fair for the component associations within the basic structure. Justice as fairness is political justice, not necessarily applicable to components of a society, but only to the basic structure of society as a whole. Principles applicable to components of society are "local justice." Local justice, domestic justice, and international justice are three levels of justice. Rawls focuses on domestic justice. 4.3. Justice as fairness is an approximation that aims at no great specificity. Details must be filled from circumstances under which citizens then dwell.

§5. **Limits to Our Inquiry**. 5.1. Rawls does not detail local justice. Rawls does not undertake general moral inquiry. Rawls limits himself to justice in well-ordered societies, and thinks his theory is realistically utopian, which means an approximation of democratic perfection. As such, the theory should prioritize problems of injustice and needed reforms. Rawls does not take up international relations, but rather adopts Kant's view (in *Perpetual Peace*) that a federation of States upholding human rights would be best. World government appears unworkable. 5.2. Justice as fairness is not a big political philosophy theory, but rather answers the narrow question of what basic structure best supports modern democratic societies.

§6. **The Idea of the Original Position**. 6.1. "Original position" is Rawls's fourth fundamental idea. Pluralistic societies cannot agree about natural law or divine edicts or even common sense. What remains is some form of collective agreement. 6.2. To be fair, the agreement must meet conditions: no individual advantages, no coercion, no fraud. Every agreement reflects to some degree its circumstances, some of which are considerations about basic structure. Rawls wants to examine the basic structure itself, and so needs a tool by which to extricate the basic structure from more diverse deliberations. The "original position" is such a tool. In the "original position," one imagines that none knows his own details or those of others, not race, sex, gifts, heritage, religion, or any other specifics. This is Rawls's "veil of ignorance." All deliberators are free and equal citizens of the society under construction. The original position extracts accidental and historical advantages from the shared conversation about basic structure. 6.3. The "original position" is a generalized treatment of the idea of social contract, seeking hypothetical and nonhistorical agreement (what the bargainers would agree, not what they do agree). 6.4. Original position agreements clarify public deliberation by enforcing their equality and specifying the sorts of reasons the conversation can accommodate. If hypothetical agreements can be reached, those are likely to carry over to actual circumstances, if we care about the fairness of that circumstance. 6.5. Original position parties are symmetrically situated (equal). No historical benefits distort their rationale for choices.

§7. **The Idea of Free and Equal Persons**. This is Rawls's fifth fundamental idea. "Fundamental ideas" become conceptions when one specifies the elements of the idea in some way. 7.1. Free and equal persons, as political actors, have a sense of justice and goodness employed over their whole lifespan, adapting to circumstances as these mutate. 7.2. "Free and equal person" is a political (not a moral, philosophical, metaphysical, or psychological) concept. 7.3. Equality indicates that all those who are equal have the minimum requisite capacities to participate in fair societal cooperation for mutual advantage over the span of a lifetime. A fair and just society is not a "community" because its members do not share values and non-economic purposes. Society coerces; communities do not coerce. Granting pluralism of sentiment precludes communal existence. Communities exist within society, but society cannot be a community. 7.4. "Freedom" consists in, first, having moral capacity to conceive (and re-conceive) the good, and believing others share this ability. Shifts in personal identity do not affect one's political status. 7.5. Second, freedom consists in the ability to make claims upon one's political institutions on the sole basis of one's citizenship. 7.6. The free and equal citizen has long been a subject of political comment, and differs from the idea of a human being.

§8. **Relation between the Fundamental Ideas**. 8.1. Rawls's five fundamental ideas interact and cross-referentially explain one another; they also have a sequence. 8.2. These ideas are not deduced from one another. 8.3. Other ideas (such as theological edicts or natural law) might organize just societies. Rawls explores the idea of fair democratic social cooperation, and cannot say before discussion whether it will prove best. It will prove best if it coheres when elaborated, and balances our various thoughts about political justice against one another (that is, the theory offers wide reflective equilibrium).

§9. **The Idea of Public Justification**. This is Rawls's sixth and final fundamental idea. 9.1. Public justification has three satellite ideas: overlapping consensus, reflective equilibrium, and free public reason. Public justification is the way pluralistic democracies authorize ideas about society's basic structure. No overarching comprehension is required or permitted; public justification is political only. Public justification draws from ideas extant in the public realm. 9.2. Public justification means that when a citizen makes claims upon society, all agree as to the right of the claiming citizen to make his claim. He is justified by shared public sentiment, which tells the citizen which arguments will count and which will not be countenanced. 9.3. Public justification must be possible for essential issues of constitutional import: government structure, powers of branches, limitations on acts with respect to basic rights and freedoms. Where citizens can agree on these, then broader agreement becomes possible. 9.4. Public justification, as Rawls draws it, avoids reliance on any particular moral or theological or philosophical perspective, focusing rather on what can be agreed by all, despite their various broader perspectives (which he calls "comprehensive doctrines").

§10. **The Idea of Reflective Equilibrium**. 10.1. A considered judgment is one made under optimal conditions for reason and justice to predominate. 10.2. Our judgments diverge from those of others. Our own judgments often conflict with one another. Eventually, we must abandon some of our judgments, if we are to reach consensus. 10.3. If we consider the alternatives broadly, then when we bring our various judgments into line with one another, we reach wide reflective equilibrium as an individual. 10.4. When all members of a society share the same wide reflective equilibrium, then that society has "full reflective equilibrium." Finding that quantum of judgments on which we can agree is the best a society can do.

§11. The Idea of an Overlapping Consensus. 11.1. Though all citizens share the same view of justice, they need not do so for identical reasons. 11.2. Justice as fairness appeals broadly because it pertains only to basic structures, it demands no particular overarching viewpoint, and its ideas are familiar. People of all stripes can endorse it. Many people's viewpoints are unsystematic; they endorse the consensus for various reasons at various times. 11.3. Five facts about mankind underlie overlapping consensus: 1) reasonable pluralism, 2) one can maintain a comprehensive doctrine only by coercing citizens (oppression), 3) democracies require support of, at a minimum, a substantial majority of citizens, 4) certain fundamental ideas characterize any workable democracy (reasonable citizens disagree, for they encounter persistent obstacles to good judgment such as conflicted evidence, the weight of that evidence, vagueness, and the role of experience in judgment, and the ambiguities of human existence), and 5) reason is insufficiently consistent to produce, even after conscientious debate, consensus. 11.5. These facts do not lead to philosophical skepticism. Pluralism attaches wherever sufficient numbers of human coexist. 11.6. There is no guarantee that an overlapping consensus can be reached in a given society. Constitutional democracy is worth defending, because it proves, overall, just and workable. One does not try to weave a path through existing comprehensive doctrines, but rather to develop a conception to which they, for their multifarious divergent reasons, may consent. The world in not inextricably cruel and prejudiced. Goodness and equity subsist alongside miseries. There is room for hope.

Part II: Principles of Justice

§12. Three Basic Points. 12.1. Rawls lays out where he is headed in the rest of his book. He wants to answer the question, What principles and institutions should govern social cooperation in a democracy that aspires to treat citizens as free and equal? 12.2. Rawls assumes that most people are born into the social system in which they will live their entire lives. Inequities trouble the system. How are these inequities (for example, of birth, class, education) consistent with free and equal citizenship? 12.3. Justice as fairness promotes values of political liberalism. One enters society by birth and leaves by death. Power is coercive, but also resides in the citizenry, and so amounts to self-coercion among equals. How can citizens legitimately coerce one another? Liberalism answers that coercion is valid when exercised under a constitutional structure that all recognize as reasonable. This does not answer all legislative questions, but hopefully addresses all questions about basic structure. 12.4. What just principles best protect free and equal citizens from social and economic inequalities? We seek a principle of distribution that is just.

§13. Two Principles of Justice. 13.1. Rawls has revised these statements after criticism from H. L. A. Hart, whose criticisms were most penetrating. First, every citizen claims equal access to basic liberties. Second, where inequality exists, the structure of society must contain opportunities open to all equally, and that structure must be biased to benefit those who have least (the "difference principle"). (Rawls describes differences between the difference principle and the "maximin" principle, in footnote 3.) In application, these principles must be satisfied in the order they are presented. 13.2. "Fair equality of opportunity" means that skill and motivation alone, not class or wealth, determines who receives an opportunity. Any free market economy must be constrained to prevent concentrations of wealth and power. Education must be equally available, regardless of family income. 13.3. Basic liberties are several: freedom of thought, conscience, voting, participation in party politics, association, personal integrity, and the rule of law. 13.4. One can develop lists of essential liberties by historical review or by analysis. 13.5. First principles of justice apply only to a society's basic structure or constitution. One must have a society of structural equality before one can apply the difference principle of redistribution. Reasonably favorable conditions must pertain in the society in question. 13.6. Rawls judges constitutional equity and providing for basic needs of all to be essential. The difference principle and fair quality of opportunity" are not constitutionally essential. Principles of justice are established in four stages: 1) adoption of fundamental principles with the veil of ignorance protocol, 2) constitutional convention for adopting a specific constitution, 3) legislation by the constituted bodies, and 4) administration of adopted laws and interpretation by courts. 13.7. The idea of a loyal opposition captures the constitutional circumstance. While opposed in perspective, both the majority and its loyal opposition share a constitutional framework for their disagreements. The difference principle requires reciprocity.

§14. The Problem of Distributive Justice. 14.1. Distributive justice asks the question how the institutions of society must be arranged in order to provide a fair system across generations. Allocative justice asks how to divide up a particular bundle of goods. 14.2. The basic structure of society, to be fair, must be such that when every one honors the rules in good faith, the distribution of goods that results is viewed as fair. This is "pure background procedural justice." 14.3. Some rules are required to keep any system just trans-generationally. Background institutions must use inheritance rules and redistributionist taxes that keep wealth shared enough to maintain political liberty and equal opportunity over time. The NBA lets the worst teams draft the best players to keep games interesting and relatively equal. 14.4. The difference principle requires nothing more unusual than taxation schemes of the ordinary sort. The difference principle also respects the earnings of gifted or motivated workers.

§15. The Basic Structure as Subject: First Kind of Reason. 15.1. The primary focus of justice as fairness is basic structure. Free and fair agreements contain small injustices, which over time aggregate into basic unfairness. We cannot, as did Locke, presume that fair actions never aggregate into injustice. 15.2. Inheritance laws must be changed to benefit less advantaged people, to keep equality and fairness intact. We must also govern the sorts of contracts people make with one another. 15.3. Once one regulates the basic structures and contracting in the background to insure fairness, then one can let people relate as they will, secure in the knowledge that no dramatic unfairness will erupt.

§16. The Basic Structure as Subject: Second Kind of Reason. 16.1. Which inequalities in society deserve to be substantively addressed? Inequalities created by social class, native abilities, and luck, insofar as these affect fundamental life prospects of individuals, are the sorts of contingencies that justice as fairness addresses. 16.2. Educational institutions must teach citizens they are free and equal, as well as the structure of justice. Society also induces hope when it offers help with basic inequities. Society nurtures some abilities, which then come to fruit. 16.3. Rawls summarizes the last two sections.

§17. Who are the Least Advantaged? 17.1. Primary goods are those things a citizen needs as a free and equal person living his whole life as a member of a cooperative society. 17.2. Five kinds of primary goods are: 1) basic rights and liberties, 2) freedom of travel and occupation, 3) powers of whatever offices the citizen holds, 4) sufficient income to execute chosen ends, and 5) self-respect confirming worth of the individual and self-confidence. 17.3. Less advantaged persons have insufficient access to primary goods. Generally, the least advantaged are that class with the lowest income expectations. 17.4. The concept of primary goods derives from the idea of free and equal citizens, not by averaging what groups within society might prefer.

§18. The Difference Principle: Its Meaning. 18.1. Citizens who cooperate in a society produce goods to be distributed. The wealth of those with more in a society is justified only to the extent that the cooperative wealth produced in collaboration with the less advantaged groups also improves the lot of those less advantaged. Rawls offers Figure 1, a two-axis graph, as an explanation of the basic structure and the difference principle. 18.2. Rawls explains his less-advantaged-group (LAG: y-axis), more-advantaged-group (MAG: x-axis) graph. The more efficiently MAG/LAG cooperation is structured, the more both groups benefit. 18.3. A steady state economy would also continue to benefit the less advantaged groups to the same extent the more advantaged are benefitted. 18.4. Why do slavery and the oppression of women not define less advantaged groups? Rawls wants his theory to be ideal, not historical. The least advantaged are those in society who have less income and wealth. 18.5. Rawls further considers gender and race as disadvantaging factors, and argues that the primary goods index should suffice for women and descendants of slaves. 18.6. Justice as fairness fails if, in the end, it does not redress gender and racial inequalities.

§19. **Objections via Counterexamples**. 19.1. Rawls considers several distortions of the relationship between less- and more-advantaged groups in his graph. 19.2. Rawls does not want to specify the exact relation of less- to more-advantaged groups in a society. That relation should emerge from the background procedural justice adjustments. Rawls does not seek strict economic egalitarianism, since some inequalities serve as incentives and otherwise make an economy efficient. 19.3. Does the difference principle work when the less-advantaged prosper more under a constitution than the more-advantaged? Rawls counters objectors in this regard. 19.4. Rawls further considers this counterexample, explaining why the less-advantaged are better off with the more-advantaged getting yet more. 19.5. The difference principle only makes sense when the background equities are well-established. It does not address the needs of particular groups, but rather the weal of society generally.

§20. **Legitimate Expectations, Entitlement, and Desert**. 20.1. In justice as fairness, what people do depends on what entitlements their constitution provides, and their entitlements depend upon what the people do. All are determined by the background structures. 20.2. Justice as fairness considers some sense of moral desert in entitlements. But moral desert proves to be something about which people cannot agree, because of their assorted comprehensive doctrines. 20.3. In games, when well-played, one team wins, but we might say both deserved to win. That is the sort of desert that applies to questions of justice. 20.4. When individuals do as the system demands, they deserve rewards, though no system can guarantee equal rewards. This is the sort of moral desert countenanced by justice as fairness.

§21. **On Viewing Native Endowments as a Common Asset**. 21.1. No one deserves anything for being born with gifts or male or privileged. One should be rewarded for training and diligence, and for applying skills to the general good. 21.2. The difference principle represents an agreement among citizens to share the common asset of differential abilities in a fair manner. 21.3. People differ. Society owns the *distribution* of various skills and abilities (though not the skills and abilities themselves). Society is a symphony, in which talented musicians perfect individual skills to play masterfully together. 21.4. The distribution principle would be agreed by deliberators in the original position (under the veil of ignorance of people's specificities). Persons so situated would agree that the distribution of talents is a common asset. Citizens must act reciprocally. Talented persons (they did not deserve their talents) devote their skills to improving the lot of less talented persons (who also did not deserve their lot).

§22. **Summary Comments on Distributive Justice and Desert**. 22.1. The work that "moral desert" does in moral schemes is performed in political justice by the ideas of legitimate expectations and entitlements. 22.2. To perform adequately, these ideas need to: authorize useful disparities (extra education, incentives), emphasize reciprocity, remediate disparities of birth and talent, make verifiably fair adjustments, and be simple and comprehensible. 22.3. Rawls argues that justice as fairness may well create a fair context for social cooperation, though final proof exceeds human possibilities. Entitlements must be earned under fair conditions. People in their religions and ideologies may want to claim more for their gifts and skills, and may even be correct in so arguing. But, given pluralism, their views cannot be publicly adopted. 22.4. Rawls previews Part III. If we cannot argue and act from the original position, perhaps our words are only words, lacking integrity.

Part III: The Argument from the Original Position

§23. The Original Position: The Setup. 23.1. The original position models the fair terms of social cooperation for free and equal citizens, and what reasons will count in deliberations of what constitutes just social arrangements. The original position also serves to make discussion of fundamental conditions more lucid. 23.2. The original position explains, not how people actually behave, but how representatives of free and equal citizens might behave under restricted knowledge (the veil of ignorance). 23.3. What counts is what is reasonable, not what is merely rational. Reasonableness is a moral idea that is mostly intuitive. 23.4. The parties in the original position are imaginary, as are the persons they represent. The original position is, in the end, a thought experiment. The parties in the original position select societal features from a list of common political ideas. One seeks some formulation of political system that serves citizens well and improves upon other alternatives.

§24. The Circumstances of Justice. 24.1. The original position presumes historical circumstances of some scarcity and the need for social cooperation to live acceptably. Citizens hold incommensurate beliefs about the world which can in no manner be wholly reconciled (pluralism). Political philosophy is ill-equipped to discover which, if any, comprehensive doctrine is best, and political agreement is unlikely (or impossible). So, political justice includes good ideas that fit, but does not describe goodness comprehensively. 24.2. The parties to the original position are trustees seeking the best interests of those whom they represent. They cannot defend comprehensive doctrines, because to do so would make the results of their deliberation threatening and unpersuasive to those represented.

§25. Formal Constraints and the Veil of Ignorance. 25.1. The original position places representatives in a particular vantage, that is, under the veil of ignorance. First principles must, in original position deliberations, be general, universal, and public. 25.2. The original position limits the sorts of arguments that count, and requires unanimity among the parties. The veil of ignorance removes special pleading from the mix, leaving all parties similarly situated (symmetrical). These limitations make the original position fair. 25.3. The original position parties are rational. None of the parties suffers bitter emotions, hatred of uncertainty or risk, or a need to dominate. In setting up the original position, we are deciding who can play and what sorts of people they are. 25.4. The idea of primary goods helps the parties to the original position decide what might be best. 25.5. The parties presume that their constituents are not governed by spite or fear or need to control others. If it turns out to be otherwise in fact, then their well-ordered society will prove unstable.

§26. The Idea of Public Reason. 26.1. Public reason means that parties agree on principles that lead to a basic structure, and principles of reasoning that illuminate just decision-making. 26.2. The parties to the original position have common sense and non-controversial scientific knowledge. No comprehensive doctrine specifics are admitted. These may be discussed, to explain oneself. But ultimately, one steps back and uses public reasoning to support one's conclusions. Political legitimacy emerges when citizens, using their own common reason, grasp the reasons for constitutional frameworks. 26.3. Only by using public reasons, acceptable to all citizens, can citizens impose on one another rules enforced by coercive sanctions. 26.4. Every deliberation, public or private, has rules. Otherwise, it is mere rhetoric or pointless talking. Forms of deliberation differ in various associations. 26.5. Citizens can leave their associations; they cannot leave the State. The State is neither an association nor a community, though both such organizations dwell within the State and give meaning to life.

§27. First Fundamental Comparison. 27.1. The maximin principle (that the inequities of society should be structured to be of maximum benefit to the least privileged members) and the difference principle appear more similar than they are. One proceeds in the original position by comparing two alternatives. 27.2. Rawls compares classical liberal theory (social cooperation with equality and reciprocity) with a utilitarian approach (producing maximum average welfare in goods and social well-being). 27.3. The first comparison compares justice as fairness with utilitarianism's foundational principle of maximum utility. The second comparison substitutes for the difference principle the principle of maximum utility. 27.4. The comparisons ultimately necessary in original position deliberations are those of justice as fairness with utilitarianism, perfectionism, intuitionism, and libertarianism.

§28. The Structure of the Argument and the Maximin Rule. 28.1. The maximin rule requires one to adopt a rule better than the one with the worst outcome. The first original position argument proceeds as follows: 1) the maximin rule prefers justice as fairness over average utility, 2) the maximin rule governs basic structure in three conditions, 3) the three conditions pertain in the original position, 4) therefore, justice as fairness would be agreed over average utility. 28.2. The three conditions of section two of the argument require comment. The first condition is that the maximin rule avoids probabilities since the parties have no basis for calculating them. The second condition is that the best worst outcome is a guaranteeable level, which the parties will measure against all other outcomes. The third condition is that the parties will avoid all outcomes below the guaranteeable level. 28.3. Concerning these conditions, using the maximin rule permits normal reasoning, but reasoning without substantive content. It is critical that the second and third conditions obtain. One need not use the maximin rule in comparing outcomes, but it helps. 28.4. The guaranteeable level is acceptable to most people; this is crucial to Rawls's argument.

§29. The Argument Stressing the Third Condition. 29.1. That parties to the original position are unable to estimate the probability of outcomes (the first condition) is important, but not crucial. The parties know reasonably favorable conditions pertain. 29.2. Justice as fairness is preferable to utilitarianism because it has a very satisfactory guaranteeable level for all, and utility requires that some people sometimes suffer restriction of their rights and liberties. 29.3. Making an agreement means that one undertakes good faith commitments that may prove strenuous. If another acceptable agreement that is less strenuous exists, that less-demanding agreement is preferable. There is no going back, once the basic structures are agreed. 29.4. Justice as fairness lacks risks that the principle of utility cannot avoid, and so is preferable.

§30. The Priority of the Basic Liberties. 30.1. Liberties have different value, some being more important than others. Some may be compromised to make all fit together. In doing so, one compromises less important liberties to preserve more of crucial liberties. No one would gamble with, say, liberty of conscience, especially when the gambler acts as a fiduciary for other free and equal citizens. 30.2. Various liberties are not exchangeable. Some are more important.

§31. An Objection about Aversion to Uncertainty. 31.1. Risk can be estimated; uncertainty cannot. In the original position, the parties face uncertainty, not risk (since they have by definition no appreciation of probabilities). 31.2. Trustees act with extreme conservatism where their wards' fundamental interests are at stake. So, the parties in the original position choose the structure that guarantees their minimum interests, rather than risk any liberties in an effort to acquire more. 31.3. Some argue that the third condition is veiled utilitarianism. The utility function in Figure 2 contains the justice as fairness norms within it. Rawls intends no judgments about utilitarianism as a comprehensive doctrine. 31.4. Rawls responds to a model of the original position by Howe and Roemer. 31.5. Some features of the first comparison (with utilitarianism) are controversial: non-use of probability, aversion to uncertainty, and that utility requires truncation of some liberties.

§32. The Equal Basic Liberties Revisited. 32.1. Liberties conflict, and so must be juxtaposed in a scheme that maximizes each. No considerations other than another basic liberty can serve to limit a basic liberty. 32.2. Basic liberties may be regulated, but not restricted, in a scheme of liberties. 32.3. The number of basic liberties should be small enough to fit together. Rawls adds the significance criterion to the original position (which differs from his earlier formulation of the problem). 32.4. Basic liberties guarantee citizens can exercise their two moral powers fully in fundamental cases, which are 1) when the citizen needs to evaluate the justice of the basic structure and its policies (equality and freedom of thought), and 2) when citizens need to conceive and bring to realization their view of the good life (practical reason, liberty of conscience, freedom of association). The remaining basic liberties (integrity of person, and legal rights) are protected by these prior two cases. 32.5. Liberties are more or less significant depending upon the role they play in the exercise of moral powers with respect to evaluating the justice of the basic structure and social policies, or conceiving and achieving the good life, or both. 32.6. Property is a basic right to the extent property is necessary for independence and self-respect. No citizen should have private property in natural resources or the means of production, or be able to pass such interest to heirs, since these must be owned by all. Such property might be granted by law, but not as part of the basic structure. The original position seeks to keep open questions about private property, other than the minimum.

§33. **The Argument Stressing the Second Condition**. 33.1. Rawls considers why justice as fairness bests utility in guaranteeing equal basic liberties. Justice as fairness secures the basic liberties, while utilitarianism leaves the liberties in flux and consideration. 33.2. Stable constitutional societies require clear public reason deemed reliable by citizens. Justice as fairness is straightforward in this. Utilitarianism makes public reason calculations very complex, and so uncertain. Public reasoning must be fair, but must also seem fair to most people, some of whom will be flummoxed by complexity. 33.3. By keeping the most divisive issues off the public agenda (religion, ideologies), justice as fairness keeps the tone of political dialogue accommodating and ready for compromise. Justice as fairness encourages reciprocity, which virtue is missing in utilitarianism. 33.4. Public civility is part of public reason. Take abortion as an example. Public reason seeks political values that might settle disputes: respect for life, guiding practices that reproduce the public population, equality of women, and no theological pre-emption of issues. Most public debate is warfare. One defies and rallies supporters, and so departs public reason. Public reason is social capital. It amasses slowly, and requires persistent repetition in present political dialogue. 33.5. The best political agreements guarantee background liberties, inculcate a moral tenor in public life, build cooperation based in respect, and leave room for divergence among citizen's lives.

§34. **Second Fundamental Comparison: Introduction**. 34.1. Rawls takes up, as his second comparison with utilitarianism, his second prong of justice: equal access to opportunity and the difference principle. 34.2. Analysis of the difference principle presumes two classes in society (more- and less-advantaged); success means that both groups prefer justice as fairness.

§35. **Grounds Falling under Publicity**. Publicity, reciprocity, and stability all argue for justice as fairness. Publicity has three levels: 1) mutual assent to principles of justice and basic structure, 2) shared general facts about the rationale for the basic structure, and 3) shared acceptance of the overall justification for justice as fairness. 35.2. If publicity prevails, then society will have no ideology. Citizens may still have comprehensive doctrines, but their overlapping consensus shares public reason. 35.3. Publicity educates the public about its order.

§36. **Grounds Falling under Reciprocity**. 36.1. Nothing in utilitarianism encourages either equality or reciprocity. Justice as fairness emphasizes equal access to opportunities and sharing the benefits with the least advantaged, and so expressly supports equality and reciprocity. Justice as fairness asks, What inequalities help all citizens? 36.2. Under justice as fairness, only those departures from equality would be permitted that improve efficiency (and hence wealth) of some while benefitting all, especially the least advantaged. 36.3. In short, inequalities that benefit one party are not allowed because of their detriment to those worst off. 36.4. Rawls sums his argument on the difference principle.

§37. **Grounds Falling under Stability**. 37.1. A stable regime self-generates support for itself. Citizens lack desire to violate or renegotiate the social structure. 37.2. The wealthy would tend to seek renegotiation whenever further gains are possible. Other considerations must temper their agitation. 37.3. A first consideration is education and rationalization of the difference principle. A second consideration is that the wealthy see themselves as privileged by the difference principle, and can, with moral warrant, do what benefits themselves, since it also benefits others less advantaged. A third consideration is that the difference principle means self-interested wrangling can vanish, because trust and cooperation prevail.

§38. Grounds against the Principle of Restricted Utility. 38.1. Restricted utility is indeterminate. Uncertainty increases disputes, destabilizing society. 38.2. Restricted utility asks the less advantaged to benefit the more advantaged in a manner that leads to dissatisfaction and hence instability. It relies on sympathy, rather than self-interest, and hence is weaker. 38.3. Critics have suggested ways in which a restricted utility principle might provide a decent life to all, without creating excessive strains of commitment. 38.4. The utilitarian concept of a minimum decent life is vague and indefinite. The difference principle maximizes benefit to the least advantaged over time. Receiving the human minimum for a decent life may not leave people abject (and revolutionary), but it may not give them a stake in society. Rawls expresses concern that lack of a stake in the least advantaged may make property-owning democracy inviable.

§39. Comments on Equality. 39.1. Rawls reviews reasons for regulating societal inequalities among citizens. 1) Lacking real scarcity, it is wrong for basic needs of some to go unmet while less urgent needs of others are well-addressed. 2) Regulation of inequality prevents one segment of society from dominating the others by manipulating laws and basic structure to their advantage. 3) Inequalities may lead some to view others as fundamentally inferior, which may lead to further vices. Inequality is intrinsically wrong, especially when linked to class status, gender, or race. 4) Open markets outperform monopolized ones, and avoid unfairness. Fair elections generate better participation than those in which wealth dominates. 39.2. Rousseau argued fundamental equality of citizens is foundational. This deep equality favors the difference principle over restricted utilitarianism's basic minimum for decent life.

§40. Concluding Remarks. 40.1. The difference principle gives substance to the idea of societal reciprocity. 40.2. Rawls argued that the original position deliberation should be deductive, but that claim needs to be clarified. Much in the original position requires intuition and further judgment; these lead the deliberation to be not very deductive. 40.3. Such is the nature of practical reason. We ask not for deductive rigor, but whether, in our judgment, a political approach helps us decide disputes, especially constitutional and distributional questions, makes our thinking more coherent, and helps those of diverse opinion to work together. If so, the regime works.

Part IV: Institutions of a Just Basic Structure.

§41. Property-Owning Democracy: Introductory Remarks. 41.1. Rawls seeks now to differentiate a property-owning democracy, such as that contemplated in his justice as fairness scheme, from a capitalist welfare state. Rawls makes only tentative and intuitive arguments here. 41.2. Rawls identifies five social-economic systems: 1) laissez-faire capitalism, 2) welfare state capitalism, 3) command-economy socialism, 4) property-owning democracy, and 5) liberal socialism. Questions pertain to all five regimes: a) is it just?, b) is it effective?, c) will its citizens conform to its demands (consider corruption)?, and d) can its functionaries perform their assigned tasks? Rawls focuses on the first question concerning justice and rightness. 41.3. Which regime meets these criteria when it is working well? Each may create internal social pressures that prevent it from achieving its stated goals. 41.4. Laissez-faire capitalism violates both equality and opportunity when these impede efficiency. Welfare state capitalism permits vast inequities in property ownership, and so reciprocity fails. State command-economy socialism violates both equality and opportunity and fails to use markets.

§42. Some Basic Contrasts between Regimes. 42.1. Property-owning democracy and social liberalism both protect equality and opportunity, and both regulate social inequality. But liberal socialism does not employ the difference principle. 42.2. Justice as fairness does not decide between these remaining regimes, but advances guidelines by which to choose. 42.3. Liberal socialism redresses inequalities after they have injured. By the difference principle, citizens under property-owning democracy never become disadvantaged, because they are equally educated and participating fully. 42.4. Welfare state capitalism tends to create an under-participating class dependent upon welfare. Property-owning democracy insures education, skills, and participation by acting proactively to disperse them throughout the citizenry, creating a fair basic background justice.

§43. Ideas of the Good in Justice as Fairness. 43.1. The concept of goodness in justice as fairness points to the direction of society; justice sets the limits of societal action. The good, however, needs to be generally shared and not be wed to any comprehensive doctrine. All acts of the State must be justifiable to all citizens on the basis of public reason alone. 43.2. Six ideas of goodness characterize justice as fairness: 1) rationality, 2) primary goods, 3) permissible conceptions of the good associated with comprehensive doctrines, 4) political virtues, 5) well-ordered society, and 6) social union of social unions within justice as fairness. 43.3. Civic humanism requires too much of citizens, since it is modeled on Greek city-states where political life consumed much adult male time. 43.4. Modern life is more than political life, and not all engage it primarily. Many devote time to associations within political society. 43.5. Classical republicanism urges that active participation in public life, devoted to public justice and good, prevents government from falling into the hands of people of less helpful aims. Some, who are appropriately gifted, should focus on politics, while others are otherwise occupied.

§44. Constitutional versus Procedural Democracy. 44.1. Constitutional democracy denies to legislatures the power to pass laws that contradict equality and opportunity. Procedural democracy has no such limitations on power, and permits majorities to pass whatever laws they prefer. 44.2. Constitutions serve not only to limit government action, but also to educate their publics. Judicial deliberations draw citizens into political discussions. 44.3. John Stuart Mill thought that man naturally has a desire to promote the long term interest of humanity. Rawls asks, What if other drives prove more potent? Putting humanity's long term interests into constitutional form serves to preserve and educate and redirect citizens.

§45. The Fair Value of the Equal Political Liberties. 45.1. Some criticize that "equal liberties" functionally means rich people rule, and poor people suffer, so those liberties are form without content. Rawls answers that the difference principle compensates the less advantaged, so their liberties become actual. 45.2. Rawls argues that by making equality and opportunity structural components of justice as fairness, he sets apart equality and opportunity from other values, thereby protecting them. 45.3. To accomplish these outcomes, policies will have to be fashioned that keep concentrations of wealth from influencing the outcome of decisions in a manner that changes fundamental equality and opportunities. 45.4. Political processes must make equal access to public office practicable, so that fair legislation becomes possible. Access to such offices is limited, by the nature of representation, so protecting such access for those of lesser means proves critical ("fair value" of equality).

§46. Denial of the Fair Value of Other Basic Liberties. 46.1. Why not secure the fair value of all political liberties? To do so would confuse. An efficient society cannot share resources equally. To allocate resources according to all liberties might obligate government to pay for cathedrals (religious liberty), which would prove divisive. 46.2. To avoid political dissension, one must delimit the scope of good to that required to keep all citizens free and equal, which is expressed in "primary goods." Perfectionists want to fund all good things maximally, but this contravenes the public good of equality and opportunity.

§47. Political and Comprehensive Liberalism: A Contrast. 47.1. Any regime encourages some forms of life and discourages others. Such is political liberalism. Justice as fairness also expresses preference for certain sorts of persons (those amenable to original position deliberations), but remains neutral as to comprehensive doctrines. 47.2. Comprehensive doctrines may be discouraged by conflicts with the principles of justice (equality and access), or because they cannot find adherents among persons convinced of justice as fairness. Every political view will exclude some inimical alternative views. Some ways of life do not fit in any society. Still, such exclusions are not arbitrary bias. They are inherent to well-ordered society. 47.3. An equitable society, such as justice as fairness, makes room for many different comprehensive doctrines. Liberalism supports individualism more strongly than communitarian schemes. The core question, however, is whether liberalism excludes collective, especially religious, identities. 47.4. Liberalism intrudes into religious life to demand that children's education include knowledge of their freedom of conscience, that each may leave his or her religious tradition with legal sanction. The interest of justice as fairness is that children should be educated to become functional citizens in their future.

§48. A Note on Head Taxes and the Priority of Liberty. 48.1. Rawls addresses a progressive head tax on talent. The greater one's natural endowment and privilege, the greater the tax. Rawls makes two decisive objections to such a head tax. First, we have no way to measure endowments that is accurate enough to value the tax. Once the tax is known, people will hide their endowments until after the tax is assessed. 48.2. Second, such a tax would force the gifted to enter vocations that enable them to pay the tax, thereby infringing their liberty to choose otherwise. The difference principle does not tax talent. It, rather, argues that if we benefit from our inordinate talents, we must do so in a way that also benefits the less talented.

§49. Economic Institutions of a Property-Owning Democracy. 49.1. How deeply must benefitting today take into account the well-being of those who come after us? Rawls introduces the concept of "just savings." 49.2. The difference principle allocates wealth among contemporaries. Just savings allocates wealth among generations. 49.3. The sum justly saved is amount that we would have had our predecessors set aside, and the sum we anticipate our ancestors will expect. 49.4. Rawls speculates about the sorts of taxes that might fund just savings: 1) one might progressively tax those who receive bequests, 2) one might progressively tax inheritance solely to prevent wealth maldistribution, and 3) one might tax consumption. To effect the difference principle, one would adjust taxes over time. 49.5. One does not have to calculate the effect of every bit of legislation for its affect upon the least advantaged; rather, one can choose a few approaches that level the playing field, and then monitor the outcomes. The difference principle needs to be of constitutional magnitude. The guarantee of a social minimum support to all citizens should also be constitutional.

§50. The Family as a Basic Institution. 50.1. Families are part of the basic structure, the part aimed at replacing societal members. Families must be accounted in all societal arrangements. 50.2. Expressly political justice does not govern associations, including the family. But political justice limits some actions of associations, those that contradict equality and opportunity. 50.3. So too, the family. Husbands and wives are equal citizens, regardless what patterns they choose in private life. Society must acquiesce at some point in the good faith and parental affection of parents toward their children. 50.4. In every association, members are equal citizens under the basic structure first, without exception. There are no private places beyond the reach of public justice. 50.5. Community property laws make an equal division of assets earned while women raise children. Any society that does less does not care about women as equals, or about the children who are its future. 50.6. Feminists (Okin) may think more features of society are gender-structured than does Rawls, and they may be correct. Women and children must be equal and have fair opportunities, just as do men. The family must produce society's replacement generation.

§51. The Flexibility of an Index of Primary Goods. 51.1. Sen objects that any index of primary goods will prove too inflexible for fairness. Sen asserts that goods are not what matters, but rather a person's basic capabilities and his relation to certain goods. 51.2. Rawls argues that his primary goods concept includes the basic capabilities of citizens. 51.3. Citizen needs are similar enough that their complement of primary goods allows comparison of their relative status. The list of primary goods is quite flexible. 51.4. Citizens provide for themselves within a fair economy, though the basic structure and background justice insure that all have the freedom and opportunity to improve their endowments. Those whose abilities fall within the normal range merely operate within the society, gathering what they need. This leads to some (not-unjust) inequalities. 51.5. Citizens unable to cooperate due to need for medical treatment are a special case. All primary goods are not private wealth. Some contemplate governmental assistance. Primary goods are received over a lifetime, and so contemplate illness and injury. 51.6. Primarily, health care will be decided legislatively, not in the basic structure. A society should pay medical expenses of the least advantaged citizens until further expenditure diminishes their well-being because diverting further funds from other projects injures their general prospects in life (by neglecting the workforce, child care, capital investments, retirement income, defense, and foreign policy). One must view claims from the perspective of one person living through all of life's various phases. Medical care that restores a person to full participation in society pre-empts other care. Some medical care (say, cosmetic surgery) is not medical care at all. 51.7. Rawls summarizes his points about flexibility of primary goods. Addressing citizens who perform above and below expectations is critical to overlapping consensus. One seeks to evade difficult disputes, simplify, and employ common sense. 51.8. Property-owning democracy promotes political liberties, equality of opportunity, and basic health care for all citizens.

§52. **Addressing Marx's Critique of Liberalism.** 52.1. Private property in Rawls's treatment is not essential, but rather a means to justice. One puts meat on the bones of justice as fairness by giving fair values to those liberties. Justice as fairness will overcome each of Marx's objections about division of labor. Well-ordered society differs from Marx's communist society. 52.2. Marx argues that no private property regime can meet the two principles of justice as fairness. Rawls responds that such is not apparent, and must be tried for proof. One ought not compare actualities with ideals. 52.3. Marx would have more workplace democracy. Rawls recurs to Mill's worker-managed enterprises, which Mill thinks might outcompete capitalist competitors. This has not happened, but possibly should.

§53. **Brief Comments on Leisure Time.** 53.1. Do those benefited by the difference principle live off welfare and play for a living? 53.2. The basic structure presumes all citizens work (say eight hours) and all have leisure (say sixteen hours). Leisure time should be included in the index of primary goods.

Part V: The Question of Stability.

§54. **The Domain of the Political.** 54.1. How much will envy and spite (which were excluded from the original position) actually affect the equality and opportunity of society? Those choosing the structure of justice as fairness will need to answer this question for their deliberations to proceed realistically. 54.2. Can justice as fairness garner ongoing public support? Will subsequent generations have a stable sense of justice that prevents acting on spite or envy, seeking to dominate or acquiescing in domination? Divisive attitudes will destabilize the well-ordered society. 54.3. Justice as fairness is not philosophical, religious, or moral imposition, but rather political formulation of fairness in society's basic structures. Political society is closed; one enters by birth, exits by death. Associations, families and personal life are non-political. 54.4. To be stable, an overlapping consensus of the major comprehensive doctrines within the society is needed. Complaints about political structure must be framed in public reason, not by reference to various groups' comprehensive doctrines. 54.5. Claims outside public reason (for example, there is no salvation outside the church) are not necessarily wrong. They are unreasonable as a mode of dialogue within a constitutional democracy, and public coercion cannot be put to the task of effecting them.

§55. **The Question of Stability.** 55.1. Our political structure must be workable. 55.2. Justice as fairness seeks not just to exist with support, but to be inherently stable. That is, justice as fairness must deal with human foibles in a way that leaves most people motivated to maintain their constitutional structures. 55.3. Justice as fairness must convince inherently by convincing citizens from within public reason. 55.4. Rawls has added the idea of overlapping consensus to his approach, and has clarified that justice as fairness is not a comprehensive doctrine and cannot be such. 55.5. Citizens view the world in two parts: a political conception such as justice as fairness, and in a more comprehensive religious or philosophic manner (a comprehensive position). Such is necessary where pluralism prevails. By this change, Rawls's theory avoids utopianism, and does not countenance the use of coercive compliance regimes.

§56. **Is Justice as Fairness Political in the Wrong Way?** 56.1. A political system is political in the wrong way when it structures itself to win assent from existing political interests. A political system is political in the right way when it offers an independent assemblage of critical moral values in the political realm accessible by public reason. 56.2. Overlapping consensus means groups with comprehensive doctrines can support justice as fairness for their own reasons, as well as public reasons. 56.3. Justice as fairness caters to itself, not to various religions or ideologies that might support it.

§57. **How is Political Liberalism Possible?** 57.1. What about justice as fairness might cause others committed to various comprehensive doctrines to support it, rather than seek hegemony of their own viewpoint? First, some of the values of justice as fairness are fundamental to all societies and every form of cooperation. 57.2. Coercion will be used only in ways that citizens endorse, since it is their own power. 57.3. Second, overlapping consensus happens in most cultures, in many different configurations. Groups endorse their own view, but also endorse political views that allow groups of different views to co-exist. 57.4. Not all comprehensive doctrines are reasonable. Doctrines that impose their view because they can may be rational, but doing so is unreasonable. No one in the original position would permit State power to be used to coerce non-adherents to a comprehensive doctrine. All reasonable comprehensive doctrines seek a government sufficiently tolerant to allow competitors to survive.

§58. **An Overlapping Consensus Not Utopian.** 58.1. Some argue that under no conditions could justice as fairness become actual. To be stable, citizens must endorse justice as fairness, regardless of the relative political strength of their own comprehensive doctrine. 58.2. People may adopt a political regime without integrating fully (or at all) with their comprehensive commitments. 58.3. Over time, people find merit in the values of justice as fairness and its weight overwhelms countervailing pressures. This contributes to overlapping consensus. 58.4. Overlapping consensus is more than mere acquiescence. Citizens consent for reasons consistent with the comprehensive doctrines. They come to view justice as fairness as desirable, even when they may have acquired power to change constitutional fundaments unilaterally.

§59. **A Reasonable Moral Psychology.** 59.1. A reasonable moral psychology is necessary for overlapping consensus to emerge. Such persons are both rational and reasonable, and wish to fairly cooperate with others. These tendencies strengthen as successes mount. Citizens recognize that pluralism is endemic and cannot be overcome with oppressive State action. Moderate scarcity prevails, and so the upside gains of social cooperation lure all potently. 59.2. Because justice as fairness is not comprehensive, it may find support among citizens, who gradually, over generations, acclimate to its structures.

§60. **The Good of Political Society.** 60.1. Justice as fairness abandons the idea of political community as a group associated under one comprehensive doctrine. Pluralism precludes such concepts. 60.2. The best one can hope for under modern conditions is a society that shares justice concepts, organizes its basic structure justly, and acts effectively to maintain justice. This is modern social unity, and for more none can reasonably hope. Citizens express their personal aspirations in a manner that includes justice as fairness. 60.3. When citizens share final ends in political society, they create the premise for political goodness. Such society is good for citizens because they know and seek justice and goodness (which are their moral powers), and have good basis for mutual- and self-respect. 60.4. Justice as fairness is also good for society. Cooperative success in maintaining a just society over generations is itself a social good. When citizens see their State as good for themselves and good for the whole, that society grows stable.

CHAPTER 4
NOZICK

LADY JUSTICE, JUSTICIA, GOES TO HER THIRD PSYCHIATRIC APPOINTMENT. When Justicia enters, a tall, handsome, plainly elegant man, with a shock of graying hair and an infectious smile, rises to greet her. The black box of conscience remains on the coffee table next to the psychiatrist's chair. Justicia leans onto the divan.

JUSTICIA: I got an email this week. You are Robert Nozick, another Harvard political professor. You wrote *Anarchy, State, and Utopia*.

NOZICK: That's right. I heard you spoke with my colleague, John Rawls. He and I often come as a boxed set. You also spent a session with Capuchin, that funny little tuxedoed monkey. Tell me what you learned.

JUSTICIA: Both were kind to me and listened well. Capuchin taught me that justice wells up from deep parts of the mammalian brain. Dr. Rawls believes my sanity may improve if I stack society's economic deck so those dealt losing hands get better cards in future games. I told them both about my identity struggles. I am sure you have read their notes.

NOZICK: I read what Capuchin and Rawls heard you say in previous sessions. Can you add anything?

JUSTICIA: I had another frustrating moment this week. I sat statuesque with my sword, scales, and blindfold at the back of the Bar Association's center downtown. The Bar convened a member town meeting to address a "legal technician" rule. The rule allows paralegals, in some areas of law (family law, at present), to complete pre-approved forms for their clients without attorney supervision, upon passing an examination, gaining years of experience, providing mandatory pro bono service, and insuring themselves. The proposal arose from a Bar study of civil legal need in Washington State that indicated 87% of civil legal needs go unmet because the citizens in need either will not or cannot hire an attorney. The Bar Association has thrice opposed the legal technician rule. The vast majority of speakers agreed with the Bar's Board of Governors, each citing some ding their own practice area might suffer if legal technicians are allowed to work. I was disheartened by the spectacular failure of imagination of some of the lawyers present, and the abject collapse of moral concern about the ugly role our legal monopoly plays in the welfare of our neighbors. That unserved 87% represents a gigantic market of potential clients (at admittedly lower rates of payment). These unserved many constitute most of Washington. The Supreme Court spanked the Bar Association for its retrenchment by passing the legal technician rule. But the Bar, ever the monopolists, continue grinding their axe. Incorrigible!

> **JUSTICE IS:**
>
> MARKETS
> AMIDST
> FREEDOMS.

NOZICK: Wow! Frosty! Do you follow all the politics of the Bar Association with such intensity?

JUSTICIA: No. But when most people cannot get meaningful access to the court system for everyday conflicts, I think my good name is compromised. What are your thoughts, Dr. Nozick?

NOZICK: First, I think you are feeling a bit better. You have not been so eloquent with my predecessors.

Just then, the black box of conscience flies open on the coffee table. Up pops John Rawls, now half a foot tall. "Don't listen to Nozick, Justicia. He'll whack you with his libertarian schtick: minimalist states, respect for individual liberty. It's good for the competent many; not so for the limping remainder. Nozick's peddling a dame hooked on Adam Smith and social Darwinism. He got her lipstick and a new hairdo. Yo, Bob. No offense. I'll sit now." *Tiny Rawls pulls the lid back over himself.*

JUSTICIA: So, your "libertarian schtick"?

NOZICK: It is not too complex. If one respects individuals, one imposes minimally. How much interference do you want from your neighbors? Interfere with others no more than that. This is just Kant, or Jesus, or Mencius. If you work circumspect intervention out for masses of people, then one conceives the minimal state. The legitimate activities of a just society consist in protecting citizens from crime and foreign invasion. Possibly, a society should provide courts.

JUSTICIA: What about everything else? Schools, poverty, pollution, regulation, social security, Medicare?

NOZICK: Leave those needs to private institutions and individuals, acting in a market context.

JUSTICIA: So, my job would be downsized.... Hey! I'll bet you oppose the legal technician rule?

NOZICK: It's government intermeddling. In my world, your job would be mostly outsourced, Justicia. Governments would abandon their monopoly and let other individuals and social institutions do things that governments attempt now. The world would be more chaotic, but more creative. Justice would be more available, and less hidebound.

JUSTICIA: So, that's my problem. I suffer megalomania. I need to do less, in a principled way. I should work less in courts and governments, and hang around homes, churches, and volunteer associations?

Justicia licks her lips and leans toward Nozick. He throws up his hands.

NOZICK: The file says you're looking for love. I am not your man. Time's up. I've got to run.

Nozick, Robert. *Anarchy, State, and Utopia.* New York: Basic
Books, Inc., Publishers, 1974.

*Robert Nozick (1938-2002) was an American philosopher, who taught at Harvard University.
He is best known for* Anarchy, State, and Utopia, *a libertarian response to John Rawls's concept
of "justice as fairness." Nozick died after an extended battle with stomach cancer.*

Preface. Nozick writes of States, their legitimate functions and philosophical arguments supporting States. Individuals have rights no State can legitimately contravene. So
potent are these rights that it may be the case that no State of any sort is justified. Nozick
promises that he will conclude that the only justified State is a minimal State. Its powers
extend only to security and enforcing contracts. Any expanded State action lacks warrant.
Consequently, the State may not coerce individuals to support others, nor may the State
interdict actions to protect people from themselves. Nozick notes that the positions he
defends he used to disbelieve. But truth in ethics may differ from what we customarily
think. Intellectually honest inquirers must entertain arguments that cut their preferred positions. Nozick will treat anarchists' claims seriously; they argue that no State is justified.
He considers John Rawls's positions advocating classical liberal democracy. He presents
his positions with their warts intact, not interposing commonplace (but usually disingenu-
ous) philosophical arrogance. Nozick describes the usual philosophical journeyman's task
of nipping and tucking non-conforming ideas to fit in conceptual spaces where they do not
actually fit. He hopes to avoid this practice, but is not optimistic. Nozick styles his book
an exploration, and he expresses his doubts as well as convictions in its course.
    Acknowledgments. Nozick thanks his employers, those who edited, colleagues who
debated with him, and Murray Rothbard, who led Nozick to anarchist theory.

PART I: STATE-OF-NATURE THEORY, OR
HOW TO BACK INTO A STATE WITHOUT REALLY TRYING.

    1.   **Why State-of-Nature Theory.** If no States existed, would we need one?
Nozick considers "state of nature" theory, describing a hypothetical man-before-govern-
ment, because doing so helps one theorize. *Political Philosophy.* Why not anarchy?
Nozick relies on Locke's state of nature formulation, which he cites, and seeks to explain
political theory in non-political terms. It does not matter that the state of nature never
existed, nor that Locke's statement of that state fails utterly. Taking the most optimistic
view of an anarchic circumstance, a State would be justified if it would improve that circumstance. *Explanatory Political Theory.* To explain the State, commencing from a non-
political and very fundamental point of beginning (say the human state of nature), would
serve to explain the State's existence. Nozick considers defective forms of reasoning in
such enterprises. He begins with Locke's description of the human state of nature.
    2.   **The State of Nature.** Locke finds men in the state of nature to be independent,
bound to harm no other, justified in protecting themselves from and punishing transgres-
sors justly. There are inconveniences in this arrangement, which for Locke justify civil
government. Against civil government, Nozick cites Proudhon's hyperbolic [but entertain-
ing] list of State misdeeds: government pries, records, extorts, and punishes, all without
warrant. Yet, private enforcement leads to vendetta, and perpetual insecurity in self-rein-
forcing cycles of violence. None knows how to end the repetition. *Protective Associations.*
How might anarchist society avoid this outcome? Nozick considers private protection associations, and points out their difficulties. In resolving these challenges, Nozick notes
that protective associations resolve, when the dust settles, to systems much like courts and
appeals. People, relying on government, forget they can act privately and contractually.

The Dominant Protective Association. In any area, competing protective associations might offer services. Conflicting, one proves dominant. Each looks like a minimal State. Some may act aggressively. *Invisible-Hand Explanations.* How does a dominant protective association differ from government? Money may arise without agreement. It is as though an invisible hand guides mankind to outcomes we never conceived (Adam Smith), of which Nozick offers numerous examples. *Is the Dominant Protective Association a State?* Deciding what constitutes a State is messy. Nozick argues that a State holds monopoly on who uses force in its geographical area. Lacking monopoly on use of force, protective associations, even the dominant one in an area, are apparently not States.

3.   Moral Constraints and the State. *The Minimal State and the Ultraminimal State.* The minimal State monopolizes force, and provides only security and enforcement of contracts, protecting all within its territory. The ultraminimal State monopolizes force, and provides security and enforcement only to those who pay for its services. The minimal State redistributes personal property, because citizens are compelled to pay for protection of others. But the ultraminimal State fails to protect all, and does so in the name of protecting the right of all not to pay for benefits to others. *Moral Constraints and Moral Goals.* Utilitarianism fails to protect rights that should be protected because rights are not an essential part of its ultimate purpose (which is the greatest good for the greatest number). One might build a form of utilitarianism that adopts rights protection as part of its prime goal, or set rights protection as a set of constraints on utilitarian choices. This latter approach shows that it would be consistent for an ultraminimal Statist to refuse to be forced to assist others, provided that he also recognizes no others can be forced to assist him. *Why Side Constraints?* Why would one choose nonviolation of rights as a side constraint, rather than make it the prime purpose of actions? Kant would have no human used as a means only, but always also as an end. Can one constrain a person's acts so that they are not used in this or that manner? Politics addresses only certain uses of others. One may not use another person as an object of physical aggression. When governments demand a sacrifice from one citizen, they benefit others at that sacrificer's expense, then cover it up with talk of "social benefit." The sacrificer is not benefitted; he is injured. No government that is neutral as between its citizens can demand such sacrifices. Citizens are not resources for the consumption of other citizens. *Libertarian Constraints.* No moral scheme can justly balance citizens' lives against one another, and decide what sacrifices lead to greater social goods. Libertarians find that separate existences mean none can aggress against another justly. No citizen can be sacrificed to benefit another. Nozick considers, but does not settle, issues related to non-aggression, innocent threats, and innocent shields of threats. *Constraints and Animals.* Some animals should be given consideration in human deliberations. Why do animals count (or humans, for that matter)? Some argue that killing animals leads to killing men. This seems factually false. Which animals deserve consideration? Why? If eating meat in no way improves health, are we justified in killing animals only for the taste preference their meat provides? Nozick does not support eating animals, but his point concerns moral side constraints, not animal rights. More meat animals exist because we eat them than would otherwise exist. So, meat-eating gives life to more animals, though they are treated as means to satisfy human preference. We could impose a side restraint that one can use animals, but not humans, if a greater good is achieved. Utilitarianism allows imposed sacrifice if the utility is great enough, certainly sacrifice of animals, and in unusual circumstances, of humans. (Bentham held that animal sacrifice counted in the calculus). Utilitarianism does not work for animals, and raises numerous questions. *The Experience Machine.* Does anything matter other than the way we feel inside? If one could choose experiences and experience them artificially in a manner that is indistinguishable from normal experience, should one do so? Humans want to act, to aspire to be something, and to experience the world's depth beyond what humans can construct. Every person would decline machines that lived for them. More matters than how we experience things. So too for animals, though to a lesser degree. *Underdetermination* *of Moral Theory*. Is there a scale of being in which humans are higher and animals lower? What if humans encounter beings higher than humans? In such circumstances, two theories (hierarchical species elitism and absolute side constrains on use of humans) account equally well for all known cases, but not for hypothetical cases (like super aliens who sacrifice humans under the species elitist theory). *What Are Constraints Based Upon?* What makes humans distinguishable from animals? In what way are we "higher"? Why is a moral side constraint concerning use of humans warranted? Most focus on reason, choice, and moral agency. But this amounts to meaningful life, which is itself a difficult concept. *The Individual Anarchist.* We are now positioned to reframe the anarchist complaint. When a State forces citizens to provide for others and coerces citizens, the State violates the moral side constraints on how individuals must be treated (as ends, even if partly as means). Therefore, every State is inherently immoral.

   4.   Prohibition, Compensation, and Risk. Some may decline to pay for protective association defense, remaining independent. How should others respond? Independents might be physically surrounded, then having no way to exit a location without trespass. Or one might allow the independent's personal vengeances, but then evaluate them within the protective association, and exact punishment from him. But an independent might kill, so no after-the-fact evaluation would suffice. So, the protective association members would insist on an adjudicative process for pre-evaluation of independent's claims to retaliations. What if the independent resists protective association activities? *Prohibition and Compensation.* Consider a person's natural rights in moral "space." A line bounds the perimeter of this space. Can none invade the space? Or can one invade upon payment of compensation for the intrusion? Nozick presumes that infringed persons make reasonable adjustments to the intrusion before calculating the intruder's compensation to the infringed person. *Why Ever Prohibit?* Nozick presumes, *contra* Locke, that a person may do anything to himself (including killing himself), except that which he has agreed not to do. Why prohibit any intrusion, provided compensation is paid? Why not prohibit any crossing of the moral line at all? Some might intrude without detection, and so avoid compensation. Prohibition might address undetected intrusions. Neither deterrence theory nor retribution theory seem to result in no violations of citizen's natural rights, but rather creates a counter-pressure against transgressions, leaving a residue of violations. Victims may over-compensate themselves, and the protective association may seek over-compensation because it wants the retributive penalties to fund itself. *Dividing the Benefits of Exchange.* What if more than one person wants to fully compensate a person for a contemplated infringement? A market in the infringement arises, in which the infringed individual might get more than full compensation for a given infringement. *Fear and Prohibition.* Some injuries may be non-compensable. Even compensable injuries may cause fear, leading to an apprehensive citizenry. A group would prohibit compensable acts that cause general fear. Some intrusions do not cause general apprehension. Those causing general fear are public wrongs; those not causing public fear are private wrongs. Compensating only direct victims of intrusions fails to address the fear of non-victims living in a regime that permits intrusions. Where full compensation for intrusions is guaranteed, why does one fear? *Why Not Always Prohibit?* Inspiring general fear warrants prohibiting fear-inspiring acts. But prohibiting all unconsented intrusions would also fill life with risk and uncertainty. One cannot distinguish a reasonable line beyond which intrusions would be impermissible. Forbidding unconsented intrusions forsakes the benefits presumed to flow from the intrusion. Allowing unconsented intrusions generates fear. Either involves significant transaction costs. *Risk.* Acts that cause no apprehension individually may be feared if a large number of such minimal intrusions were to occur. In boundary crossing, one may: 1) punish all boundary crossings, 2) permit boundary crossings where compensation is paid, or 3) permit boundary crossings provided compensation is paid to all who might suffer the intrusion. No coherent theory emerges for where lies the minimal intrusion permissible, nor for assessing which intrusions are permitted, nor for determining who gets compensated or how much the compensation should be. *The Principle of Compensation*. How might citizens compensate one another for intrusions? If by insurance payments, do we then punish when one cannot afford that insurance? When we forbid some act, must we all then compensate the coerced person for his lost opportunity? (Pollution transfers negative impacts from the polluter to the property of non-polluters. Nozick proposes a class-action tort system for assessing to polluters the costs upon the public of their activities.) Establishing classes of prohibited activities (due to their exceeding danger) proves difficult. Every act can be construed from multiple points of view. When one forbids an act, those inclined to undertake the forbidden act suffer loss. They must be compensated, to some (difficult to ascertain) extent. *Productive Exchange*. A productive exchange leaves the buyer better off than if the exchange never happened. The blackmailer sells his silence; no productive exchange occurs, because the buyer would be better off if the exchange never occurred.

   5.   The State. *Prohibiting Private Enforcement of Justice.* Private justice would be prohibited if its risks (unreliability, or over- or under-punishment, or uncertainty) are deemed excessive. But how would a protective association gain legitimate authority to prohibit? Associations aggregate the powers of their individual members, but no more. And a free rider would be motivated not to consent, since he can get what he wants, plus the benefit of the association's actions, by contracts and abstention. *"The Principle of Fairness."* John Rawls's principle of fairness argues that: a) all those who benefit from cooperation, including free riders, owe a duty to acquiesce in the rules of the cooperative many, and, b) the many may legitimately enforce their view of matters upon outliers and free riders. Nozick rejects both assertions. Hart wishes to argue that promising any action necessarily entails the right to compel compliance. Nozick answers that giving the moral realm its due weight, compulsions are add-ons, not essentials. One may, or may not, have a right to compel, based on the agreements of the parties. As to the "principle of fairness" itself, general agreement does not bind a person. He may, or may not, decline to participate in majority-chosen activities. The dissenter may have other preferred activities, even co-operative ventures he would prefer. No right to coerce attaches to unsought benefits imposed upon one by others. People must consent to cooperation and limitations. *Procedural Rights*. If, in the state of nature, a cooperative majority enforces its rules on an independent, may that independent then retaliate or demand compensation for the injury suffered? If one wishes never to punish innocents, then one can have no punishments at all, for any system has shortcomings. An ideal system exactly balances likelihood of being unjustly punished against the risk of suffering crime (by failing to punish the guilty). People would, however, differ as to the appropriate balance of innocent punishment to released bad actors. When groups adopt differing standards, each may defend their own on principle, leading to non-procedural conflict (war). Pacifists may demand non-violent opposition (and a principle probabilified for the likelihood of success would help), but the possibility of this sort of conflict describes the human circumstance. Political or military structures do not relieve one of personal responsibility to determine that one's acts (even if ordered to perform them) are morally acceptable. Our knowledge is frequently imperfect or non-existent. *How May the Dominant Agency Act?* A dominant protective association can impose justice procedures on its members, and may announce punishment for any outsiders who impose different standards. Individuals may demand to know that justice procedures are fair and consistent. Where a justice system is something less, a person may defend himself. Nozick considers the claims of a protective system when one of its own is being judged by a different protective system. Unreliable procedural systems impose risks, even when they reach occasional just results. Any person may punish offenders provided she has determined the offense was committed and stands in the best possible circumstance for determining what happened. Protective agencies may punish other protective agencies for punishing a client, even if that client is guilty. *The De Facto Monopoly*. A dominant protective association may not claim the sole right to judge, but its power makes that practically so. This is a *de facto* monopoly on questions of justice. The dominant protective association has no right to intervene in disputes among non-members. *Protecting Others.* If a protective agency forbids non-members from enforcing their rights on members, the the non-member is disadvantaged. The most efficient way to compensate the non-member would be to provide that person with protective services for free. If the protective agency is forced to pay, the fee would be only the difference between the cost to the non-member of defending himself and the cost of protective services. But this sum may be insufficient to compensate the non-member for his losses. The burden lies with the protective association that prohibits self-defense to compensate the non-member adequately. Even this *gratis* protection does not protect the non-member against other free riders, but only against members. Most people will join the protective association from self-interest. *The State.* The anarchist critique being met, we see a protective agency's monopoly of force and universal protection emerge with moral legitimacy. These are the core elements of being a State. Liability insurance would cover losses of those protected. The protective agency, where size of population and land is adequate, constitutes a State-like entity. *The Invisible Hand Explanation of the State.* The *de facto* monopoly on coercive acts of a protective association creates an ultraminimal State invisibly. How does the minimal State emerge from the ultraminimal?

6.   Further Considerations on the Argument for the State. Nozick considers objections to his construction of the minimal State. *Stopping the Process?* If, by *de facto* protective agencies, some acquire more protection than others, may the others prohibit people joining the agency? May the agency prohibit other from joining competing agencies? Nozick graphs the relations and States of two people with differing approaches to the protective association. Dangers emerge when people attempt to prevent others from joining competing protective agencies. *Preemptive Attack.* Self-defense permits preemptive attack upon States that announce intent to attack, but not upon those that merely grow in power. The intent to do wrong justifies preemption. So, Nozick's *de facto* protective association (State) does not prove that none can join competing protective associations, since one joining intends no wrong. *Behavior in the Process.* Even anarchists, who recognize that States, once created, grow, would not be able to resist their self-interest in joining a protective association. Nozick considers Locke's view of social compact, and argues, *contra* Locke, that the State emerges naturally from the human natural norm. *Legitimacy.* When does a *de facto* dominant protective association legitimately wield power? The association has no powers but those ceded to it by its members. So, it acts legitimately when victims agree its punishments are sufficient. There emerge problems as to who is authorized and how many times may one be authorized as to any given compensation. *The Right of All To Punish.* Locke argues that in the human natural state, every person has liberty to punish any violator. But who should punish? The victim is owed compensation, but not a right to punish as well. Even the delegation by all to a punisher remains a murky proposition in the state of nature. A dominant protective agency would violate fewer rights to punish (of individuals) than any other, since it is authorized by most to act for them. When it does so, it becomes a *de facto* State. Agreement upon libertarian principles, even among libertarians, seems unlikely (consider copyrights or patents). *Preventive Restraint.* Some rules inhibit the likelihood that one will injure another. Yet, such rules might incarcerate some, based upon their likelihood of offense. A rule against private justice is a preventive restraint, and common to all legal systems. Any person who is preventively restrained must be compensated for that injury. The great cost of such compensation would argue against preventive restraint itself. For poor communities, compensation would not be adequate until all members were as disadvantaged by the compensation as those restrained were disadvantaged by their incarceration.

Nozick turns to explaining why, having derived the minimal State, one should admit no more extensive State.

PART II: BEYOND THE MINIMAL STATE?

7.   Distributive Justice. No State of greater scope than the minimal State can be justified, for any such State violates its citizens' rights. Others, however, justify more extensive State on various rationales. Nozick considers the rationale of distributive justice. People acquire things by contract or gift in a vastly complex agglomeration of exchanges. There exists no central distribution point or person. What is just regarding people's property? *Section I: The Entitlement Theory.* Property justice has three topics: a) owning that which has never before been owned, b) transferring property from one person to another, and c) repairing the effects of unjust acquisition of property. To acquire property justly, one gets it originally, or one receives by fair transfer. No other just ownership exists. Just ownership depends upon historical events, not ideas. Where property was acquired by unjust means (theft, slavery, fraud, for example), steps must be taken to rectify those injustices to the extent possible. But to whom and how far back in time must one rectify? One needs a theory of just property rectification. The property distribution described by that theory should be effected. *Historical Principles and End-Result Principles.* Entitlement theory differs from end-result principles of justice. These theories take possessions as they are and adjust them according to some principle, with scant or absent regard for historical ownership. If historical entitlements matter, then achieving a "perfect" distribution (according to some end-result principle) may nevertheless be unjust to those affected and their historical right to certain property. *Patterning.* Patterned theories of property justice make some historical criterion, other than entitlement (such as moral merit, need, productivity, effort, or combinations of such criteria) the measure of just property ownership. The entitlement theory of just property is not patterned. Historical acquisition of property is much more chaotic than pattern permits. Nozick considers the pattern proposed by Hayek: to each according to the extent to which his services and goods benefit others who can pay for them. Nozick rejects Hayek's pattern for its sub-descriptive simplicity. If history matters, there is no pattern. Entitlement leaves just ownership to the just producer of property. All patterned distributive theories accept the formula "From each according to _____, to each according to _____," but fill the blanks differently. For example, Marx preferred "From each according to his abilities, to each according to his need." Nozick prefers "From each as they choose, to each as they are chosen." *How Liberty Upsets Patterns.* Patterned distributions destabilize as soon as people start making choices. Some end up with more, others less, because people differentially choose some things over others. The purveyors of those favored things prosper; those who offer less favored goods suffer (the Wilt Chamberlain example). Some work their minimum (or less). Others work overtime, generating surplus. Liberty destroys any economic preconceived pattern. Very weak patterns might avoid this rule, but such weak patterns may be satisfied by the entitlement regime. *Sen's Argument.* Nozick recounts Sen's argument. Nozick argues that individual rights do not determine a social construct, but rather operate as limitations upon choice within a given context. Nozick construes Sen's argument to support his assertion that economic patterning collapses before individual choices. *Redistribution and Property Rights.* Patterned distributions necessarily require interference with individual choice. Families, with their love and affectional redistributions, disrupt patterned economic schemes. Radicals approach loving families ambivalently; they want familial relations as a societal standard, but condemn the family as an impediment to radical purposes. (Rawls's standard of focusing on the least fortunate member is a rule loving families would never adopt regarding their children.) Both love and justice are historical. We love someone, not a set of characteristics. Patterned distribution schemes focus on recipients, not givers, for inexplicable reasons. Patterned distribution entails redistribution. Redistribution violates property rights as conceived under entitlement theory. Taxation resembles partial slavery. One forces another to work to benefit someone to whom he chooses to give nothing. Some argue for taxation only on assets above the minimum required for living. But this forces those who prefer costly entertainments to work for others, while those who relish sunsets pay nothing. Patterned distribution schemes give all a right to a portion of production, regardless of a person's participation in production. The receiver takes a part ownership interest in another's property (or time). Regimes that make such demands cannot allow emigration or opting out of the system to avoid payment. *Locke's Theory of Acquisition.* Nozick finds Locke's property theory problematical. How exactly does adding labor to an un-owned thing make that thing yours? Locke requires that taking an un-owned thing as property should not worsen the lot of other persons. But it would seem any appropriation might worsen another's position. Here enter arguments favoring private property. Private property puts things in the hands of those who use them profitably (social product increase), lets individuals make risk decisions, protects future persons by desire to hold some products back for future markets, employs unpopular persons, and so forth. Collective property rights also need a theory about why those living on or using something have a right to control it. *The Proviso.* The weaker proviso of justified property from Locke prohibits taking property unclaimed by any other, provided the taking does not exhaust the total supply of any possession necessary to others surviving (nor acquire from others a similar monopoly by purchasing their interests). *Section II: Rawls' Theory.* Nozick praises Rawls's book, *A Theory of Justice. Social Cooperation.* Nozick quotes Rawls, to the effect that social cooperation, which improves the lot of all, creates issues of social justice of the distribution of that economy's wealth. Nozick asks what is it about cooperation that raises social justice issues? Nozick imagines ten Robinson Crusoes on ten separate islands, each faring as he may fare. Would these non-cooperators not make claims of justice against one another, were they to become able to communicate? Nozick takes the Robinson Crusoes scenario as a pure entitlement example. One can never theoretically separate a product from its producer. The contributions of individuals can always be teased out. In the end, individuals work, make exchanges in a market, and possess what they choose to possess (for good or ill). Even Rawls does not believe the relative contributions cannot be parsed. Rawls allows for differential rewards, provided that these benefit the worst off people. *Terms of Cooperation and the Difference Principle.* Rawls's "original position" puts disinterested individuals under very specific circumstances of self-ignorance (the veil of ignorance) in a position of choosing societal first principles. Such persons would choose, according to Rawls, equal rights and duties, and the difference principle, which asserts that extra benefits are justified only to the extent such an unequal distribution benefits the least advantaged in society. Nozick asks why Rawls focuses on groups rather than individuals, and then assaults the inner logic of the difference principle. There is nothing inherently just about worse off people demanding as much as they might get. Why would the well off not demand the same? Worse off people should accept the difference principle, which leaves them worse off, because without it, they would be worse off still. *The Original Position and End-Result Principles.* By denying persons in the original state self-knowledge, one guarantees that their view of what they ultimately want will prevail (end-state principles). Having no history, people in the original position could not choose principles based on historical wisdom. Rawls, using his original position, can never get to anything like our usual sense of justice, which is historical and involves entitlement. Rawls's original position deciders could never choose entitlement as a principle, for it would always look to them like a proposition to tailor justice to benefit oneself. *Macro and Micro.* Rawls argues that the difference principle applies only to the macrostructure of all of society, and not to individual circumstances where counterexamples may abound. Is justice an emergent feature of macrostructures? Are there micro-structural counterexamples that tell against Rawls's scheme? Nozick believes the difference principle is inherently unfair. Nozick argues that there are no forms of justice that apply only to macrocircumstances, but not microcircumstances. One cannot exclude micro counter-examples.

Rawls's difference principle is an end-result criterion. It asserts that any process or feature of society that fails to benefit the least advantaged citizens fails of justice, and so is an extraordinarily potent form of end-result criterion. Nozick considers "organic" schemes where an unjust distribution can emerge merely by deleting some people and their distributive shares. A "nonaggregative" scheme maintains the proportions within a group, but fails to maintain proportions between groups. Nozick contradicts a speculation of Thomas Scanlon that no schemes intermediate between the difference principle and strict equality exist; he does so by offering such intermediate positions. Nozick asks whether each successive generation in Rawls's veil of ignorance would themselves choose the same principles as did the first generation. If not, where does it all end? *Natural Assets and Arbitrariness.* Rawls objects to entitlement theory because it allows shares of wealth to be distributed by arbitrary factors (birth, talent, education, luck). Where lies choice in Rawls's scheme? Some choose to do much with little. How are their efforts honored? Rawls nullifies the effects of natural endowments and social contingencies. Why? Perhaps Rawls seeks to nullify arbitrary factors in justice (the positive argument), or that Rawls seeks to counter an argument that natural endowments should not be nullified (the negative argument). *The Positive Argument.* Four arguments may support the idea that natural differences among people should be nullified. A) if people do not deserve what they receive naturally, and natural endowment determines other societal benefits, then property should not be distributed according to natural gifts. Rawls rejects this argument expressly. B) Property distribution should conform to a predetermined pattern, and natural distribution is not patterned. Therefore, property should be distributed in a patterned, not natural, manner. But it is possible that natural gifts and distribution according to, say, service to others, might correlate. So, one cannot exclude all patterns that are arbitrary morally. C) Version C holds that any moral arbitrariness in a pattern of property distribution infects and discredits the entire pattern. Nozick argues that not all theories of justice are patterned (consider Nozick's account of entitlement). There is no product man uses that is not the previous product of human choice and activity. That is, there is no manna. And every patterned distribution would be transformed into a different pattern by human trading and preferences, even if it were justly patterned to begin with. D) One can find no unified underlying theory that explains all facets of any patterned distribution of property. The attempt to do so leads one to disparage non-fitting facts to achieve consistency. Does Rawls's positive argument fare better if one places equality, which matters so much to Rawls, at its center? This argument goes: since property ownership should be equal, barring important moral reasons to deviate, and since people's natural gifts differ for no particularly moral reason, therefore, differing natural assets should not cause property ownership to be non-equal. Nozick argues that there exists no inherent reason that all should hold equal possessions. *The Negative Argument.* Some might argue against Rawls that people's possessions are legitimate, even when that possession depends upon their natural gifts and the results of those gifts. Nozick replaces Rawls's talk of desert with talk of entitlement. People are entitled to be themselves, with their gifts, even if they do not deserve such blessings. That someone's skills and gifts are arbitrary says no more than that procreation is arbitrary. Which sperm succeeds is arbitrary. Surely, something of significance (something non-arbitrary) comes of procreation, since it is the fount of human life. *Collective Assets.* Rawls claims that each person has an equal claim on the natural abilities of the human race, viewed as a pool. Nozick counters that Rawls's principle makes envy part of its root. Does the need to rectify past injustices warrant a State more expansive than the minimal State Nozick prefers?

    8. Equality, Envy, Exploitation, Etc. *Equality.* Equality is frequently an assumed good, but rarely argued for as a good. Under an entitlement theory, one cannot decide how property should be distributed among citizens until one knows how they got the property. Entitlement theory does not favor equality or inequality, but rather history. Nozick criticizes Bernard Williams's argument for universal health care, noting that he fails to argue for its equality, but rather assumes that equality. Deep in Williams's argument is the conviction, unexamined, that society should provide for member's important needs. He cares little how members came to have their wealth or lack of it. *Equality of Opportunity.* The weak version of equality is equality of opportunity. One cannot take from others property they justly own to benefit others. One must convince the holders of that property to contribute it. Life is not a race. No single goal governs. People trade for what they want. Perhaps it would be fine if people with lesser opportunities magically got better opportunities. But no one is being injured when people choose what they want. Taking other people's things to make some people's lives better is just theft. The only rights that exist are some particular right of a person over some particular property conjoined with the right to make agreements with others. No more general property rights exist. *Self-Esteem and Envy.* Envy distorts equality. Self-esteem and equality may have a nexus. When one has a skill, another better skilled person may, unintentionally, cause the first to feel inferior. All fine performance is relative to the skill of those performing the task. When many agree about which skills are important, then those who perform in those tasks poorly may well come to view themselves as worthless people. Self-esteem operates by comparison. When the comparison pales, self-esteem moves to another, more relevant comparison. Things that are actually important (enlightenment, holiness, caring) do not lend themselves to comparisons at all. Eliminating bases for comparison might intensify envy, as people cling more and more to less and less distinction. Self-esteem might be maximized by having a large number of dimensions of excellence and different standards by which to evaluate those excellences. *Meaningful Work.* Self-esteem is not uniformly damaged by taking orders from superiors. Meaningful work includes a chance to use one's talents independently in worthwhile work, where the worker participates in some larger goal that is part of a larger process. Non-meaningful work deadens all of a worker's life. Many people choose less money for more meaningful work environments. Meaningful work, then, can be created. If it proves less efficient to work meaningfully, the workers may bear the costs, or the consumer, or a government might order all work to be meaningful. *Workers' Control.* Workers might directly control their factories. Such factories would suffer certain predictable problems, such as decision-making cutting into work time, raising capital with a differently-interested workforce, and losing workers to non-worker-controlled industries able to pay more. If consumers support worker-controlled production, they might pay more for such products. Though possible, most workers do not form worker-controlled companies, and unions do not capitalize such enterprises. Why? *Marxian Exploitation.* Marxist theory finds exploitation in every society where investment occurs and wherever some are supported by the work of others. The theory argued that workers were forced to work for capitalists because they could not wait for other avenues. But now, many workers have capital themselves and could wait. Do they lack entrepreneurial skills? If so, they could hire those skills. New ventures are risky. Many workers do not want the risk of new ventures, but, oddly, want a share of those that succeed. They decline, however, to give back a portion of their wages when ventures fail. Marxism treats entrepreneurial risk inadequately. Marxist economics finds value in the socially useful product, measured by the labor hours to produce it. But the caveat "socially useful" reintroduces markets and consumers into the equation, and the labor theory of value collapses into market responses. Most workers prefer a steady wage to bearing the uncertainties of markets. *Voluntary Exchange.* Whether an exchange is voluntary depends upon the choices of others. Some are sometimes left with only one choice. This does not make the choice involuntary. One has rights, but only as to persons who themselves have a right to participate in the "righted" relationship. *Philanthropy.* Some contribute to causes they prefer. But would it not be more efficient, and eliminate free riders, if government coercively redistributed to provide for those causes? Why would one opt out of non-compulsory schemes? Wealthy persons might opt out because without compulsion of all citizens, the problem addressed will persevere, or because without compulsion of all, his gift costs him more than before. *Having a Say Over What Affects You.* Some argue that a larger State is required to let people have a meaningful say in issues affecting their lives. Most people value having a say in what affects their lives. Yet this say has limits, limits determined by others' entitlements. None has a say in who another marries, or whether one retires. *The Nonneutral State.* Perhaps a bigger state could equalize political power among citizens. People use government to secure and preserve the economic benefits, to the detriment of others. A minimal State offers citizens the least opportunity for corrupting influence. *How Redistribution Operates.* Redistributive programs primarily benefit the middle class because when redistribution is proposed, the economic elites buy enough votes from middle class voters to defeat redistributionist schemes. This then benefits some middle class voters, but not the poor.

9.   **Demoktesis**. The minimal State withstands all anarchist and moral arguments for a more extensive State. Assymetric rights cannot be legitimately derived. Can one continue the story of the minimal State in a manner that exposes the nature of present more extensive States? *Consistency and Parallel Examples.* People cling to their evaluations of things. If one offers a parallel, the parallel must be close, or the hearer will agree but distinguish the circumstance. If one offers a deduction, the hearer will dismiss a premise rather than change his prejudgement. People like to say there are infinite solutions to any given set of facts, but this is not so, and has not been proved to be so. So, what happens in ethical argument? We ask the hearer to state the moral fundaments in his own thinking that lead to his moral conclusions. *The More-Than-Minimal State Derived.* Societal living has benefits, both those others give a citizen, but more the pay one receives for benefitting others. Nozick indulges some economic analysis about "internalizing positive externalities." Property consists in multiple rights to a thing, but not all rights (for example, right to use the property criminally). Some rights are shared, and philanthropy and communalism may reduce destitution. The more-than-minimal State may arise if people sell shares in themselves, parting out their various capabilities (or rights). Each sale reduces the absolute freedom of the seller. If all is done voluntarily, there is nothing unjust in this circumstance. But some deem it intolerable, and opt out. The many hold and sell shares of themselves, and the process becomes very inefficient. So there is a great conclave, where large shareholders only speak. All are owners; all are owned. The large group shares all things. But malcontents moan. And some children claim they never opted into the social corporation. So, the outliers want to buy land but not participate in the corporation. The corporation decides to brook no dissent. So, we have the modern State in its multitude of powers. The grand State arose without anyone (except the outliers) being forced, and justly. Another tale might be told: Tale of the Slave. Again, Nozick derives the modern State, this time beginning from a patently unjust circumstance, that of slavery. *Hypothetical Histories.* One might also reach the modern State by a process of boycott, with those seeking the more-than-minimal State refusing to do anything with those who refuse that State. Hypothetical histories do not justify States that in fact arose unjustly.

PART III: UTOPIA

10.   **A Framework for Utopia**. Only the minimal State is justified. But is it not underwhelming? How does it compare to stupendous projects of utopian imagination? *The Model.* A utopia seeks the best of all possible worlds. Yet few would be able to agree about its structure. So, to become a reality, utopia must be optimal in some restricted sense. (Utopia contains ambiguity. A minimax principle would build institutions that bad men can exploit less flagrantly. But such a principle would make some goodnesses more difficult to bring to fruit. A maximax principle would seize every goodness, but is infused with such wild optimism that a misstep is inevitable. Since institutions exist, perhaps one should speak of a utopian principle for evaluating institutions, not for designing them.) If any leave an optimized world, then it is no longer optimal. So, the utopian again redesigns.

Are there any worlds agreeable to all? What might be characteristics of such a stable utopia? Its inhabitants, each free to imagine, can imagine no better arrangement for living. In a utopia, inhabitants admit no person who does not make them better off. This makes a market in members among stable utopias. But some people in some societies may get more than they give. Or one may get more from a different society than the one that most values her. Sometimes, the mere fact of social participation is held dearly, or the person values the company of diverse others in and of itself. Nozick proposes to investigate this interesting model. *The Model Projected Onto Our World.* This possible worlds model most closely corresponds to a world of diverse flexible communities that welcome people, let them leave when necessary, and foster social experimentation and diverse approaches. Nozick calls this the "framework." These communities will encounter difficulties: communities might not find the members they prefer, communities might have conflict with one another, members might find transition costs prohibitive when they seek to move from one community to another, and communities might attempt to keep members ignorant of better alternative communities in order to retain members. A diversity of communities would permit individuals to choose among them for those which most closely align with their own values and preferences. *The Framework.* Many paths lead to any utopia. First, people are diverse. No one sort of community could serve all people. Any utopia consists in many utopias. Utopia is a framework for utopian pursuits. Utopia is a meta-utopia, a theoretical structure within which pursuing what matters most is encouraged. Second, every actual society entails trade-offs as one recognizes that not all goods can be simultaneously achieved. Utopian communities will sport different systems of trade-offs. *Design Devices and Filter Devices.* Third, people are complex. Given complexity in and between individuals, no blueprint can be conceived that would state an ideal society. One may design societies and filter ideas that comprise those designs, but in the end one never knows what will work until one puts it into practice. Some communities will prosper, others will fail. *The Framework as Utopian Common Ground.* The utopian goal is to create communities people want to live in. Nozick distinguishes three sorts of utopians: imperialists, who impose their structure; missionaries, who attempt to convince people; and existentialist, who just hope somewhere they can live the utopia they imagine. *Community and Nation.* Communities are not nations; different rules apply. A community may refuse to allow members to opt-out. Nations may not. Nations impose themselves on citizens. Communities are chosen, and in communities one may not avoid offensive co-participants, and communities may own the land they share, giving them rights of control. *Communities Which Change.* What if one joins a community, invests one's life, and then the community changes its values and orientation? Nozick suggests that compensation for members who must leave should be written into the community's original contract. *Total Communities.* Communities will have differing goals and involvements of members. Social bonds grow from shared goals. *Utopian Means and Ends.* Critics disparage utopian means to establish communities that differ from the larger society's norms. Yet, we desire a structure that welcomes people less than perfect, and makes them more ideal. Critics also demean utopian goals in establishing better communities. The most telling criticisms aim at the inflexibility of utopian plans and the utopian penchant for ignoring predictable problems. Nozick wants to specify that the framework must leave freedom to experiment with communities of all sorts. The many details of the framework remain open. Nozick considers some of the problems that will have to be addressed. *How Utopia Works Out.* Nozick's framework substitutes a process for an end state. It is in communities, which Nozick declines to describe, that particular visions of the good life are explored. That is where life lies. Nozick cannot decide if this view is utopian or antiutopian. *Utopia and the Minimal State.* The minimal State is legitimate, and no more extensive state is justified. Considering utopian schemes, one arrives at the same location from a different vantage. So, the minimal State inspires the dreams of visionaries. It respects our rights. It honors our choices and cooperation. States should do no more, and no less.

CHAPTER 4
NIETZSCHE

LADY JUSTICE, JUSTICIA, GOES TO HER FOURTH PSYCHIATRIC APPOINTMENT. When Justicia enters, a dark-haired man of penetrating eyes waits. His profuse moustache, to which a portion of a recent meal clings, projects from his lip. He averts his gaze from Justicia. The German philosopher taps a tuneless rhythm on the black box of conscience that rests on the coffee table at his left hand. Justicia settles herself. Silence ensues. Justicia clears her limestone throat.

JUSTICIA: Are you Friedrich Nietzsche? An email said Nietzsche was coming, the author of *Genealogy of Morals*? Are you that Nietzsche?

NIETZSCHE: I died in psychiatric lockup. Now I find myself resurrected as a psychiatrist. I thought *I* was irony's master. I am humbled.

Nietzsche resumes his silent reverie, staring at his knees. Justicia waits. And waits. Finally, she speaks.

JUSTICIA: The others have been anxious to talk. Is silence a new kind of therapy?

NIETZSCHE: I do not wish to converse with the Great Harlot. In your name, history's giants have fallen.

JUSTICIA: Perhaps I should leave...? I do not intend to perturb you.

NIETZSCHE: Utterly clueless, aren't you? You are a marble statue and I am dead. Some power fabulously greater than either of us has arranged this little session. That door will not open until we have suffered this hour.

The lid of the black box of conscience rises a bit. Nietzsche slaps it down. A tiny voice squeaks, "Mein Gott."

JUSTICIA: I am accustomed to psychological discombobulation. I am seldom, however, hated.

NIETZSCHE: An oversight of the middling many. If the ruck saw with clarity, they too would despise you.

JUSTICIA: Explain yourself, sir. And wipe that cheese out of your moustache.

Nietzsche chews his lip hairs, extricating cheddar. The lid of the black box of conscience flies back and Adolf Hitler, now six inches tall, leaps up. A drop of blood trickles from a little Luger hole in Adolf's skull. "It is I. I am the explanation. I rid Germany and her neighbors of imbeciles and homosexuals and dissidents and communists and the Jewish Menace. The pure blood of the Germanic peoples coursed unblemished. Until you intervened, witch. The sad herd of Jew-loving weaklings gathered itself, all doped up on your opiate of justice, and ruined the best nation in human history. And her best leader. Me! Der Führer." *Hitler daubs at his leaking skull. Nietzsche firmly closes the lid and sighs.*

NIETZSCHE: Adolf dogs me. He is my conscience. He reminds me that stupendous insights become sewage in the mouths of tiny souls. My thought has been forever sullied by Hitler's gargantuan fractured ego, and my sister's betrayal.

JUSTICIA: That must be hard for you, Friedrich. Tell me more about your sister.

NIETZSCHE: Don't psychobabble me, Lady Justice. Hitler's confusions compare favorably to your own. You miss the most obvious thing. Great people differ from normal people. The few are eagles. But the milling millions are lambs. Proud, soaring raptors pick off lambs at will, tearing them limb from limb for food or entertainment. Still, the mutton-horde cannot bother itself even to look up. They are tame, so weak-minded they adopt customs and adhere to those impositions without bleating. The flocks dwell in slave morality and suffer bad conscience. Knowing that eagles soar effortlessly above, they nevertheless praise resistance to raptors in putrid morality tales. Eagles invent the universe as they go. No one and nothing binds them. The will-to-power of great men supervenes, subjecting all. Great men stare into a god-free abyss. Eventually, the abyss stares back, sucking the mire of humanity from each giant's innermost depths. Supermen exude pure, distilled nothingness. In *Übermenschen* lie the hope of, and the only value in, mankind.

> **JUSTICE IS:**
>
> EAGLES
> EATING
> LAMBS.

JUSTICIA: You exalt maniacs! Are you not praising Agamemnon, Alexander, Augustus, Khan, Innocent III, Napoleon, Stalin, Mao Zedong, Pol Pot, Amin, and their ilk? They caused cascades of death and untold suffering.

NIETZSCHE: Silence, Harlot! You berate your superiors. You utter the mind of muddlers.

JUSTICIA: I will speak! You have helped me today. I recognize an opponent. That clarifies things for me.

NIETZSCHE: As I said when we started. Raw irony. Forced to "clarify things" for the confused stone woman.

Justicia opens her mouth to rejoin, but the clock ticks. Nietzsche vanishes in a puff of vapor.

Justicia puts her hand to her heart. Yawning absence aches there. She knows Nietzsche cannot fill her void. She wonders what might.

Nietzsche, Friedrich. *Beyond Good and Evil, (Jenseits von Gut und Bose).* Translated by Walter Kaufmann. New York: Modern Library, 1992.

Friedrich Nietzsche (1844-1900) was one of Germany's most controversial and influential philosophical lights. He held the chair of classical philology at University of Bonn, Switzerland, which he resigned in 1879, after ten years, due to deteriorating health. Nietzsche wrote the bulk of his works in the six years before he was institutionalized because his mental health collapsed.

On the Prejudices of Philosophers. What is the value of truth? Perhaps no one has yet been truthful enough about what truthfulness is. It may be that what we take for goodness is inextricably linked with deception, selfishness, and lust, that good and evil may be essentially one. Philosophers who think such thoughts deliberate dangerous possibilities. The core issue is not whether a judgment is true, but whether it is life-promoting and species-preserving. False judgments appear to be essential to mankind, as in math, language, and imagined absolutes by which we evaluate reality. Untruth is a condition of life. Men survive by use of falsehoods. A philosophy that risks these sorts of thoughts places itself beyond traditional morality, beyond good and evil. Most philosophers of history simply have it wrong; they were guided invisibly by their instincts into wrong-headedness. They have frog-perspectives, seeing the world each from their own little ponds. Kant, Plato, the Stoics, Descartes, Berkeley, Locke, Spinoza, even Schopenhauer--all of the greatest minds are subject to the error. They failed to see that any philosophy that believes in itself creates the world in its own image. This is the philosopher's *will to power*. Even science is subject to this error. Physics is an exegesis of the world, not an explanation. Psychology has gotten stuck in moral prejudices, and avoided the depths of the will to power and the doctrine that all good impulses derive from wicked ones. Unlike these many, philosophers of the "dangerous maybe" skip over common morality.

The Free Spirit. The free spirit, who is the philosopher of the dangerous maybe, lives in simplicity, superficiality, and falsehood. He has a will to know, but also a will to ignorance. This ignorance *refines* knowledge, and is not its opposite. The free spirit, who is a choice human being, seeks a citadel and a secrecy where he is saved from the crowd, because all contact is bad contact except with one's equals. Nietzsche himself strives to be hard to understand. It keeps his thought inaccessible to the rabble. Such independence is for the very few; it is a privilege of the strong. If the crowds learn of the free spirit, they see his acts as follies and crimes. But there are heights of the soul from which even tragedy ceases to look tragic, and the free spirit inhabits these heights. In the pre-moral period, the value of an action lay in its consequences. In the moral period, the value of an action was reinterpreted to lie in the intention of the actor. The free spirit stands at the threshold of the extra-moral period, in which the value of an action lies in what is unintentional in it. This is the challenge of the free spirit— to overcome morality. This is the work saved up for the finest and most honest and most malicious consciences of the present, who are living touchstones of the soul. These philosophers of the future are free spirits.

What Is Religious. Christianity overturned the values of antiquity. Christian faith is a sacrifice of all freedom, pride, and self-confidence of the spirit. Christianity creates enslavement and self-mockery and self-mutilation. It is a neurosis. Unlike the Italians, Germans have little talent for religion. The Old Testament had a fearsome God and the people cowered before him. But Christianity glued the New Testament to the old and sinned against the spirit by infecting it with the small-soul smell. This Christian superficiality may derive from reaching beneath it, and finding terrifying realities. Man may not yet be artist enough to look so deeply. The choice individual might find a use for religion in pacifying his followers. Nevertheless,

Christianity has been the most calamitous sort of arrogance yet; it has made of the European the small, almost ridiculous herd animal, something sickly and mediocre.

Epigrams and Interludes. There are no moral phenomena at all, but only moral interpretations of phenomena. Where lies courage, the choice man finds the courage to rechristen his evil as what is best in himself. To the tyrant in such a choice man, not only reason but also conscience bows.

Natural History of Morals. All philosophers have to date been seeking a rational foundation for morality. This is a false and sentimental view. The will to power explains the world, but knowledge of this fact is veiled. Men make up most of the world. We are accustomed to lying, or, put more virtuously, we know inadequately how much of an artist we are. The Jews first inverted values, working a slave rebellion as to moral issues. The Jewish/Christian formulation of morality amounts to advice concerning the danger that lies in the individual: prudence, prudence, prudence, mixed with stupidity, stupidity, stupidity. Mixing races has resulted in a weaker sort of human being. And loving one's neighbor is based upon fearing him. Fear is the mother of morals. European morality is the imperative of herd timidity, with its democracy and femininity. Higher moralities are possible. The philosophers of the dangerous maybe have a different faith, and one that views European morality with nausea.

We Scholars. Scholars have declared their independence from philosophy. Philosophy has castrated itself, reducing itself to mere knowledge theory. This is philosophy in its death throes. A genuine philosopher lives unphilosophically and unwisely and imprudently. Scientists share the sentiments of other scholars. All work to annihilate the uncommon man. The "objective" man is a minion, working for the uncommon man, and not the goal of manhood. Objectivity is a form of nervous exhaustion and sickliness. Europe needs a new caste to rule for a long, terrible millennium. We need a fight for the earth, and a compulsion to large-scale politics. The problem with the European scholar is his insipid skepticism. The skepticism of audacious manliness is virile. Its proponents are harder than human people might wish. They feel genuine nausea over everything that is enthusiastic or idealistic. Such men create values. They determine the Whither and For What of man. These philosophers of the dangerous maybe are men of tomorrow and the day after tomorrow. They are the enemy of the ideal of today. They are the bad conscience of their time. The greatest among them are the loneliest, most concealed, most deviant, human beings beyond good and evil, the master of his virtues, he that is over-rich in will.

Our Virtues. The values of a philosopher of the dangerous maybe differ from those of the European herd. This means, first, that there may be moralities of various colors, and, second, that some moralities might be superior to others. Proponents of inferior moralities always denigrate proponents of superior moralities. Moralities must bow to the order of rank. It is immoral to say that what is right for the superior man is also fair for the inferior. The morality of herd Europe is the product of semi-barbarism linked to mingling of classes and races. We must reject hedonism, pessimism, utilitarianism, and Aristotelianism. Each leads to a pity of the downtrodden sufferer. The pity of the choice man is not for the poor, but for the miniaturization of man caused by these misled philosophies. Man is both creature and creator, paradoxically (and painfully) united. The British Utilitarians have caused the most havoc. They are boring. If talk of morality were ever to become interesting to large numbers, we might find exactly how seditious moral talk can be. The general welfare cannot guide all men; such morality is detrimental to the higher men. Their morality must be allowed. The herd concern with stamping out cruelty must be itself quashed. All drama is rooted in cruelty. Even seeking knowledge involves a form of self-cruelty. We must, rather than avoid cruelty, translate man back into nature by erasing the interpretations by which philosophers have painted man as other than he is. Deep down in every man is an unteachable granitic core, insensitive to learning. The worst evidence of the putrefaction of European values is feminism. The great art of woman is lying, with her emphasis on appearance and beauty; woman is demeaned by teaching man of her equality and seeking such. Woman is properly a man's possession, and a woman's power comes by her will to power from that position. Feminism defeminizes women, making of her a mere clerk with almost masculine stupidity. She should bear strong children. Feminism makes women boring.

Peoples and Fatherlands. Choice men have overcome the fragmented structure of European politics and thought to prepare the way for a new synthesis of European culture, men like Goethe, Napoleon, Beethoven, Stendahl, Schopenhauer, even Wagner. Soon one will come who will be master over the strong in Europe. They will unify Europe, and avoid national identity. The mixing of classes and races in Europe has created a supra-national, nomadic type of man, one who is extremely adaptable. Though this has leveled the European, made of him a mediocre multi-purpose herd animal, these same conditions make it more likely a highly exceptional and dangerous human being will arise. He will find Europe peopled with persons ready for slavery before a tyrant. Nietzsche then turns to analyze components of the European culture. First, he examines Germanness. Germans elude definition; they lack a center. Germans are developing, good natured and vicious. In German music and language, the result lacks melody. German is best heard in Luther's Bible. The European Jews could easily overwhelm the German culture, for theirs is the toughest and purest race in Europe. They resist change and prevail under bad conditions. Anti-Semites should be expelled from Germany, for fear they might jolt the Jews from their thirst for assimilation into Europe. Second, the English philosophers have manufactured a world of mechanized dolts. The French have Europe's most spiritual and sophisticated culture, which suffers by voluntary and involuntary Germanization. Third, Mediterranean music makes one imagine a music with no knowledge of good and evil. The Germans are better positioned for the coming of the leader of the future because they are closer to barbarism than the French.

What Is Noble. Aristocratic societies have created all improvements in mankind. By standing upon the backs of lower men, choice men (masters) have enhanced themselves, creating the continual *self-overcoming of man*. Admit the truth. Powerful barbarians subjugated those who could be subjected. The nobles were more whole human beings, which meant also more whole beasts. A vital aristocracy accepts slavery as its due and the price of its ascension. Mutual respect befits equals, but if the principle is extended between classes, the result is cultural disintegration. Life is will to power. Aristocrats exploit the underling classes. This is as it should be. Morality is of two sorts: master morality and slave morality. The problem is that in higher cultures and even in individuals, these two moralities exist side by side. Nobility creates values; it does not acknowledge them. What is good for the aristocrat is good. With respect to the lower classes, the aristocrat is beyond good and evil. He does as he pleases. Slave morality concerns utility. Goodness in slave morality is whatever is not dangerous to slaves. Good and stupid grow closer together. Noble humans fail to understand vanity. The aristocratic commonwealth is a breeding ground for aristocrats, which noble characteristics pass as acquired traits to their children (Lamarckism). Language depends on shared experience to invest words with meanings. Mixing peoples diminishes linguistic understanding. Thus there is constant heritable pressure creating herd-persons, and a pressure contrary to the emergence of extraordinary individuals. The noble tends to the ruination of his soul. He is masked, and needs to be so. What most separates peoples is their various senses of cleanliness. The four noble virtues are courage, insight, sympathy, and solitude. One writes philosophical books to conceal what one thinks. Man invented "good conscience" so, despite his nature, he could enjoy his own soul. Gods enjoy laughter and could learn some humaneness from humanity.

From High Mountains: Aftersong. Nietzsche indulges a convoluted poem about loneliness and solitude.

Nietzsche, Friedrich, *On The Genealogy of Morals: A Polemic. By way of clarification and supplement to my last book, Beyond Good and Evil. (Zur Genealogie der Moral).* Translated by Douglas Smith. Oxford: Oxford University Press, 1996.

Nietzsche offered On the Genealogy of Morals *as a clarification of* Beyond Good and Evil.

Preface

§1: Humans do not know themselves and this state of affairs is necessarily so.

§2: The subject of this book is the origin of moral prejudices. Philosophers' ideas must be unified and interdependent, not isolated or fragmentary.

§3: The question that has bothered Nietzsche from childhood is the origin of the notions of good and evil. The question became for him another: What caused man to invent the ideas of good and evil? What is their purpose?

§4: Nietzsche's thoughts on good and evil were spurred by his rejection of the theses of Paul Ree's book, The Origin of Moral Sensations (1877). Ree was Nietzsche's friend.

§5: Valuing compassion leads mankind toward great danger, toward a new Buddhism or nihilism. Nietzsche rejects Schopenhauer.

§6: Morality itself (the morality of compassion) may itself be the force that prevents human progress, and "good" men may be a narcotic that by which we live presently at the expense of the future.

§7: No other philosophers have been willing to join Nietzsche in his philosophical views.

§8: Nietzsche's *Zarathustra* and *Beyond Good and Evil* present difficulties in reading. They require a now-lost reading skill: rumination.

First Essay: 'Good and Evil', 'Good and Bad'

§1. The English philosophers are enigmas and are by this fact interesting, unlike their books. They do not seek truth because some truths do not appeal to them.

§2. The English philosophers justify their concept of "good" by reference to utility, forgetting, and habit. Their thought is essentially unhistorical. The "good" was so designated by the powerful and imposed by them upon the common people. There exists an emotional gap between the powerful and the common. There is no necessary connection between good and compassionate action. Only when aristocratic value-judgments declined did the "good equals compassionate" connection grow prevalent.

§3. The English philosophers also err when they argue that the origin of good and evil has been forgotten.

§4. Certain etymological speculations provide Nietzsche with insight into a lost history that supports his view. Words associated with the aristocracy recall "good," while words associated with common people recall "evil" or "badness." This is a fundamental insight.

§5. The etymological argument is fleshed out. The Aryan race was the conqueror of the non-Aryans in Germany, but now finds itself in an inferior position.

§6. Some aristocracies became priestly, which made "everything more dangerous." With the priests, humans became more interesting animals, because the soul became deeper and more evil.

§7. The Jewish priesthood took revenge on the aristocrats by inverting (*transvaluing*) their values. The Jews made the powerless into the good, putting the world as it should be on its head. This is the *slave revolt in morals*, not yet two thousand years old.

§8. The Jewish conspiracy of revenge culminated in Jesus. Cleverly, the Jews rejected him, creating in him a most dangerous bait by which to perfect Israel's *transvaluation of all values*.

§9. Slave morality has won. The church propagated the poison, but has itself become so repellent that it now hinders the progress of the poison.

§10. The slave revolt in morals began when resentment became creative, ordaining values. Slave morality is reactive; aristocratic morality is spontaneous and self-generative. The man of resentment (that is, the slave) does not deal with others uprightly. The slave's soul squints. In the end, slaves must become more clever than aristocrats (the nobles) because slaves practice deceit.

§11. The evil of slave morality is the noble aristocracy. The bad of the aristocracy is an afterthought. The aristocracy is exemplified historically by the Romans, Arabs, Germans, Japanese nobility, Homeric heroes, and Scandinavian Vikings. They have customs among themselves, but in the wilderness are wild, committing a horrific succession of crimes as though they were student pranks. Blonde German animalism is the soul of all the aristocracies. The real goal of culture is to domesticate the noble aristocracies.

§12. The smell of the entrails of a failed soul is worse than any other of life's displeasures. European man goes constantly downhill, becoming more tame. He wearies us—this is nihilism, to be weary of man. Nietzsche prays to see a noble man, a reason to retain faith in mankind.

§13. Nietzsche proffers the memorable analogy of *lambs and eagles* (or large birds of prey). Doing is everything; no "being" exists metaphysically behind the doing. Slave morality argues that eagles can become lambs, and then blames eagles for failing to do so. Slave morality is self-deception, for it makes weakness an incapacity, to which the slave knows no alternative, a path of merit.

§14. The workshop of slave morality (where weakness is transformed into merit) is described. Impotent failure to retaliate becomes goodness; craven fear becomes humility. Submission to those one hates is obedience. Patience is hesitation at the threshold. In the theory of salvation, God beats those whom he most loves. Revenge and hatred are cloaked as justice.

§15. The Kingdom of God and a life lived in faith, hope, and love will require an eternity in compensation, so much is given up in so living. Nietzsche indulges long Latin quotations from Aquinas and Tertullian.

§16. The battle between noble and slave morality has raged for thousands of years. Slave morality has prevailed. Now the battle has been psychologized; noble men fight the inroads of resentment within themselves. The battle is a battle between Rome and the Jews. In Napoleon, a man out of time, the ideal of the noble aristocracy emerged in flesh and blood. Napoleon was a synthesis of the inhuman and the superhuman.

§17. Aristocratic morality, presently in abeyance, will flare up again. We should wish for this most strongly. Nietzsche includes a note to the academic community proposing that it set its program to consider the issues Nietzsche has been raising. His morality challenges the presupposition that good for the many is superior to good for the few. The fundamental task of the philosopher henceforth will be to establish the hierarchy of values.

Second Essay: 'Guilt', 'Bad Conscience', and Related Matters

§1. Man is an animal entitled to make promises. In promising, the healthy operation of active forgetfulness is suspended, and a man exercises a memory of the will. To do so presupposes that man himself has become regular, calculable, and necessary in his future acts.

§2. Man is regularized by the strait-jacket of the morality of custom. When this process has run its course, the sovereign individual results, who is entitled to make promises. The sovereign individual is the ultimate completion of man and he bestows respect or contempt on others. This bestowal is responsibility, and the sovereign individual's instinct for it is his conscience.

§3. The noble conscience is purchased at the price of remembering. The technique of memory is pain. Only what hurts incessantly is remembered. Consider the harshness of ancient punishments. The fruits—reason, seriousness, emotional control—were purchased at tremendous cost.

§4. Bad conscience (or guilt) derives from relationship between creditor and debtor. Guilt (*Schuld*) leads to debt (*Schulden*). There exists an ancient idea of the equivalence of damage done and consequent pain inflicted on the doer.

§5. A promisor pledges something to show the earnestness of his promise. Ultimately, he pledges his body. The creditor accepts this arrangement because, upon default, he gets to exercise the power of the masters—doing evil for the mere pleasure of it. A contract entitles the promise-maker to a right of cruelty.

§6. Breach of contract caused displeasure; the extraordinary pleasure of inflicting suffering on the breacher compensates the injured party. This cruelty was, in ancient times, a part of every festivity. Seeing suffering is exceeded only by causing it; the agony makes a festival.

§7. The progress of slave morality is one of man learning shame. Man learns disgust of life. Man learns to be ashamed of all his instincts, to pinch his nose as he examines himself. The problem of evil and suffering now argues against existence, but in noble morality it argued for life. Suffering causes outrage, not because of the pain, but because of its meaninglessness. Man invented gods so there would be no meaningless or hidden suffering. By inventing gods, man justified his evil. In noble morality, suffering was a show for gods. Philosophers invented free will so that the world would be brimming with plots and subplots and never become tiresome to the gods.

§8. Responsibility and guilt derive from the thinking that accompanies commerce. This may be the earliest form of thinking, and constitutes thinking *per se*. Man is the animal that measures. Society derives from these measuring, economic relations. The great generalization of moral justice, that any debt can be repaid, is the ground of slave morality.

§9. Society and its members are creditor and debtor. The criminal breaks his promise to the community, is cast out, and suffers the fate of a warring outsider.

§10. As society grows more powerful, it reduces punishment for criminals. The measure of a creditor's (society's) wealth is how much harm it can sustain without suffering. So, justice began with the dictum, "Every debt can and must be paid," and it ends with society ignoring the debts of those unable to pay. Justice cancels itself out, as does every good thing on earth. The self-cancellation of justice is grace. And grace is an attribute of noble morality.

§11. Anti-Semitism, especially as stated by Dühring (father of anti-Semitism) is slave morality and resentment. Bad conscience derives from resentment. Justice tempers and diverts the rage of slave morality against the criminal. It does so by establishing law. Life, outside law, naturally operates by means that, within law, would be deemed criminal. Dühring's cliché, that each will must recognize every other will as equal, leads to the destruction and dissolution of man. Equality exhausts man, and leads to nothingness.

§12. Moral theorists have heretofore proceeded naively, believing the current use of a practice reflects its ultimate origin. For example, punishment exists to exact revenge or work deterrence. This theory is false. Everything gets reinterpreted in a process that manipulates past forms to present desires. The *will to power* uses everything to work its own interests. Form and meaning are fluid; they do not signify progress toward a goal. Progress would be to sacrifice the mass of humanity to promote a single stronger species of man. The democratic prejudice against the aristocracy is "misarchism" (Greek for hatred of power). Misarchism leads one to neglect the fact that activity is essential. The will to power reshapes everything; it gives form to life.

§13. To consider a particular example, punishment has enduring customs, but fluid meanings. In Europe, punishment has a synthesis of sometimes contradictory meanings; it is beyond definition. Ideas without actual historical context can be defined. Historical ideas cannot. Nietzsche lists some European meanings of punishment.

§14. Slave morality presumes that punishment creates a sense of guilt (bad conscience) in criminals. This is empirically false. Punishment hardens the criminal. The justice system does to the criminal just what that system punishes the criminal for doing, a fundamental hypocrisy. In prehistory, under noble morality, the aristocrat did not view the criminal as guilty, but only as one who caused harm. The criminal received punishment like a piece of his fate.

§15. Punishment increases fear, inculcates prudence, and urges control of desire. It tames man, but does not make him better. Punishment, insofar as it tames a man, makes him worse.

§16. Bad conscience arises when man's wild instincts are turned by society back upon man himself. Instincts that are not externally vented turn inwards—"soul" develops in man. The great and sinister sickness of this—man's suffering from man, from himself.

§17. The State derived when Germanic aristocrats seized power violently and suddenly. There was no social contract. A living structure of domination was created. This structure crushed the freedom of the slave masses. This repressed mass freedom gave rise to slave morality, the origin of bad conscience.

§18. Slave morality exercises the will to power against itself, psychologically. In aristocrats, the will to power takes others as its object. A slave is voluntarily divided against himself in his complicated and self-defeating motivations. The value of selflessness derives from slave bad conscience.

§19. A sense of obligation to the primordial forefathers of one's race-community grows as the prosperity of the community grows. Ultimately, this growth makes gods of the forefathers.

§20. Empires that seek to be universal seek to impose deities that are universal. For example, Christianity exports global guilt. Atheism may release mankind from guilt, and generate a second innocence.

§21. Bad conscience gets entangled with the concept of god. The growth of guilt, of obligation, to the progenitors (now deified) grows, so the impossibility of compensation becomes plain. So, Christianity had a stroke of genius: God pays himself back, out of love (incredible proposition).

§22. The slave invents an absolute idea—the idea of God and human sin—and proceeds to torture himself with this idea. Man is a sad, insane beast. Slave morality is fixated on this idea, and has lost touch with the animalistic activity. The earth is a mad house.

§23. God-concepts need not defile man, as does the Christian concept. The Greek gods were used to keeping bad conscience at bay.

§24. The West is heir to slave morality, which comprises centuries of self-mutilation of human conscience. Any attempt to reverse this state of affairs may now be impossible. It would require a different kind of spirit, a sublime wickedness, a self-assured intellectual malice, which belongs to great health. This "man of the future" will liberate us from the Christian god and the nihilism that God engenders. He is the Antichrist.

§25. The Antichrist is Zarathustra.

Third Essay: What is the Meaning of Ascetic Ideals?

§1. The meaning of the ascetic idea: for artists, nothing or too much; for philosophers, an instinct for high spirituality; for women, the charming flesh of a pretty animal; for the masses, struggle against pain and boredom by the fiction of being too good for this world. You don't understand. Humans must have goals, even if the goal is nothingness. The will has a horror of vacuum.

§2. Wagner adopted the ascetic ideal at the end of his life (much to Nietzsche's disgust). Wagner inverted himself. Luther's wedding (an unfinished Wagner opera) would have been a disgusting hymn to chastity. Luther himself, however, had the courage of his sensuality, which he called "Protestant freedom." Those who worship chastity are unsuccessful swine. What are these swine to us?

§3. Parsifal (a character in Wagner's opera) frees a king by the power of compassion. Did Wagner want us to take Parsifal seriously? Perhaps Wagner used Parsifal to laugh at himself—this is the height of artistic greatness. But if we take Parsifal seriously, he represents hatred of knowledge, spirit, sensuality, and a return to the sickly ideals of Christianity and obscurantism. The young Wagner preferred Feuerbach's healthy sensuality to the blood of the redeemer.

§4. The artist must be separated from his work. An artist is not his work. Parsing the psychological origin of artistic works is vivisection of the spirit. An artist is the womb or manure in which a work of art grows. As with pregnancy, the bloating and pain must be forgotten before the child can be enjoyed. So, an artist is a step back from reality. Homer is not Achilles; Goethe is no Faust. The artistic whim is to reach over into the real. Parsifal (for Wagner) was one such fateful and disastrously misleading reach.

§5. Artists are the valets of men of true conviction. For example, Wagner is subservient to Schopenhauer. What does it mean when a true aristocrat like Schopenhauer acclaims the ascetic ideal? Wagner adopted Schopenhauer because the latter elevated music theoretically. Music was, to Schopenhauer, the most authentic and original of the arts. It spoke the language of will itself. And so, the musician rose in value too suddenly. The musician became the ventriloquist of God, speaking metaphysics. The ascetic ideal could not be far behind.

§6. Kant defines the beautiful as what pleases without interest. This is consistent with Kant's emphasis on impersonality and universal validity. But this thought, adopted by Schopenhauer is grossly off-track. To Schopenhauer, the beautiful suppresses desire and interest. Stendahl shows Schopenhauer's error. Stendahl says that beauty arouses the will. So to answer his question [of §3:5: What does it mean when a true aristocrat acclaims the ascetic ideal?], a philosopher who praises the ascetic ideal wishes to be freed from a form of torture.

§7. Philosophers have affection for the ascetic ideal, so much so that married philosophers are a study in comedy. A philosopher who affirms the ascetic ideal merely affirms himself as a philosopher. He is not denying his existence. He is making the world safe for him and his philosopher kind.

§8. Nietzsche considers philosophers. They value the ascetic not as a negation, but as freedom to be themselves, undisturbed by the world's concerns. They are leashed dogs, one and all. Philosophers dislike hatreds and friendships. They avoid big words and Truth, which they find boastful. Their chastity is seeking fertility in the spirit, in making the world think like them. Philosophers disdain their worldly existence, preferring universals. Schopenhauer fits this model. But he was wrong.

§9. Philosophy needed the ascetic ideal to find its self-confidence. Having found confidence, it learned pride, and taught it to the whole world. We are proud toward God, whom we view as a spider weaving his moral web behind causality. We are even proud toward ourselves, dissecting our souls. Good things now were previously bad; sins have become virtues.

§10. Philosophers, and the contemplative spirit generally, have throughout the ages been compelled to conceal themselves from the culture. They have disguised themselves in the form of the spiritual man of an earlier age: the shaman, priest, prophet, magician, and even the ascetic ideal. Philosophers have even come to believe the ascetic ideal, since they were forced to represent and believe it. Without doing so, their existence was not possible. But they were caterpillars. Have things changed? Is there enough boldness and spiritual will now for the philosophers to spread their bright and dangerous wings on the earth?

§11. The ascetic priest helps us understand the essay's question: What is the meaning of ascetic ideals? The ascetic ideal is a bridge from this life to another existence, calling one to retrace this life's path back to the point of beginning. Seen from outside, the ascetic ideal leads one to assume all earthly life dwells in profound frustration and disappointment concerning life as a whole, and derives pleasure only from its own pain. The ascetic priest does not reproduce biologically, and yet life itself does not let the ascetic priests die out. Ascetic priesthood serves life itself. Ascetic priests seek not to control a piece of life, but life itself. They deny life, and replace it with a jealous atrophy, pain, self-mutilations. Ascetic priests imagine their agonies are triumphs. *"Crux, nux, lux"* (Cross, nothingness, light): the ascetic priest holds all as one.

§12. If one could induce an ascetic priest to philosophize, he would seek error. For example, Vedanta (Indian) philosophy denies subject and object, pain, and diversity. They are wrong. Kant argues that the only way to know the "intelligible character of things" is to note that it lies entirely beyond our grasp. It is good to see differently, because this prepares one for objectivity. But objectivity is not disinterested daydreaming, but rather gathering arguments for and against to be deployed as weapons. Philosophers must abandon their old view of objectivity with its observer without perspective. Perspectival seeing and knowing are the only kinds of seeing and knowing that exist. The more perspectives the better. To suspend perspectives (feeling) is to castrate the intellect.

§13. Paradoxically, the ascetic priest, in his negation of life, is attempting to protect himself by desperate means. Why is the ascetic priest sick? He has abandoned his essence. He was destined for courage and wonder, but now wallows in despondent disinterest.

§14. What is of greatest concern is that the ascetic priest's disgust and compassion will breed, producing global nihilism. This could happen now. Everything has the smell of the asylum, the hospital. Weak people greatly undermine life. They poison an aristocrat's trust in life, in himself. Weak people conspire against the well-constituted man, whom they hate. Women in particular are unsurpassed in their refinement of sickness. Everywhere the sick wrestle the healthy. The sick's favorite sound is righteous indignation. They seek to make the aristocrat doubt his right to good fortune and feel disgrace. The sick should not infect the healthy.

§15. The ascetic priest exists to tend to the sickly. Such ministration cannot be the task of the healthy, the aristocrat. The ascetic priest defends the herd, for he can summon contempt more easily than hatred. The ascetic priest wounds before he heals, and then poisons the wound before binding it. In the herd's desire to have its pain anaesthetized lies the root of the ascetic ideal. The herd says, Someone must be to blame for the fact that I do not feel well. And the ascetic priest enters the scene to say, That is correct. The cause of your sickness is you yourself. Thus is the direction of the herd's resentment changed from outward to inward.

§16. Life itself has a healing instinct, and it inoculated the world to some degree from the ascetic priests by destroying them through themselves. Human sinfulness is not a fact, but an interpretation of facts, as is spiritual suffering.

§17. Is the ascetic priest a physician? No, he only combats the sick man's listlessness, not the causes of it. Christianity anesthetizes. All the great religions struggle against listlessness of epidemic proportions. The listlessness is physiological, the result of miscegenation of races, classes, climate, racial old age, blood-poisoning, malaria, syphilis, and so forth, but is treated only psychologically and morally. This is in fact what a religion is and does. Religion depresses life and makes consciousness impossible. Buddhist and Indian religions urge a state beyond good and evil.

§18. The priestly ascetic also prescribes for listlessness a resort to the work. Mechanical activity can occupy a person's mind wholly. Also, the priestly ascetics organize the herd's instinct to congregate. The strong tend to disperse and join forces only with reticence. The weak congregate naturally.

§19. The means of ameliorating the listlessness of the herd so far discussed have been honest. We now turn to the guilty means: excess of emotion. How can an excess of emotion be generated? Only by dishonest lies. The honest liar knows he lies. The ascetic priest lies to all, especially himself.

§20. The ascetic ideal influences even the philosopher to mistrust himself. Florid and voluminous emotion alleviates listlessness. The ascetic priest harnesses such emotions like a "pack of wild dogs." Such excesses provide only temporary relief, each such treatment serves only to make the patient sicker. The ascetic priest generates emotional excess by manipulation of guilt. The parishioner's listlessness lifts temporarily while being castigated for his sins, and so he cries for more and more agony.

§21. Excess of emotion tames, weakens, discourages, pampers, and emasculates a person. It spreads physical illness: ruined nervous system, epilepsy, paralysis, depression, hysteria, somnambulism, death-wishes. The ascetic ideal's imposition of sin, and the emotional explosions that attend it, are a ruinous European pandemic.

§22. The ascetic priest ruins not only the physiology, but also the mind. Consider the New Testament. Nietzsche has no love for it, for its characters are weak. In the Old Testament, one encounters great men, heroic deeds, strong hearts. New Testament figures vomit their inner stupidities, and imagine intimacies with God. Luther found the church insufficiently German. He wanted to talk directly to God, and he did so. The ascetic ideal lacks good manners, because it flees moderation.

§23. The ascetic ideal has ruined many other things besides physiology and mind, but that is beyond the scope of this work. Why has an effective opposition ideal not risen to fight the ascetic ideal? Nietzsche says he is terrified. Some suggest that science is such an opposition ideal. But science has no self-confidence. Science is an elevated form of the ascetic ideal. Scientists should be shaken to consciousness.

§24. Are the anti-cultural freethinkers the opposition ideal? First, they are believers, not in God, but in their ideals. Belief establishes a probability of illusion. Believing in truth leads to the ascetic ideal. For in the ascetic ideal, which has dominated philosophy for so long, God is metaphysically the truth, and the truth is divine. But God may be our most ancient lie. If one denies the ascetic ideal, not as the cultural freethinkers do, but in fact, then a new problem comes to the fore: what then is the value of truth? The value of truth must be called into question.

§25. Science is not the opposition to the ascetic ideal. Science aids the ascetic. The two have the same foundation: an overestimation of the value of truth, the conviction that truth itself need not be questioned. Art is a better candidate for the opposition to the ascetic ideal, though some artists corrupt themselves by serving the ascetic ideal with their works. Science can itself be viewed as a problem, What is the meaning of science? Science, by dethroning man from the center of all things, has made his spiritual needs even greater, further diminishing man's self-respect. Kant severed the transcendentalists from theology, for which they thank him heartily. But the transcendentalists themselves, worshipping the great question mark in their agnosticism, nevertheless serve the ascetic ideal, depreciating man.

§26. Is modern historiography a spirit opposing the ascetic ideal? No, it is ascetic and even nihilistic. It is dominated by armchair blowhards who disgust, offend, and try one's patience. Nietzsche has great respect for the ascetic ideal, provided the proponent honestly believes it. These scholars merely pretend. They excite the herd sentiments of the people, and stultify the German mind.

§27. So, we leave the search for the opposition ideal. The only enemy of the ascetic ideal is the man who pretends this ideal without really holding it, for those people make others suspicious. We call it atheism where the spirit works against the ascetic ideal. But even atheism is not the opposition, for it still seeks truth, and so is one of the final forms of the ascetic ideal. What will destroy the ascetic ideal? What defeated the Christian God? Christian morality defeats itself. Christian truth draws one conclusion after another, and now draws its final conclusion—against itself.

§28. Apart from the ascetic ideal, man has no meaning, a condition from which man suffers. Meaninglessness, not suffering, troubles mankind. The ascetic ideal gave suffering a meaning. As such, the ascetic ideal saved the human will from self-destructive nihilism. But the will which the ascetic ideal saved is the will to nothingness. A man prefers to will oblivion than nothing at all.

CHAPTER 6
JESUS

LADY JUSTICE, JUSTICIA, GOES TO HER FIFTH PSYCHIATRIC APPOINTMENT. *When Justicia enters, a pungent, dark-skinned, oily man sits in worn peasant clothes, waiting for Justicia. His eyes lock on hers, and a subtle smile tickles his face. The man rises and kisses Justicia's cheek. Oddly, his gesture seems appropriate. Justicia sits.*

JESUS: I was elsewhere. Now, I am here. I do not know why.

JUSTICIA: This is my psychiatric appointment. You are here to help me. Did you not read the previous sessions' notes?

JESUS: I am a peasant. I cannot read. I do not write. Are you unwell, Justicia?

JUSTICIA: Not exactly. I am confused. Ummm. No, that is not entirely correct either. I am troubled in my heart, by an absence, an ache. I can tell I am missing something, but cannot put my finger on exactly what that something is.

JESUS: I have observed the hearts of friends closely. Perhaps that is why I am here. Tell me of your heart.

JUSTICIA: I am a statue, just carved rock. But I also dwell in every person's feelings. So, a lot of folks' agendas get attached to me. I get confused over what I am about, in my deepest self. I feel like I am missing something. I have my toga, the sword of retribution, the blindfold of impartiality, and the scales of equity. But a piece is missing.

JESUS: Tell me what bothers you most.

JUSTICIA: That's a good question. I am most bothered when I peek from behind my blindfold and it seems that my sword falls more heavily on poor people than rich, more on dark people than white, more on men than women, and more on immigrants than citizens. I am also bothered when I find heavy little magnets on the bottom of my scales with the names of gigantic businesses on them, making my scales tip against common people. I remove those magnets fastidiously, but they just keep showing up. Oh, yes. I am nonplussed when god and I get saddled with drumming up rationale for the most recent war.

Jesus laughs.

JESUS: You have not changed, Justicia. You are exactly as I remember you from Palestine.

JUSTICIA: We knew each other? In the Middle East?

JESUS: You were younger then. King Herod kept you locked in his closet, and made you dance for his friends. But we spoke. I met you by the River Jordan when you were having a walk. My friend John introduced us. We spoke of deep things.

JUSTICIA: I am embarrassed. I have utterly forgotten this exchange. Forgive me. What did you tell me?

JESUS: I told you what I believed at the time. I told you that things will never be right in your heart until a new world breaks into this one. The world must be transformed. Only unimaginable power could work such a change. I thought the big event would happen on my watch. Then I thought it would come to pass just after I died. It turns out I was wrong.

The black box of conscience slides open. Judas Iscariot stands, a six-inch simulacrum of a man whose neck is slightly askew. "I told you. You were wrong, Jesus. You could have ruled Jerusalem, if you had encouraged Peter's sword. Instead, you let those bastard Romans crucify you. How did that help? With you gone, we disciples were useless. It all came to nothing. I checked out early. I was the only wise one." *Jesus nods and settles Judas back in the box.*

JESUS: Judas is right, at least partly. But he lacks faith, except for his faith in coercion.

Jesus sighs.

JUSTICIA: I am remembering bits of our conversation at the Jordan now. You said something about the poor being in charge.

JESUS: Yes. Hearts matter most. People who have suffered have the best hearts. They shine. They make the world taste better. If broken people were in charge of human relations, you would have a better time of it, Justicia. Humans would find sympathy and give compassion. Humans would kill and brutalize less often. Judas was so very wrong in his convictions. One cannot compel good faith by cunning and murder. The future belongs to peacemakers and those who seek forgiveness. Money and frenzy and public praise ruled the past. The future I value belongs to humble people. One wins this battle by patient non-violent resistance. One can wield good faith as a sword.

> **JUSTICE IS:**
>
> HEARTFELT
> DIVINE
> INTERVENTION.

JUSTICIA: That sounds so right to me. But your kingdom has not happened. Aren't you a tad disappointed?

JESUS: No. I was wrong about timing. I may yet be vindicated. We will see, eh?

A muffled voice from the black box of conscience hollers, "Naivete. Damned foolishness."

JESUS: Judas could be right. Still, I hope.

Jesus wept.

Justicia turns to comfort Jesus, but the Palestinian has vanished.

Jesus, the Galilean.   An excerpt from Lancaster, *Gethsemane Soliloquy: An Epitome of the Reliable Sayings of Jesus*, Shoreline, Washington: St. George's Hill Press, 2017.

Yeshua, known to most westerners as Jesus, profoundly changed the Roman Empire. Yeshua's ongoing influence, through advocacy by and opposition to the church, is global. Since Yeshua wrote nothing, we lean upon the church's transmission of Yeshua's message, which has, more than infrequently, lacked care and evidenced disregard for Yeshua's historical legacy. The lengthy essay, Gethsemane Soliloquy, *takes up the challenge of sorting the reliable from unreliable sayings of Yeshua in the New Testament's synoptic gospels. Here, I present only my epitome of what Yeshua taught, having removed from the tradition sayings I deem unreliable.*

In Gethsemane on the night before his execution, Yeshua implored his disciples to watch with him. They napped instead. What might Yeshua have said to his somnolent peasant companions?

THE GETHSEMANE SOLILOQUY

Slumber. So much weakness, my friends. You sleep; events crash over you, heedless. It has been so from the beginning. Even now, you do not grasp the good news. The kingdom of God is upon us, breaking into this world. In our work together, we have ushered the kingdom's leading edge: the sick are well, the lame walk, the dead rise, the possessed are freed, sins are forgiven. Yahweh is about to right the scales of justice and invert our diseased social order. I am to be his strong right hand in so doing. I am the Son of man of the prophet Daniel's vision.

I know you have wished I were a messiah. You would have me mount an insurrection and throw off our odious Roman yoke. You aim too low, my friends. You would shed blood for nominal gains. You would have more of the same, only more to your liking. You would be satisfied with mere political retribution. The onrushing kingdom of God is not an earthly dominion. The Son of man is no mere messiah. Yahweh's kingdom is a realm where the words of peaceful men crush the wiles of the violent. It is a kingdom that rewards those who give all. In the kingdom, the weak find power and the low find exaltation. The arsenal of the kingdom is the heart, not the sword. Let nothing hinder you. Give yourselves utterly to Yahweh's inbreaking kingdom. Hear me! Perhaps you would do so, if only you were awake.

Vindication. Tonight, if Judas's absence is as I suspect, I will suffer torments fashioned by my religious enemies. Take a deep breath. Be unafraid. Stoke your patience. Yahweh will act to vindicate me. If I am muzzled, stones will shout. If I am bound, my shackles will crumble. Even if this body dies, my Father will resurrect it. Yahweh's kingdom is inexorable. We shall meet again. Then I shall exercise Yahweh's power. Doubt will flee. Faithless men shall perish. The repentant shall prevail.

Kingdom. The kingdom of God is not a bigger and better version of human empires. The kingdom of God shatters what has been. The kingdom of God is Yahweh's square peg in humanity's round hole. Human rulers marshal armies and erect earthworks. In a day, fields are strewn with the dead and realms are won or lost. The kingdom of God is otherwise. It starts tiny, hidden, beneath notice. Yahweh's kingdom is like a tiny mustard seed that becomes, once grown, a gigantic bush. In the end, God's kingdom overwhelms utterly, transforming all things. God's kingdom is yeast in a loaf. Unseen, it changes everything from within. In the kingdom, even fruit trees bear out of season.

The kingdom of God takes for its army the human heart; its razor weapons are compassionate action, forthright speech, and resilience. We, in our wanderings, have taken the good news of the kingdom of God to all the Jews of Galilee and Judea. Yahweh intends, however, to take as his citizens any who demonstrate confidence in Yahweh, and reject any who lack that faith. Yahweh's kingdom is bursting its Jewish container. All faithful persons, Jew and gentile alike, will be gathered in my harvest. All chaff will be consumed in fire. A new world dawns.

Do not worry. I have chosen you. You will not die before you see this kingdom of God in its glory. You will see me exercising divine power as Son of man. You will stand beside me, as will all poor, maimed, downtrodden, blind, lame, broken-hearted, peacemaking, diseased, faithful disciples. Yahweh's kingdom is a peasant movement. Be proud to be part of it. Seize it for yourself now. Do not delay. For Yahweh's kingdom thunders toward us with breathtaking rapidity. Do not be overtaken unawares!

John.   John announced Yahweh's judgment at the Jordan River. He baptized for the forgiveness of sins, and ignored Temple sacrifices. Yahweh cherishes repentant sinners. I am wholly aligned with John. Yahweh sent John. Yahweh bypassed the Temple and its religious authorities. It would perhaps be more accurate to say that Yahweh, tasting their vile perversions, spat the Temple and its functionaries from his mouth. Those vipers have hidden their evils; they skulk in shadows. They make their students worse than themselves. Yahweh will expose them. Their sins will be broadcast to all. Then they will be consumed in divine fire.

Hearts.   Yahweh wants your hearts. All men violate God's laws in some way. Only hatred of Yahweh himself will not be forgiven. Many believe that if they comply with religious laws, Yahweh will love them. They are wrong. Yahweh loves pure hearts. God wants mercy more than compliance, and generosity more than alms. All sins emerge from distorted hearts. That is how men become putrid within. Their visible sins reflect ugliness of heart. People proud of their religiosity are the worst: they pray so others can see, they give to be praised for generosity, and they fast for publicity. Do not imitate them. Pray privately, simply, and quietly. Give in secret; don't even take note of your generosity in your own mind. To do so is dangerous. Fast invisibly. Stay focused on your heart. Introspect. Measure your words; do not blurt. Putrid hearts are easy to come by; pure hearts require some attention to detail. A man's heart is a tree; taste its fruit to know the man. No price is too great when purchasing a pure heart. In the economy of God, to lose much is to gain all.

To know Yahweh is to drown in your inadequacy. Humble people let their inner putrefaction drain away as they cling to God. Humble people become salt, making life tasty. The kingdom of God belongs to people who embrace their inadequacy. This humility comes more easily to people who cannot equivocate their shortcomings. God's kingdom brims with poor people, mourners, quiet persons, people who show mercy, peacemakers, people who ask questions and seek God, people who seek forgiveness readily, people who give to children, people who are persecuted, repentant tax collectors and whores, people who forgive readily, children, people of childlike simplicity, and people who rely upon God for daily needs. These persons are more likely to have hearts pleasing to Yahweh. A man of pure heart builds his life on a solid rock; putrid-hearted men build on sand. The inwardly-ugly will be washed away in the onrushing cataclysm of the kingdom.

Some matters pose grave risks to your heart. Learn the pressing dangers of anxiety, money, talking, and clamor.

Anxiety.   Avoid anxiety about food and houses and clothing. Yahweh knows your needs. He cares for all creatures. How much more God cares for you! Stay focused in the present. Of tomorrow you know little and control less. Ask God, confident of his affection. Wait patiently.

Money.   Love of money pollutes a clean heart. Hearts follow desire. Riches tempt one to forsake God in favor of self-assertion. Those who amass wealth already have their reward. Do not aggregate possessions or envy others' things. To love money is to hate God. Wealth is transient; God is immutably forever. If you need excess, hoard joy in God. Yahweh rejects the rich. They have no place in his kingdom. Avoid wealth. If you suffer the misfortune of having wealth, give it away. Stay poor. Keep your heart safe.

Talk. The voice exposes the heart. Never boast. If you find yourself boasting, start over again cleaning out your heart. Your spirituality is plastic; what was once in good shape can again become distorted. Beware! All are inclined to pretend more than is true. Just do what I tell you. Let your life do your talking.

Clamor. Remember! When things get tough or we reach a critical juncture, I go to the wilderness or a mountain and spent time alone. Noise erodes the heart. Quiet restores it.

Suffering. The world gushes suffering like a ruptured pipe. Yahweh relieves suffering as a sign of the inbreaking kingdom. I have healed, exorcized, and repaired sufferers. So too have you, my friends. Still, many more suffer than we have helped. Faith heals. Encourage faith. Pray Yahweh will hasten the kingdom, where suffering of innocents shall cease.

Opponents. Do not emulate evil people. Those who think themselves right with God usually are not. If a person proclaims his righteousness, he stinks to Yahweh. Evil people clamor to lead, but cannot see the way themselves. Religious hypocrites are the worst. To mislead others, they utter words that would please Yahweh, were the words issuing from pure hearts. Religious hypocrites impose convoluted religious rules of their own invention, but ignore those very rules themselves. Evil people do not care about the suffering they propagate. Their doubts about Yahweh lead them to demand signs and omens. They ridicule obvious good when it suits their purposes. Evil people make others sin by discouraging and misguiding them. Evil people will be damned for that! Always, evil people corral money. Jerusalem authorities have remodeled Yahweh's Temple into a livestock trading pit. I went to the Temple and kicked over money changer tables, preached a fiery sermon, and brought Temple functions to a halt for a brief period. Temple spirituality is deficient; if you cannot surpass Temple righteousness, you will never enter the kingdom of God.

Evil people ensnare opponents in word tangles. Evil people are never satisfied in their intellectual wrangling; they flip-flop for convenience and without blushing. Corrupt authorities seek to exercise control as though such belonged to them and not to Yahweh. Evil people are, with respect to God, usurpers. They demand animals to kill, thinking themselves meticulously obedient by so doing. Meanwhile, Yahweh demands mercy and justice and faith, all flowing from pure hearts. He is ignored. Evil people accuse people who do good of stinking motives. Evil people think themselves favored by Yahweh. Whores and Roman soldiers will enter the kingdom of God first, and the Temple establishment last, if at all. Theirs is a perilous position. Jerusalem authorities hate prophets; they murder them. It has always been so. Now they intend to kill me, or so I expect. Yahweh will dismantle the Jerusalem authorities and their Temple. Nothing on Temple mount shall stand when the kingdom breaks over it.

Confront evil people. You do not need to seek them out, but when evil people accost you, speak plainly and truthfully. Do not fear calling them disparaging names, provided the names suit them. Do not let your anger rule you, but use your anger to make your voice unmistakable. You have seen me confront opponents over and over. Speak to them frankly. If they plan evil for you, receive those evils humbly. Ask the evildoer if he would prefer another stab at you. If they steal from you, offer them more from your wallet and do not ask for reimbursement. If you are pressed into forced labor, do twice as much as demanded. In the end, love evil people, as you would yourself wish to be loved. Doing so leaves their hearts to stew. Some may change their paths, which would be a great joy for Yahweh. But if not, you have shielded your own heart from their reeking vomit.

Recognize evil people without judging them. One's vision blurs when examining one's own sins, but grows telescopic inspecting the faults of others. To avoid judging evildoers demands balance. One must recognize evil people to avoid following them. One must recognize evil people to confront them. But yours is not to condemn. Yahweh judges. Speak plainly to evildoers of their deeds. Keep your heart from slamming the door on perpetrators.

Unanticipated repentance remains possible. Barring that, God will judge soon enough. Their damnation lies beyond those concerns appropriate to humble, open-hearted seekers of Yahweh.

Law. Give political governments what they ask for, if the request is indifferent. Reserve your heartfelt loyalty for the kingdom of God. Among political persons, much evil resides. Know you may be called to confront that evil.

Religious governments are much more dangerous. In Jerusalem, they preserve Yahweh's laws, but hedge them all around with manmade prescriptions and pointless distinctions. Keep God's law; break human law when necessary. Remember! As the Son of man ushers in the kingdom of God, Yahweh's law will fall to the wayside, utterly fulfilled.

One must find some perspective about divine law. When God says, Keep the Sabbath holy, does he mean that one cannot do good on the Sabbath? No. The Sabbath exists to help, not injure, man. One is free to work hard on the Sabbath doing good, despite Temple rules.

Men cannot bind or release divine law. Even with a Temple-sanctioned divorce, one has not ceased to fornicate when he remarries. God binds marital partners. Man cannot unbind them. The law forbids murder. The kingdom, however, demands more. Anger is heart-murder; so too, impudent insults. Lust is heart-adultery. Swearing is abusive god-mongering; just say "yes" or "no." Do not let conflicts lie. Resolving disputes matters more than Temple compliance. Honor your parents. No priest can relieve you of that obligation. Look within. Who loves God more?--the Jew who keeps divine ordinances, or the gentile who saves a crime victim's life? This is no easy question. Do both.

All the hundreds of rules in the Torah boil down to two: Love Yahweh wholly, and your neighbor as yourself. God sees every person individually. He embraces the sacrifice of a poor person donating a pittance. He scoffs at the ostentatious largesse of the rich.

You will experience this change of perspective regarding the law as a violent upheaval. That it is!

Mission. You have walked with me from Capernaum, around Galilee, and south, up to Jerusalem. We have seen remarkable healings and exorcisms, announced the kingdom, encouraged repentance, confronted opponents, and loved one another. We have had good days and bad days. Capernaum scoffed at us. Five thousand picnickers cheered our message. If you have been paying attention at all (which is not in evidence tonight), you know that Yahweh sent me on this mission. I called you to join me.

You noticed that my understanding of our task changed midstream. When we began at Galilee's lakeside, I believed that I would preach and train you. When I sent you out to the countryside without me, I expected a great groundswell of enthusiasm to erupt. Yahweh would act, so I thought. The kingdom would roll over us, and I would be installed as Son of man in the clouds with power. But you went and returned. Believe me, you did well! Still, Yahweh checked his divine hand. I struggled to understand, and slowly understanding dawned. I saw that the Son of man must suffer, as did Isaiah's suffering servant, as did the prophets, as did John. Only then is the Son of man qualified to supervise the kingdom of God. I surmised that my tormentors would be Jerusalem authorities. I resigned myself to my restated role, though not without my own measure of objections and trepidation. You, however, did not receive this mission revision politely. Peter, you corrected me, and I rebuffed you. Judas harbored his disappointment, and tonight seeks to compel me toward a messianic insurrection which he imagines preferable. He is wrong, but cannot be deterred, if I read Judas aright.

So, the time is upon us. I will suffer. You will fear and flee in disarray. But then, the kingdom will arrive in power. I will call you to myself.

I remind you now of other matters we have discussed in the course of our travels and work with the poor of the land.

Preaching. Our mission is to tell people about the kingdom of God. Its time is now. That is why I left home. That is why you left your fields and nets and families, and followed me. We just tell people the news. What happens after that is a matter for them to work out. We are lamps in darkness. When we go places, we let people know what we need. If they welcome us, we stay. If not, we leave. We do not coerce. Do not worry about money as you go on your way. Yahweh provides. So long as you follow me, you will have no permanent home. You must teach others to announce the news. The harvest needs workers.

Family. This journey is a demanding one. Every fellow traveler must realign priorities. Families and jobs must take second place. The family of God has become our first task. When your father or mother needs burial, you may not be able to help dig. If your family disapproves of your choice to follow, let that be. The kingdom brings conflict aplenty. You must stay focused on the kingdom. That may mean that you never have sex again. That may mean you seldom parent your children. You give up nothing when you follow me that Yahweh will not more than compensate.

Rest. We have rested along the way when necessary. We have also sought solitude.

Competitors. Those who heal in the name of the kingdom, leave them be. But do not be fooled. Only those who are with us are with us.

Honors. Some of you have requested honors. Honors, in the kingdom, belong to those who serve. Have you been paying attention?

Forgiveness. Set no limit to forgiveness. When a brother sins, confront him. When he repents, forgive him. Just keep forgiving and forging onward.

Children. Children matter. They always have access to me. Open your arms to children. In Yahweh's kingdom, all citizens resemble children.

Giving. Give freely. Do not ask for terms or reimbursement. If someone asks, give.

Discipleship. Your path will be mine; prepare to suffer. Yahweh has linked glory and suffering inextricably. You will be disparaged. Find encouragement in one another.

Prayer. I have often prayed. Do so yourselves. Find a quiet place and immerse yourself in Yahweh. Pray also with others. Yahweh hears. Persistence matters. Faith and persistence move mountains.

Sadness. I have been sad, even tonight. I have asked Yahweh to grant me a different path. He has not done so. I accept that outcome. Shortly, Yahweh will vindicate our faith and suffering. I shall overcome whatever our opponents do to me. Have faith.

Now I must be going. Wake, friends!

Judas, is that you, there in the shadows?

CHAPTER 7
CONFUCIUS

LADY JUSTICE, JUSTICIA, GOES TO HER SIXTH PSYCHIATRIC APPOINTMENT. *When Justicia enters, a ramrod straight-backed Chinese man, impeccably dressed in fine silks, waits. His long salt-and-pepper hair has been pulled severely to the back of his head, and dangles in a braided queue. The gentleman rises and bows silently. His hand subtly points to the divan for Justicia.*

CONFUCIUS: I am K'ung Ch'iu of a venerable Chinese family. Your people call me Confucius.

Justicia lays her blindfold, sword, and scales on the floor next to her divan. She reclines, sighing.

JUSTICIA: You wrote *The Analects*? The work is still widely read. You're famous.

CONFUCIUS: I am humbled. I must note, gracious lady, that my students wrote most of that book. My <u>fame</u> is perhaps now limited to fortune cookies. As during my life, most who read me, forget me.... I have perused your session notes, though there were none from that peasant, Jesus. Tell me how this process is going for you so far.

JUSTICIA: Jesus urged me to hope that Yahweh of Israel, his god, will intervene dramatically to set straight the jumbled pieces of this fractured world. I guess I have to say, I am just not that religious.... It seems to me that righting the global social world is a messy job that belongs to the human community. Their greatest challenge, actually. Mankind is presently wandering dazed in a bramble of ill-deliberated change and rampant overpopulation. Malthus vindicated.

CONFUCIUS: I agree. Why do you focus on human conduct, Justicia?

JUSTICIA: Because humans control conduct, at least to some extent. Humans do not command earthquakes, the sun's diurnal transit, the generational cycle of butterflies, or even the price of tea in China. Forces beyond us govern those. But, at least occasionally, humans control their actions. I focus on doing the do-able. On good days, humans can choose useful new conduct, and by diligent practice embed new habits.

CONFUCIUS: I see. Tell me more. *Confucius strokes his sparse chin hairs.*

JUSTICIA: All modern societies have grown ponderous and impersonal. Institutions crush meaningful community life in favor of supposed efficiency. We compel people to waste away performing robotic economic activity. Families have shrunk--from vibrant bushes brimming with third cousins and laughing uncles, to hard-pruned nuclear husband-wife-children bonsais, to scraggly single-parent-family poles, and now to lone people living in twiggish isolation. Humans must redirect themselves.... How do you see these matters, Confucius?

CONFUCIUS: In my time, I urged all to seek heaven's path. A man strives to grow benevolent, to tame himself for insight and utility, and to stop being small. One honors one's parents. One performs rites punctiliously. I taught....

The black box of conscience, on the coffee table next to Confucius, creaks open. Another dignified Chinese man stands, barely topping six inches. "I am Mo, a student of Confucius a century after his death. With all due deference, I do not see matters as does my esteemed Master. One owes filial devotion not just to one's parents and one's own elders, but to all mankind. What matters is not so much what is just and right, but love. Heaven requires that our love should lack boundaries. Honor and esteem must extend to all. I apologize for my hubris in contradicting you, Master." *Mo bows and sits. The ebony lid closes over him.*

CONFUCIUS: Mo may be right. I worry, however, that love of all may become esteem for none. Still, I never really questioned the class structure of my time. To honor men of lower classes....

JUSTICIA: And women?

CONFUCIUS: Now you push me too far. Women are...

JUSTICIA: Never mind. Mo interrupted you. Please continue. How would you have me make the world just?

CONFUCIUS: In my time I would have advised: Your rulers have lost the Mandate of Heaven. Small men repress gentlemen of benevolence and insight, seizing control of matters for which the small are ill-equipped. So, the people suffer. One must rely on the best people. The gentleman helps others find and do the good; small men seek profit. Deeds count more than words. Care for and esteem your elders. Perform those tasks the culture deems worthy. Seek *jen*, which is human-heartedness, benevolence, virtue, love, magnanimity. Cling to what is good in the past. Embrace the helpful new thing. Spit out evil. Be wise enough to recognize each when you encounter it.

> **JUSTICE IS:**
>
> GENTLEMEN
> RULING
> BENEVOLENTLY.

JUSTICIA: You are sage. The Chinese kings must have valued you greatly.

CONFUCIUS: Regrettably, my kings rejected me. I hoped they might seek my counsel. But, alas, I was reduced to eking my living from students' fees.... Back to you. The session notes indicate you are seeking companionship.

JUSTICIA: I once thought so. But this psychoanalysis is teaching me. The absence I feel lies within me. A consort will not help. I must fill my gaps myself. So, I am searching.

CONFUCIUS: As are we all. I see our time is up.

Justicia gathers her sword, scales, and blindfold. She hikes her jeans up stony hips, and departs.

Confucius (K'ung Ch'iu). *Analects* (Lun yü). Translated by D. C. Lau. London: Penguin Books Ltd., 1979.

Confucius (K'ung Ch'iu) (551-479 B.C.) was a Chinese political theorist and teacher of a social ethic. The Analects is a book of aphorisms, compiled by students of Confucius. It consists in twenty short chapters, each of which contains various sayings of the Master or his more important students.

How does the *gentleman* differ from the *small man*? The gentleman knows the Way (*tao*) and virtue (*te*), and seeks to perfect his own character, to be as good a man as possible. The small man knows his own profit and much anxiety. The gentleman is above all *benevolent*, seeking goodness for its own sake and working for the benefit of others. Different dangers plague the various periods of life: in youth, feminine beauty; in middle age, bellicosity; in old age, acquisitiveness. But where the gentleman seeks to grow in benevolence throughout life, increasing age brings increasing self-mastery. These things help the gentleman grow in benevolence: the rites (where those rites may have merit), music, excellent friends who are virtuous, trustworthy, and knowledgeable, knowing and keeping within one's limitations, circumspection in one's language, balance in one's opinions, and constant learning. The gentleman does not impose on others what he himself does not desire. (Book XV, §24.) The obligation to love others decreases as one's intimacy with persons diminishes. The obligation to love declines as one moves from family, to neighbors, to fellow villagers, to members of one's own class, and finally to members of other classes. The gentleman exhibits flexible intelligence, inquisitiveness, courage, a thirst to question and learn (especially about himself and his short-comings), self-restraint, even-handedness with others, tolerance, trustworthiness, and an orientation toward action. Ultimately, a gentleman must enter government office, and there be a moral beacon by working for the welfare of the common people. The welfare of commoners is the measure of a ruler. None of Confucius's teaching is innovative, according to Confucius. He merely transmits what antiquity taught him.

CHAPTER 8
MOSES

LADY JUSTICE, JUSTICIA, GOES TO HER SEVENTH PSYCHIATRIC APPOINTMENT. *Justicia arrives early, to find an empty office. From nowhere appears a wild-haired irascible little man of piercing eyes. A smell of burnt flesh wafts with his pungent body odor. Justicia begins to sit, but the hoary oracle gestures for the marble icon to remain standing. Moses juts his hands over his head. Loud Hebrew bursts from his mouth. His blessing complete, the prophet points where Justicia is to sit. She removes her sword, and stashes her blindfold and scales near her feet. The black box of conscience sits on the coffee table next to Israel's divinator.*

MOSES: I have read your file. You have been talking with some tremendously confused people. Small wonder your mind is a mess.

JUSTICIA: Perhaps you can help me. I seek guidance.

MOSES: My message is simple. The hard part lies in your will. You are stone statuary. But does your constitution match your physical stuff, or are you yet one more among billions of flabby wafflers.

JUSTICIA: I see so many alternatives! They muddle me. Shall I believe Rawls or Nozick, Jesus or Nietzsche? And there's that cute little capuchin. The issues are many, and solutions elusive.

MOSES: Cease whining! Your troubles spring from delusions of competence.

JUSTICIA: I, sir, have been revered by a hundred billion humans.

MOSES: Idiots all. Your troubles, Justicia, are not psychological. They are voluntary. You rebel.

JUSTICIA: Me? A rebel? I have been working my stony little butt off sorting myself here....

MOSES: To what end. You rummage through conceptual trash, a starving mongrel gorging on rancid pork. Humans cannot fathom justice, much less sort its myriad issues. Yahweh has spoken: 613 *mitzvoth* (that is, commandments) given once for all men and times. Your job, Lady Justice, is to enforce those rules. If you imagine otherwise, you err.

JUSTICIA: As I recall, your idea of the administration of justice is monosyllabic. Murder—death. Fornication—death. Burning a pigeon instead of a dove—death. Parking tickets—death.

MOSES: I have occasionally winked at peccadilloes. But overall, you get the picture. Why would any community suffer those who flout its strictures? Tolerance amounts to communal suicide....

The black box of conscience flips open. A six-inch tall Mohandas Gandhi arranges his tiny little towel to obscure his bits. "Moses, yours is not the lone conception of god. Multiple divine perceptions tickle human fancies. Yours is not widespread. Neither is it terribly coherent. Justicia, resist my friend's absolutist bill of goods. He means well. He really does. But his approach to divine ethics makes war, not justice. It is peace that matters, not theological conformity. Moses, my beloved brother, make room in your heart for the rest of us." *Gandhi sits. The ebony lid closes over him.*

MOSES: Blasphemer.... You know, I love Gandhi, but would be rid of him, if I could. If he lived in my time, we would stone him. Cast his fractured corpse upon a heap of dung.

JUSTICIA: Harsh. Is there no room for compassion, understanding, flexibility, inclusion?

MOSES: I include those who conform. Ours is a harsh world, Justicia. In morality, latitude breeds lassitude. Is your abundance of confusions not the fruit of your journey toward ethical subjectivism? Yakking of many beckons cacophony of all. Would people not prosper if they knew boundaries, rigidly enforced limits?

JUSTICIA: Rugged specificity would help some, but crush others. Millions or billions would die.

MOSES: As generations passed, survivors would wax obedient. Rebellion would drain from human fiber. Tractability to divine command would set the habits of billions. There are those of other times who sing a tune like mine. There was that scrunch-faced little senator from Wisconsin, McCarthy. And the evangelical proponents of American Prohibition. And Seyyid Qutb, al Qaeda's Muslim Brotherhood theoretician. And those eremitic desert monks. And Calvin. I just love Calvin. I am not the lone voice of divine rigor.

> **JUSTICE IS:**
>
> COMMANDMENTS
> AND
> SANCTIONS.

JUSTICIA: This conversation leaves a black pit in my rocky stomach, Moses.

MOSES: And therein lies the problem, Justicia. Look in a mirror! You are the henchman of Hobbes's Leviathan. Buck up. Get a grip. Execute those who merit termination. Make the world safe for the obedient. God has spoken.

JUSTICIA: I feel the same intensity from you I found in Nietzsche--dark and scary.

MOSES: The dung heap for him too. Nietzsche was insane. He believed himself to be god.

JUSTICIA: Are you different? You quake with absolute conviction, and suffer adamant certainty how others must live.

MOSES: Yahweh scorched me in unquenchable fire, spoke from his Sinai bush. Do you not smell the cinders?

Justicia opens her mouth to object, but Moses vanishes. His smoky odor lingers.

Torah. **Authors unknown. Revised Standard Version, translated by the Committee for Translation of the Division of Christian Education of the National Council of the Churches of Christ in the United States of America. Camden, New Jersey: Thomas Nelson & Sons, 1946 (NT), 1952 (OT).**

The Torah, consisting of the Jewish scriptures commonly known in English as Genesis, Exodus, Numbers, Leviticus, and Deuteronomy, were stitched together from ancient fragments, various law codes, and oral traditions extant during the prophetic period of ancient Israel (8ᵗʰ - 6ᵗʰ centuries B.C.). The text emerges from ideological contests between groups with two major views of the essence of Judaism: monarchists who emphasize the control of Palestine by Israeli rulers consistent with the Abrahamic covenant, and the priests, who emphasize lifestyle conformity (law) and ritual worship consistent with the laws of Moses.

A core concern in the Torah is to explain why Yahweh permitted Nebuchadrezzar of Babylon to destroy the Israeli monarchies and torch Jerusalem, including the Temple (586 B.C.). The Babylonians deported Israel's artisans and intelligentsia to the Mesopotamian valley in the Babylonian Exile of 587 B.C., with other deportations related to various Jewish uprisings. These dispersed Israelis were permitted to return to their land in 538 B.C when Cyrus of Persia defeated Babylon (for which Cyrus is revered; see Isaiah 45:1-3). Not all the exiles returned; those remaining behind formed the first of the Jewish Diaspora communities.

Though these texts are sacred for Christians and Jews, and authoritative for Muslims, this epitome treats the Torah as evidence of the political and ethical development of the tribal communities comprising Israel during their transition from semi-nomadism to fixed royal and priestly governments in Palestine, whose indigenous peoples Israeli tribes conquered, in the midst of several epochs of significant external threats from the north (Assyrians and Hittites), the West (Babylon and Persia), and the south (Egypt).

GENESIS

Elohist Creation Myth.
Creation week. God (Elohim) creates the world in six days. The result pleases God. God creates man, both male and female, and grants them hegemony over earth and its creatures. God dedicates each seventh day to rest (Genesis 1:1-2:3).

Adam Cycle.
Garden of Eden. Yahweh forms man from earth, and establishes the territory. Yahweh puts man in charge of all things except man is not to eat the fruit of the tree of the knowledge of good and evil. Yahweh's hand fashions all animals, but none are perfect companions for man, who is lonely. Yahweh forms woman from man's rib and establishes their permanent bonding. A serpent tempts woman to eat from the forbidden tree. The woman induces man to likewise eat. Yahweh evicts man and woman from his garden. Yahweh gives each their name, Adam and Eve, and skin clothing (Genesis 2:4-3:24).

Cain and Abel. Cain and Abel, sons of Adam and Eve, dispute when Yahweh prefers Abel's animal sacrifice. Yahweh chastises Cain. Cain murders Abel, then dissembles to Yahweh about it. Yahweh marks Cain and makes him a nomad, wandering east of Eden (Genesis 4:1-16). Cain's progeny are enumerated, the last being also a slayer as was Cain, his ancestor (Genesis 4:17-24). Seth is born to Adam and Eve, and men begin to worship Yahweh (Genesis 4:25-26).

The generations of Adam. The Elohist creation of man (Genesis 1) is recapitulated (Genesis 5:1-2). Adam's descendants are named and their lengthy lifespans enumerated, including Methuselah's 969 years (Genesis 5: 3-32).

Giants Among Men. Divine creatures mate with human women. The progeny are giants, who were famous (Genesis 6:1-4).

Noah. [This story weaves Yahwist and Elohist accounts without complete harmonization.] Yahweh finds all mankind wicked and condemns the race, along with the other animals, to death, except for Noah. Noah's sons are named (Genesis 6:5-10). The condemnation story begins anew. God (Elohist) gives Noah design specifications for building an ark. God instructs Noah to gather mating pairs of every animal, along with his own family and food, into the ark, so that all might avoid the universal flood God plans. Noah complies. The ark loading instructions recommence; seven pairs of each animal are now required (Yahwist). The flood term is specified: forty days and nights of waters. The story bumps again to the original two-by-two plan for animal refugees. The flood lasts 850 days. The flood ensues, wiping out all life but Noah's refugees (Elohist). God withdraws the waters. Noah tests for land with a dove. Noah, his family, and the animals depart the ark. Noah builds an altar and offers animal sacrifice to Yahweh, which pleases him. Yahweh promises never again to destroy all life. God (Elohist) instructs Noah's family to fill the earth with mankind. Noah's progeny can eat of all things, but not flesh with blood in it. Causing injury or death to a man requires like response, because man is made in God's image. God sets the rainbow as a sign of his promise never to drown all life (Genesis 6:5-9:17).

Noah's son, Ham, sees Noah naked, when Noah fainted in a drunken stupor. Shem and Japheth, Noah's two remaining sons, cover their father without looking. Noah condemns Ham's children, among them Canaan. Canaan will be the slave of the others. Noah dies at 950 years of age (Genesis 9:18-29). The descendants of Noah's sons are named. The sons of Japheth become the coastal peoples. The sons of Ham become Egypt and Palestine (Canaan) and Babylon, and Assyria. The sons of Canaan become the tribes of Palestine whom the Israelites would defeat in their conquest. The sons of Shem become the people east of Mesha [possibly related to Moabites, who had a king Mesha] (Genesis 9:18-10:32).

Babel. Mankind has one language with few words. The people of the Shinar plain decide to build a tower to heaven, and succeed. Yahweh disapproves of their hubris, for they believe man is unstoppable. Yahweh confuses their language, driving them off from the city, which was named Babel because that is where man's many languages derived (Genesis 11:1-9).

Abram's Ancestors. Shem's descendants and their lifespans are named (Genesis 11:10-25).

Abraham Cycle.

Haran. Terah (Abram's father), Abram, Sarai (Abram's wife), and Lot (Terah's grandson) move from Ur to Haran, though they had planned to move as far as Canaan (Genesis 11:26-32).

Covenant. Yahweh blesses Abram and sends him to a land Yahweh will show him. Abram will be a blessing to all mankind. Lot accompanies Abram to Canaan, which land Yahweh promises to Abram's descendants. Abram builds an altar near Bethel and worships Yahweh there in Canaan (Genesis 12:1-9).

Egypt. Abram flees Canaan to Egypt to avoid a famine. Abram fears Egyptians may kill him because Sarai is beautiful. So Abram has Sarai say she is Abram's sister. Pharaoh's sons take Sarai, and plagues come on Pharaoh's house. Pharaoh gives Sarai back to Abram and sends Abram and his family away (Genesis 12:10-20). [Compare Genesis 26:1-11 and Genesis 20:1-18.]

Covenant. Abram returns to southern Palestine, growing rich, then travels to Bethel, to the site of his first altar to Yahweh.   Abram's and Lot's cattle are competing, so the two divide the land among them, Lot taking the Jordan Valley (which contains wicked

Sodom), and Abram taking Canaan (Genesis 13:1-12). Yahweh promises all of Palestine to Abram's descendants (Genesis 13:14-18).

Rescuing Lot. Local kings of the Jordan Valley and Dead Sea regions war. The king of Sodom is one loser. Lot and his family and goods are taken as booty. Abram takes 318 men, chasing Lot's captors. He recovers all and brings them back to Sodom. Another local king praises Abram there, and Abram declines that king's bribe (Genesis 14:1-24).

Vision. Yahweh promises to protect Abram. Abram complains because he and Sarai have no son. Abram's heir will be a stranger. Yahweh promises Abram abundant offspring and a son. Abram offers animal sacrifices which Yahweh specifies. In a dream, Yahweh says to Abram that his descendants will be deported for 400 years but will emerge wealthy after Yahweh intervenes. Yahweh promises Abram's descendants the land from the Nile to the Euphrates (Genesis 15:1-21).

Ishmael. Abram, at Sarai's request because she has borne no children, weds Hagar. Hagar lords her early pregnancy over Sarai. With Abram's consent, Sarai abuses Hagar, who flees. An angel intervenes, promises Hagar's son numerous descendants, and names the child Ishmael. The angel foresees Ishmael's contentiousness. When Ishmael is born, Abram is eighty-six years old (Genesis 16:1-16).

Covenant of Circumcision. Yahweh appears to Abram, again promises him many descendants, and changes his name to Abraham. This covenant, that from Abraham will come many kings and nations, is to be everlasting. Yahweh promises loyalty to Abraham. Yahweh will deliver Canaan to Abraham's descendants. Yahweh commands that all of Abraham's descendants shall be circumcised, as a sign of this covenant. Yahweh changes Sarai's name to Sarah, and promises her a son. Abraham scoffs about the age of this child's father and mother; he thanks Yahweh for Ishmael. God corrects Abraham; he speaks of Isaac and promises him many descendants. Abraham circumcises all the males of his household (Genesis 17:1-27).

Sodom and Gomorrah. Abraham entertains three divine men at Mamre, who promise on behalf of Yahweh that Sarah will bear a son, though ninety years old. Sarah laughs, but denies it when challenged. The men leave to destroy Sodom and Gomorrah for their wickedness. Abraham bargains with Yahweh that for the sake of a few good men, the cities should be spared. Yahweh accedes. The Sodomites abuse Lot when they demand sexual intercourse with the "men" who are being entertained by Lot. Lot offers the locals his daughters, to no avail. The men strike the rioters blind. The men remove Lot and his family from Sodom, and tell them to flee without looking back. Lot's wife looks, and becomes a pillar of salt. Sodom and Gomorrah are destroyed by brimstone and fire from heaven (Genesis 18:1-19:29).

Lot's Incest. Lot's daughters lack husbands. They get Lot drunk and have intercourse with him. The two resulting children become the Moabites and the Ammonites (Genesis 19:30-38).

Abraham's Self-Serving Lie. Abraham tells King Abimelech that Sarah is his sister. Abimelech weds Sarah. God intervenes, condemning Abimelech with illness, relenting when Abimelech protests his innocence if only Abimelech will restore Sarah and get Abraham to intercede on Abimelech's behalf. Abimelech confronts Abraham about his lie. Abraham discloses that Sarah is his half-sister. Abimelech returns Sarah with funds and livestock. Abraham prays for Abimelech and his family, who are healed (Genesis 20:1-18). [Compare Genesis 12:6-20 and Genesis 26:1-11.]

Isaac. Yahweh visits Sarah, who bears Isaac. Abraham is 100 years old at the time (Genesis 21:1-7).

Ishmael Cast Out. Ishmael mocks Isaac. Sarah complains. Abraham casts Hagar and Ishmael out of the family. Hagar and Ishmael wander in the desert, and Hagar despairs. They will die of thirst. God intervenes and she sees a well and survives (Genesis 21:8-21). [Note similarities with Genesis 16.]

Well Agreement. Abimelech seeks Abraham's promise to deal squarely with him, because God favors Abraham. Abraham consents. Abraham contests use of a well. He gives Abimelech seven lambs in exchange for sole use of the well. Abraham lives peacefully with the Philistines (Genesis 21:22-34).

Sacrifice of Isaac. God commands Abraham to take Isaac to Moriah and kill him as a burnt sacrifice. Abraham takes Isaac to the Moriah, binds him on the wood for the burnt offering, and takes his knife to kill Isaac. An angel intervenes, and tells him God is just testing his loyalty. A ram is caught nearby in a thicket, and Abraham sacrifices that animal in Isaac's stead. Yahweh blesses Abraham, and promises that all nations shall be blessed by Abraham (Genesis 22:1-19).

Nahor's Children. Milcah bears children to Nahor, one of whom is the father of Rebekah (Genesis 22:20-24).

Sarah's Burial. Sarah dies. Abraham asks the Hittites for a burial place for his family members. Abraham requests the cave of Machpelah, which he purchases and buries Sarah there (Genesis 23:1-20).

Rebekah. Abraham sends a servant to find a wife for Isaac from Abraham's people, so Isaac will not marry a Canaanite woman. At Nahor in Mesopotamia, the servant waters camels, and Rebekah assists him. The servant goes to Sarah's family home and tells his errand. Bethuel, her father, gives Rebekah as Isaac's wife. The servant gives Abraham's gifts to the family. Rebekah consents to go to Isaac as wife. When they arrive, Isaac makes Rebekah his wife (Genesis 24:1-67). [Compare Genesis 29:1-14.]

Abraham's Death. Abraham marries Keturah, who bears him sons. Abraham sends them away from Isaac with gifts, and gives all he has to Isaac. Abraham dies at age 175. He is buried with Sarah (Genesis 25:1-11).

Abraham's Descendants. Ishmael's descendants are named. Isaac's descendants are named: Esau and Jacob (Genesis 25:19-20).

Jacob Cycle.

Esau and Jacob. Yahweh intervenes to make barren Rebekah conceive. Esau and Jacob are born, Esau first, struggling from the beginning. Esau is a hunter, and Jacob a quiet man. Isaac loves Esau; Rebekah loves Jacob. Esau sells his birthright to Jacob for a bowl of lentil pottage and some bread (Genesis 25:21-34).

Isaac's Self-Serving Lie. [Compare Genesis 20:1-7 and 12:1-20] Yahweh tells Isaac to stay in Palestine, despite the famine, and promises to Isaac what Yahweh promised to Abram. [Note that Abraham kept Yahweh's "charge, commandments statutes and laws," not merely obeyed Yahweh. Compare Deuteronomy 4.] Isaac represents Rebekah as his sister and Abimelech saw him fondling her. Abimelech confronts Isaac because someone could have had sex with Rebekah (Genesis 26:1-11).

Gerar Wells. Philistines fill Abraham's wells, jealous of Isaac's wealth, and send Isaac away. Isaac moves to Gerar and redigs Abraham's wells. Isaac finds a springing well, and the Philistines want it. So Isaac digs another, which the Philistines also want. So Isaac digs a third well, and that well the Philistines do not claim (Genesis 26:12-25).

Appearance at Beersheba. Yahweh appears to Isaac and reiterates his promise of many descendants and blessing. Isaac worships and digs a well (Genesis 26:23-25).

Agreement with Abimelech. Abimelech comes to Isaac seeking a promise that Isaac will not harm his people, because Yahweh is with Isaac. They feast. Isaac digs a well and finds water. Again, Beersheba is named (Genesis 26:26-33). [Compare Genesis 21:22-34. On Beersheba, compare Genesis 21:31.]

Esau weds Judith. Esau weds Judith, who made life bitter for Esau (Genesis 26:34-35).

Jacob Defrauds Esau. Isaac goes blind with age. Isaac bids Esau to prepare a meat meal for him, so he can bless Esau. Rebekah overhears, and sends Jacob to kill a kid and prepare it for Isaac. Esau is hairy, and Jacob is not, so Rebekah puts the kid skin on Jacob's hands and back, and dresses Jacob in Esau's clothes. Jacob takes his meal to Isaac, claims to be Esau, and seeks the blessing. Isaac is suspicious, because the voice is that of Jacob, but the hands those of Esau. Isaac asks again if he is Esau. Jacob lies again. Isaac draws Jacob near for a kiss, and smells Esau's scent on the clothing. Satisfied, Isaac blesses Jacob, believing him to be Esau. Esau returns from hunting. Isaac is furious to have been fooled, but cannot undo his blessing. Esau wept. Esau plans to kill Jacob when Isaac dies. Rebekah learns of this plan, warns Jacob, and sends Jacob away to Haran until Esau relents (Genesis 27:1-45).

Jacob Weds Leah and Rachel. Rebekah does not want Jacob to marry a Hittite woman. Isaac sends Jacob to his uncle's house to select a cousin to marry. Esau sees what Isaac did with Jacob, and weds Mahalath, daughter of Ishmael. On his trip to find a wife, Jacob dreams. A ladder rises from earth to heaven with angels going up and down. Yahweh reiterates his promise of many descendants who will be a blessing to mankind. Yahweh promises to travel with Jacob wherever he goes and to bring Jacob back to the land (Genesis 28:10-17). Jacob takes the rock he used as a pillow, and sets it up. He calls the place Bethel, and vows that if Yahweh does as he promises, providing for Jacob and bringing him back to the land, then Jacob will worship Yahweh his whole life and dedicate one-tenth of his possessions to God (Genesis 28:18-22). Jacob arrives in the east at a well. Inquiring, he learns that a daughter of Laban, Rachel, is watering animals there. [Compare Genesis 24:1-67.] Jacob kisses Rachel and told her who he is. Laban hires Jacob, and introduces his elder daughter, Leah, whose sight is poor. Jacob serves Laban for seven years for Rachel's dowry. Laban, however, when the wedding night occurs, gives Jacob Leah, not Rachel. Jacob does not notice until morning. Jacob receives Rachel as wife, but he serves another seven years to earn her. Leah, whom Jacob does not prefer, bears him three sons, but Rachel remains barren. Rachel has Jacob impregnate her maid, Bilhah, so Bilhah can bear Rachel's children in Rachel's place. Leah gives Jacob her maid, Zilpah, who bears Jacob sons. [Compare Genesis 16:1-6.] Rachel wants some mandrake (aphrodisiacal herb, which root promotes conception in African folklore), and so bargains with Leah: herbs in exchange for sex with Jacob. Leah bears more sons. God makes Rachel fertile, and Joseph is born (Genesis 27:46-30:24).

Jacob and Laban Defraud One Another. Jacob asks for his wages for his fourteen years of labor. Laban promises Jacob all the spotted sheep and black lambs, then removes such from the flock and sends them away with a son. Jacob artificially puts spots on the strongest of the flock and takes the best animals from Laban. Jacob and Laban fall out, and Jacob returns to Canaan with Rachel and Leah and his household and possessions. Rachel steals Laban's household gods. Laban chases Jacob, but God warns him not to speak with Jacob. Laban complains of the stolen gods, and Jacob promises that the thief will be killed, not knowing the thief was Rachel. Rachel hides the gods in a saddle and then sits on them, claiming to be menstruating. Laban does not find his gods. Jacob complains about his hard service for Laban. Laban refuses to acknowledge that Jacob deserves his wages and daughters. The two make a covenant for Yahweh to decide between them if they break their promises. They sacrifice and feast, then Laban goes home (Genesis 30:25-31:55).

Jacob's Homecoming. Jacob sees an army of angels. Messengers report that Esau approaches Jacob's company with 400 men. Jacob fears Esau, and so, splits his group into two so that if Esau intends ill, one might survive. Jacob asks Yahweh for protection. Jacob sends waves of gifts for Esau before him, hoping to appease Esau. Jacob sends his wives and children across the Jabbok ford. That night, Jacob wrestles with a man until dawn, the man putting Jacob's hip out of joint. Jacob refuses to yield unless the stranger blesses him. The man changes Jacob's name to "Israel," he who prevails against God. For this reason Israelites do not eat the sinew of the hip in the hollow of the thigh to this day. Jacob leads his family to Esau, prostrating himself. Esau embraces Jacob and they weep. Jacob introduces his family. Esau tries to return Jacob's gifts, but Jacob insists, and promises to meet

Esau at Seir. After Esau's departure, Jacob takes his group to Succoth instead and settles (Genesis 32:1-33:20).

Shechem Rapes Diana. A Canaanite prince rapes Leah's daughter Dinah, and then wants to marry her. [Note anachronism at 34:7: "in Israel."] Shechem asks forgiveness, and his father wants Jacob's family to marry among the Canaanites and join the people. Jacob deceives Shechem. He says he will consent to join the people and let Shechem marry Dinah only if all the males of the city are circumcised. They agree. On the third day after circumcision, when none could fight, Jacob's sons kill all the city's males, including Shechem and his father, Hamor. They take the city's flocks and wives and children as booty. Jacob complains because the excess of their revenge will make trouble with the surrounding Canaanites (Genesis 34:1-31).

Worship at Bethel. God sends Jacob to Bethel to worship him. Jacob has his family members put away their foreign gods and purify themselves. [Note polytheism.] God terrorizes the surrounding cities so they do not attack Jacob. At Bethel, Deborah, Rebekah's nurse, dies. God appears to Jacob and renames him Israel [compare Genesis 32:28] (Genesis 35:1-15).

Rachel Dies in Childbirth. Rachel gives birth to Benjamin, and dies. Rachel is buried in Bethlehem (Genesis 35:16-21).

Reuben's Offense. Jacob's son, Reuben, has sex with Bilhah, Jacob's concubine. Jacob finds out (Genesis 35:22).

Jacob's Descendants. Jacob's descendants are named, twelve in all (Genesis 35:22-26).

Jacob Dies. Jacob dies at 180 years of age. Esau buries him (Genesis 35:27-29).

Esau's Descendants. Esau's descendants are named (Genesis 36:1-5).

Repetition of Genesis 13:5ff. The story of Jacob and Esau dividing the land east and west is recapitulated (Genesis 36:6-9).

Recapitulation of Esau's Descendant, and List of Edom's Kings. Esau's descendants are again named, their chiefs identified, along with the kings of Edom, who ruled before any Israeli kings ruled (Genesis 36:9-43).

Joseph Cycle.

Attempted Murder of Joseph. Jacob's favoritism toward Joseph, the son of Jacob's old age, causes rifts between Joseph and his brothers. Jacob makes Joseph a long robe. Joseph dreams of sheaves and heavenly bodies, implying that Joseph will become head of the family, though young. Joseph joins his brothers in tending flocks. The brothers conspire to kill Joseph. They throw him in a pit to die, but relent and sell Joseph to traders passing by (for twenty shekels of silver). They spatter Joseph's coat with blood; Jacob assumes Joseph has been eaten. Joseph is sold to Potiphar, Pharaoh's guard captain (Genesis 37:1-36).

Tamar and Onan. Judah has children by a Canaanite woman, Shua: Er and Onan. Er dies, being wicked. Judah asks Onan to impregnate Er's wife Tamar; Onan has sex with her, but withdraws his penis before ejaculation to prevent pregnancy. Yahweh is displeased and kills Onan. Judah promises his youngest son as Tamar's husband. Tamar grows impatient. She dresses herself as a prostitute and seduces Judah. In payment, Judah promises a goat, leaving his staff in pledge of payment. Judah sends the goat to the harlot, but she is gone. Tamar conceives twins. When the family learns she is pregnant, they move to burn her. She blames Judah, who confesses that he did not give her his youngest son as a husband. The twins juggle in birth which is first out, one protruding a hand to which a scarlet string is tied, the other then emerging (Genesis 38:1-30).

Joseph Imprisoned. Yahweh makes Joseph prosper in Egypt. Joseph becomes Potiphar's household overseer. Joseph is handsome and Potiphar's wife repeatedly attempts to seduce Joseph, which advances Joseph refuses. One day she grabs Joseph, who flees, losing a garment in the process. Potiphar's wife claims Joseph sexually assaulted her.

Potiphar imprisons Joseph. Yahweh makes the jailkeeper favor Joseph, putting Joseph in charge of the jail (Genesis 39:1-23).

Joseph's Dream Interpretations. Pharaoh's baker and butler are imprisoned with Joseph. The butler dreams and Joseph correctly interprets it; he will be released. Joseph asks the butler to speak to Pharaoh of Joseph's plight when he is released. Pharaoh's butler dreams and Joseph correctly interprets it; the butler will be hanged. The butler forgets his promise to Joseph when he receives his freedom (Genesis 40:1-23).

Two years later, Pharaoh dreams. Pharaoh dreams of fat and thin cows emerging form the Nile. The butler remembers that Joseph interprets dreams, and refers Pharaoh to Joseph. Joseph interprets Pharaoh's dream as predicting seven prosperous years followed by seven years of famine. Joseph recommends that Pharaoh set aside a significant reserve during the prosperous years for the lean years coming. Pharaoh puts Joseph in charge of his household and Egypt. The store of grain grows large. Famine arrives, and only Egypt has bread (Genesis 41:1-57).

Jacob's Family Moves to Egypt. Jacob sends ten of his sons to Egypt to buy grain; Benjamin stays behind. Joseph recognizes them, but they fail to recognize him. Joseph accuses them of spying on Egypt. Joseph demands that they produce Benjamin. Joseph holds Simeon hostage, and lets the other brothers return to Canaan with grain. Joseph puts the grain money in their sacks. Jacob refuses to let Benjamin go to Egypt for fear he will be killed. When the grain runs out, Jacob sends the brothers, with Benjamin (reluctantly), to Egypt for more. They take gifts and double the money. Joseph makes a feast for the brothers. The brothers fear, and tell Joseph's steward of the error regarding the money on their first trip. The steward says he received their money last trip. Joseph greets Benjamin, then weeps in his chamber. They eat and drink. Joseph gives them grain, their money again, and puts a silver chalice in Benjamin's sack. The brothers depart. Joseph sends men after the brothers, asking why they have stolen. The chalice is discovered, and the brothers return to Joseph. Joseph releases the brothers, except for Benjamin. Judah asks Joseph to release Benjamin because of Judah's promise to Jacob regarding his safety. Judah asks to replace Benjamin. Joseph reveals himself to his brothers. Joseph says that God sent Joseph to Egypt ahead of the famine to prepare a way for the family to survive. Joseph asks Jacob and all the clan to come to Egypt. God speaks to Jacob at Beersheba, telling him to move to Egypt, and promising to bring Jacob back up from Egypt after death. Jacob and his family move to Egypt. The family members who move to Egypt are named, seventy members in all. Joseph and his father are reunited. Pharaoh settles the family in Goshen. Jacob blesses Pharaoh (Genesis 42:1-47:12).

Joseph Enslaves Egypt. As the famine worsens, the Egyptians and their neighbors lack funds to buy grain. So, Joseph barters with them for their cattle, then their land, then their persons as slaves. Joseph establishes the rule that twenty percent of all harvests belong to Pharaoh (Genesis 47:13-26).

Jacob's Death. Jacob's family prospers in Egypt. Joseph swears that Jacob's body will not be left in Egypt, but will be carried back to Canaan. Jacob adopts Joseph's sons as his own. Jacob blesses Joseph's sons, Ephraim and Manasseh, but out of birth order. Jacob insists, despite Joseph's objections. Jacob predicts the histories of his sons, emphasizing the preeminence of Judah. Jacob reiterates his desire to be buried in the family cave at Machpelah. Jacob dies (Genesis 47:27-49:33).

Jacob's Interment. Pharaoh lets Joseph and his retinue take Jacob's body to Machpelah for burial. Joseph's brothers fear that now that Jacob has died, Joseph will exact vengeance upon them. Joseph reassures them (Genesis 50:1-21).

Joseph's Death. Joseph sees his great grandchildren born, then dies. He exacts a promise from his brothers to carry his body back to Canaan when God takes them from Egypt (Genesis 50: 22-26).

EXODUS

Persecution in Egypt.

Political Threat. The descendants of Jacob are enumerated by tribe. They experience a great increase in population as time passes (Exodus 1:1-7). The Egyptian administration fears the Hebrews because of their numbers and dubious political loyalty. So, Jacob's descendants do hard labor. Still, they grow in number. The administration tells the midwives to kill all the Hebrew sons. The midwives refuse and God blesses them. Finally, Pharaoh orders that all Hebrew sons shall be thrown into the Nile. Only the daughters shall live (Exodus 1:8-22).

Moses's Childhood. A Hebrew couple bears a son. The mother hides him for three months from officials. Then she makes a basket and sets him adrift on the Nile. Pharoah's daughter discovers the child. She hires the Hebrew mother to nurse him and Pharaoh's daughter adopts the child and names him Moses (Exodus 2:1-10).

Murder. Moses murders an Egyptian who beat a Hebrew, then hides the body. Moses learns that he had been seen in the act. Pharaoh learns of the murder. Moses flees to Midian [Saudi Arabia along the Gulf of Aqaba] and hides there. Moses helps some women water their flock, and ingratiates himself to their father, Jethro. Moses marries Zipporah, Jethro's daughter, who bears him a son (Exodus 2:11-22).

God Hears. Israel groans in its slavery. God recalls his covenant with the patriarchs, and sees their plight (Exodus 2:23-25).

Yahweh Sends Moses to Pharaoh. While Moses tends sheep, Yahweh appears to him as a flame in a bush at Mt. Horeb [southern Sinai peninsula]. Yahweh commands Moses to remove his shoes, for the place where he stands is sacred. Moses refuses to look. Yahweh tells Moses that Yahweh will fulfill his promise to Israel to give them Canaan, a land of milk and honey. Yahweh will send Moses to Pharaoh to bring the Hebrews out of Egypt. Moses quibbles. God commands him to deliver the people back to Horeb, where Moses shall again serve Yahweh. Moses asks who sends him, and what he should tell the Hebrews. Yahweh says his name is "I am who I am." [Possibly a play on the Hebrew word "hayah," which means "to be" and the tetragrammaton YHWH.] (Exodus 3:1-17). Yahweh tells Moses to have the Hebrews tell Pharaoh they need to go three days into the desert to sacrifice to Yahweh. Though Pharaoh will refuse, Yahweh will compel Pharaoh to let the Hebrews go into the desert. All the Hebrew women are to steal silver and gold and clothing from their masters. Moses objects that the people will disbelieve him. Yahweh turns Moses' staff into a snake, Moses hand becomes leprous and then normal again, and Nile water will become blood. Moses continues to quibble, saying that he speaks poorly. Yahweh grows angry with Moses, but gives him his brother, Aaron the Levite, as mouthpiece (Exodus 3:18-4:17). Moses returns to Egypt with his family and the blessing of Jethro (Exodus 4:18-20). Yahweh tells Moses to tell Pharaoh that Yahweh will kill his first-born son, if Pharaoh refuses to release Israel. But Yahweh will harden Pharoah's heart so he refuses to let the Hebrews go (Exodus 4:21-23). Zipporah circumcises her son, and touches Moses's feet with the foreskin (Exodus 4:24-26). Yahweh sends Aaron into the wilderness to meet Moses. Moses tells Aaron all that Yahweh commanded, and shows him the signs provided (Exodus 4:27-28).

Escape from Egypt.

Hebrew Consent. Moses and Aaron tell the Hebrews what Yahweh said and show them the signs. They believe and worship Yahweh (Exodus 4:29-31).

Confrontation with Pharaoh (First Version). Moses and Aaron ask Pharaoh's permission to let the Hebrews worship in the wilderness. He refuses and increases their burdens, denying them straw for their brickmaking without reducing their daily quota. The people complain to Pharaoh, to no avail. They turn on Moses and Aaron, and Moses complains to Yahweh. Yahweh reassures Moses that he will intervene. Yahweh tells Moses to reiterate Yahweh's promises to deliver them and give them Canaan as their own. The people ignore Moses. Their spirit is broken. Yahweh commands Moses to go again to Pharaoh. Moses objects that the people are not listening to Moses. Yahweh insists (Exodus 5:1-6:13).

The Levi Tribe Named. The members of Moses's and Aaron's family are named, identifying Moses and Aaron (Exodus 6:14-27).

Confrontation with Pharaoh (Second Version). Yahweh tells Moses to command Pharaoh to let the Hebrews go. Moses objects about his speaking deficits, and is given Aaron to speak on his behalf. Yahweh will harden Pharaoh's heart, and Yahweh will make great signs and release the Hebrews from the Egyptians. *Rod Transformation.* Before Pharaoh, Moses casts down his rod and it becomes a snake. Egyptian sorcerers do the same, but Moses's rod eats the magicians' snakes (Exodus 6:28-7:13). *Nile Blood.* Moses turns the Nile and other waterways to blood before Pharaoh. Pharaoh's sorcerers do the same, and so Pharaoh refuses to let the Hebrews go. *Frogs.* Moses brings a plague of frogs from the Nile, but again the magicians do the same, and so Pharaoh still refuses. Pharaoh asks for leave to comply with Yahweh's demand on the following day, and Yahweh kills the frogs. But Pharaoh breaks his promise to let the Hebrews go into the wilderness to serve Yahweh. *Gnats.* Moses brings a plague of gnats [or possibly lice], and Pharaoh's sorcerers cannot match this feat. Still, Pharaoh persists. *Flies.* Moses brings swarms of flies on the land, which is ruined by them. Pharaoh tells Moses to take the people and go to sacrifice, but to do so nearby. Moses says the people must go three days into the wilderness. Moses consents to ask Yahweh to remove the flies, and Yahweh does so. But Pharaoh again refuses to make good his promise. *Cattle deaths.* Yahweh promises to make Pharaoh's cattle die, but none of the cattle of the Hebrews. Still, Pharaoh refuses. *Boils.* Moses throws ashes in the air before Pharaoh, which causes boils on man and beast throughout Egypt. Still, Pharaoh persists. *Hail.* Yahweh sends heavy hail, and only sheltered men and cattle survive. The crops and trees are destroyed by hail and lightning. There is no hail on the Hebrews. Pharaoh promises to release the Hebrews, but when the hail and lightning stop, he changes his mind. Yahweh tells Moses to tell Pharaoh that Yahweh has hardened Pharaoh's heart, so Pharaoh can learn Yahweh's abilities. *Locusts.* Moses promises to bring locusts, so Pharaoh bargains: the men may go worship, but the flocks and women and children stay behind. The locusts come, and Pharaoh relents. Yahweh removes the locusts, but Pharaoh changes his mind. *Darkness.* Moses brings darkness over Egypt, except for the Hebrews, for three days. Pharaoh promises to kill Moses if he sees him again. Yahweh asks the Hebrews to seek silver and gold from neighbors so that when they leave Egypt they will leave with Egyptian wealth. (See Exodus 12:35-36.) *Passover: Death of the First-Born.* Yahweh promises that he will kill the first-born children of the Egyptians and their cattle, except for the Hebrews. Yahweh instructs the people of Israel: this month is the first month of your year. Each household shall sacrifice a one-year old male lamb. Put some of the lamb's blood on the doorposts and lintel of your house, eat all of the lamb roasted with unleavened bread. Eat with your clothes and shoes on, staff in hand, in haste. For Yahweh will pass through Egypt killing the first born, but will pass over houses with blood on their doorways. The day shall be a memorial of the Exodus forever. Eat unleavened bread for seven days and those who eat leaven shall be cut off from Israel. Moses instructs the Hebrews. Israel complies. Yahweh strikes the first-born dead. Egypt mourns, and Pharaoh expels the Hebrews (Exodus 6:14-12:36).

Principle of Redemption. 600,000 of Jacob's descendants leave Egypt, after 430 years in that country. Yahweh watches over Israel, and so the people keep the night of watching forever. Yahweh reiterates the Passover rules: no foreigners shall eat the meal unless circumcised, all the sacrificed lamb must be consumed in one house only, and no one can break the bones of the lamb. This rule applies to all Israelis and all strangers as well. Yahweh demands consecration of the first-borns, man and beast. Redemption of the first-born sons and asses is possible, if redeemed by sacrifice of a lamb. [This principle takes a fundamental place in Christian soteriology.] Moses prescribes the requirements of the feast of unleavened bread which commemorates Yahweh bringing the people out of the land of Egypt. The historical root of phylacteries is described (Exodus 12:37-13:16).

Sinai.

Red Sea. Yahweh leads Israel toward the Red Sea, not directly toward Canaan, fearing the people would anticipate war and flee back to Egypt. Moses takes Joseph's remains with him. Yahweh leads the people as a pillar of fire by night and a pillar of cloud by day. Yahweh again hardens Pharaoh's heart so Yahweh can get glory over Pharaoh. Pharaoh pursues the Hebrews with an army. The Israelis fear as Pharaoh's troops drew near, and complain to Moses. Moses encourages the people that Yahweh will fight for them. The pillar of cloud stands between Pharaoh and the Egyptians. Yahweh divides the waters of the Red Sea by a strong east wind, and the Hebrews go through on dry land. Pharaoh pursues with his troops. Yahweh brings the waters back and drowns Pharaoh's army. The Hebrews see the dead Egyptians on the seashore, fear Yahweh, and believe in Yahweh and Moses (Exodus 13:17-14:31). Israel and Moses sing a song: Yahweh is a great man of war; he destroyed the Egyptians; who is like Yahweh among the gods? [Note polytheist backdrop.] The people of Canaan tremble for Israel comes; Yahweh will be pre-eminent forever. The defeat of Pharaoh's army is recapitulated, and Miriam sings to Yahweh (Exodus 15:1-21).

Into Sinai. Moses leads Israel into the Sinai. The water at Marah is not potable; Yahweh gives Moses a stick to purify it (Exodus 15:22-25). Yahweh promises that, if the people obey Yahweh's laws, he will not strike them with the illnesses which he inflicted on the Egyptians. [Note the progression in the terms of Yahweh's covenant with Israel; compare Genesis 12:1-3, with Genesis 26:3-5, with Exodus 15:26 for their increasing emphasis on fidelity to laws, rather than land and descendants.] (Exodus 15:26-27).

Israel Complains. The Hebrews complain about hunger, accusing Moses of dragging them into the wilderness only to starve. Yahweh promises to rain bread on the Hebrews daily, to test their willingness to obey Yahweh's laws. On the sixth day, there will be twice as much to gather, so that the people may rest on the seventh day. Moses tells the people and Aaron instructs them. In the evening quails invade the camp and in the morning edible hoarfrost covers the ground. Every person gathers according to their needs, and what is left spoils by the next morning. When the sixth day arrives, twice as much bread appears, and Yahweh commands them to take a solemn rest. The bread and quail do not spoil on the Sabbath day, though it does so on other days. Some of the people go out to gather on the seventh day. Yahweh castigates them for working on the Sabbath, and commands every man to stay in his place on the Sabbath. Israel calls the daily bread manna. Moses keeps a jar of manna to remind the people of Yahweh's care for them throughout the generations. Israel eats manna for forty years, until they come to the border of Canaan (Exodus 16:1-36). The people move camp, and they lack water. Israel complains to Moses. Yahweh tells Moses to strike a rock at Horeb with the staff he used on Pharaoh, and water will gush. Moses does so, and then criticizes the people for asking if Yahweh is among them. The place is called Meribah (Exodus 17:1-7) [Compare Numbers 10:2-13].

Battle with Amalek. The tribe of Amalek attacks Israel. [Amalekites live in the Negeb of southern Palestine, per Numbers 13:29.] Moses sends Joshua to fight the Amalekites. When Moses holds up his staff, Israel prevails. When the staff falls, Amalek prevails. Aaron and Hur help Moses hold up the staff, and Israel wins. Yahweh promises that war with Amalek will last forever (Exodus 17:8-16).

Jethro's Advice. Moses's father-in-law visits, bringing Zipporah and Moses's two sons. Moses relates all Yahweh has done to Pharaoh and for Israel. They sacrifice to

Yahweh. Moses sits judging the disputes of the people from morning to evening. Jethro offers advice: You will wear yourself out. Appoint trustworthy men to decide most cases, and you take the difficult ones to Yahweh. Moses sets up such an administration of the people. Jethro goes home (Exodus 18:1-27).

Moses on the Mountain (First Version).

Three months after leaving Egypt, Israel crosses the Sinai to the mountain, where they camp. Yahweh appears to Moses, and tells him to tell Israel to keep Yahweh's covenant by obeying his laws. If they do so, Israel will be God's special possession and they will be a sacred kingdom of priests. [Note the continuing drift of the covenant terms.] Moses tells the people. Yahweh will present himself as a cloud on the mountain in three days. Let the people wash their clothes and prepare, but none are to touch the mountain on pain of stoning. Sex is forbidden until the divine encounter. On the third day, Yahweh appears on Mount Sinai in fire and smoke. Moses goes up on the mountain. Yahweh shows some confusion about his previous commands to the people, which he and Moses straighten out. Moses is to bring Aaron back up the mountain with him, after Moses instructs the people.

DECALOGUE (EXODUS VERSION). [Compare Exodus 20:1-17, Leviticus 19:3-18, and Deuteronomy 5:6-21.] God speaks the Decalogue to Moses, ten core rules for attitude and action: worship Yahweh only, no manmade gods, no frivolous oaths, keep the Sabbath, honor parents, avoid murder, avoid adultery, avoid theft, avoid lying about neighbors, avoid envy of the lives of others (Exodus 20:2-17). The people fear, and Moses comforts them. God tells Moses that he has shown himself to the people so that they will not make little gods or fancy altars from which their genitalia can be seen (Exodus 20:1-25).

Ordinances. Further laws are specified concerning: Hebrew slaves and manumission, selling daughters into slavery, penalties for killing men and sanctuaries for murderers, striking parents, death for stealing slaves, death for cursing parents, paying the costs of assault, penalties for injuring slaves, penalty of equal harm for injury to a pregnant woman ("eye for eye"), manumission if owner puts out eye or tooth of his slave, rules for ox goring, open pits, and ox assaults on oxen, penalties for stealing ox or sheep, killing thieves, animal grazing trespass, negligent fire, theft from bailors of personal property, breaches of trust, lost bailed goods, loss of borrowed goods, marriage for seducing virgins, death for sorceresses, death for bestiality, death for worshipping others than Yahweh, death for harming strangers, widows, or orphans, usury and credit security, reviling God, cursing rulers, making tithes, offering the first-born, eating dead flesh, making false reports, collaborating with the wicked, following crowds to do evil, perverting courts of justice, showing partiality to the poor in courts, returning lost or endangered property of enemies, showing partiality to the rich in courts, avoiding bribes, oppressing strangers, fallow fields every seventh year, resting on the seventh day, speaking the names of other gods, keeping the three feasts (unleavened bread, harvest, and planting), no sacrificed blood to be offered with leavened bread, leave no sacrificed fat until morning, offer first-fruits of the fields, and boiling kids in mother's milk (Exodus 21:1-23:19).

Conquering Canaan. Yahweh will send an angel before Israel. If Israel obeys him, then Israel shall take Canaan a little at a time over a period of years as the people grow in number. Israel shall possess land from the Red Sea to Palestine, from the desert to the Euphrates. Israel must drive out the natives before them, and make no agreements with them. Their gods will be a snare to Israel (Exodus 23:20-33). Yahweh invites all the elders of Israel onto the mountain, but only Moses can come near to God (Exodus 24:1-2).

Book of the Covenant. Moses writes down Yahweh's instructions, making a book of the covenant with Yahweh. Moses sets up twelve pillars representing the tribes of Israel. Half the blood of sacrifices is thrown on the altars. Moses reads the book of the covenant to Israel, who swear obedience. Then Moses throws the other half of the sacrificial blood on the people, declaring it to be the blood of the covenant with Yahweh (Exodus 24:2-8).

Moses on the Mountain (Second Version).

Elders on the Mountain. Moses and the seventy elders of Israel go up on the mountain. All see the God of Israel standing on a clear sapphire pavement. Yahweh calls Moses to give him the stone tablets of his laws, written by God. Moses asks the elders to wait for him, and puts Aaron and Hur in charge. Cloud covers Mount Sinai for six days. On the seventh day, Yahweh calls Moses up. Yahweh manifests as fire atop the mount. Moses is gone forty days (Exodus 24:9-18).

Tabernacle Instructions. Yahweh instructs Moses to seek voluntary contributions of valuables from the people as material for Yahweh's sanctuary. The sanctuary will be called the tabernacle. The tabernacle shall contain an ark holding the law tablets, a table on which sits the bread of the Presence, and a lampstand and snuffers. The inner sanctuary of the tabernacle shall be ten curtains, all set within a larger tent with a wood frame. Inside the inner sanctuary, a veil of fine linen shall segregate the ark and mercy seat from the holy inner sanctuary, and that place shall separate the holy from the most holy place. A wooden screen overlaid in gold shall be the door. The tabernacle shall contain an altar, ash pots, and a grating. The tabernacle shall contain a courtyard with a perpetually-lit lamp, tended by Aaron and his sons forever (Exodus 25:1-27:21).

Aaronic Priesthood. Aaron's male descendants shall be priests to Yahweh. Aaron shall wear holy garments, including a breastpiece, ephod [elaborate linen apron], robe, plate, and coat. Aaron, as high priest, shall bear the divine condemnation of Israel upon his heart. The sons of Aaron shall wear coats, girdles and caps of great beauty, with linen breeches (Exodus 28:1-43). [Consecration: First Version] The protocol for consecrating Aaron and his family is specified: clothe them as instructed, then sacrifice a bull and two rams before the altar. Aaron's costume shall descend to his sons (Exodus 29:1-34). [Consecration: Second Version] A seven-day protocol for consecrating Aaron and his descendants as priests is specified: sacrifice a bull daily for seven days; a lamb shall be offered every morning and every evening forever. Yahweh shall consecrate Aaron and his sons. Yahweh shall dwell with Israel and be their God (Exodus 29:35-46). Aaron shall burn incense morning and evening on the incense altar (Exodus 30:1-10). All of the Hebrews, rich and poor alike, shall pay one-half shekel at the time of census to support the tabernacle, which sum shall be called atonement money. A bronze washing laver shall stand near the altar for priests to wash themselves. Make a unique sacred washing perfume to anoint the tent and its contents and the priests, but for no other purposes. The formula for incense is specified (Exodus 30:11-38). Yahweh appoints Bezalel and Oholiab to make the tabernacle and its contents (Exodus 31:1-11).

Keep the Sabbath. Hebrews who decline to observe the Sabbath shall be put to death. As God rested on the seventh day, so shall the people, so they know that Yahweh makes them holy (Exodus 31:12-17).

Tablets of Law. Yahweh gives Moses two stone tablets on which Yahweh has, with his own finger, written the law (Exodus 31:18).

Golden Calf.

Apostasy. Moses's long stay on the mountain makes the people fearful. They fashion a golden calf and worship it, saying the calf brought them up out of Egypt. Aaron leads this apostasy. Yahweh tells Moses to go down to the people. Yahweh wishes to destroy Israel, but Moses reminds Yahweh of his covenants with Abram, Isaac, and Jacob. So Yahweh relents. Joshua says he hears singing in the camp. When Moses arrives, he is furious. Moses breaks the tablets of the law. He burns the golden calf, grinds it down, mixes it with water, and makes the people drink it. [Compare Deuteronomy 9:16-21.] Moses confronts Aaron, who says the evil in the Hebrews made him fashion the calf. Moses sends the sons of Levi out to kill three thousand men, which they did. Moses blesses the Levites. In the morning, Moses offers to ask Yahweh's forgiveness. Yahweh declines to kill Moses, but promises to settle accounts with those who worshipped the calf. Yahweh sends a plague upon the people (Exodus 32:1-35).

Moses Pleads for the Hebrews. Yahweh sends the people on, but does not go with them. His anger is too great. Israel grieves, and refuses to adorn themselves. Moses pitches the tent of meeting, and Yahweh's presence enters there. Yahweh and Moses speak as a man and his friend, face to face. Moses pleads for Israel. Yahweh agrees to keep faith with the people. Moses asks to see Yahweh. Yahweh says no man can see his face and live. Yahweh hides Moses in a rock cleft and shows Moses his back (Exodus 33:1-23).

Yahweh Renews the Covenant. Moses cuts two new tablets of stone for Yahweh's use. Moses goes up the mountain alone. Yahweh proclaims himself patient and forgiving, but punishing the guilty to the fourth generation among sinners. Moses worships. Yahweh promises to do more marvels in Israel. Yahweh will drive out the tribes of Palestine and give the land to Israel, if only they will make no contracts to coexist with the natives. Tear down their altars. For Yahweh is jealous. Israel shall make no molten gods. Israel shall keep the feast of unleavened bread. First-born belong to Yahweh. Keep the seventh day for rest. Observe the feast of weeks, the wheat harvest, and the feast of in-gathering. All males must appear before Yahweh three times yearly. No leaven shall be offered with sacrifices. Boil no kid in its mother's milk. Offer first fruits of the ground. [Compare Exodus 21:1-23:19.] Moses writes the ten words on the tablets, and comes off the mountain after forty days. [Compare Exodus 31:18.] Moses's face shines from talking with God. The people fear Moses. Moses relates what Yahweh said on the mountain. Moses begins wearing a veil when among the people, except when telling them what Yahweh has said. Moses reiterates the importance of keeping the Sabbath holy for solemn rest. Those who work on the Sabbath shall be killed. One cannot even make a fire on the Sabbath (Exodus 34:1-35:3).

Fabricating the Tabernacle.

Tabernacle. Moses tells the people that Yahweh wants a voluntary offering for materials to build the tabernacle. The people respond generously, so much so that Moses has to tell them to stop. Moses gives Bezalel and Oholiab the task of fabricating the tabernacle, along with others who are moved to do so: curtains, framework, veil, ark, table lampstand, incense altar, anointing oil, burnt-offering altar, washing laver, and court (Exodus 35:4-38:20).

Materials. Moses sums the gold, silver, and bronze employed in the fabrication. The ephod, breastpiece, robe, coats, and Moses' crown are made. The tabernacle is completed. Moses blesses the people (Exodus 38:21-39:43).

Worship. Moses erects the tabernacle, at Yahweh's command. Sacrifices are offered. Yahweh's cloud covers the tent of meeting, and his glory fills the tabernacle. Even Moses cannot enter. When Yahweh's cloud moves on, the people follow it. Otherwise, they stay where the cloud of Yahweh hovers, cloud by day and fire by night (Exodus 40:1-38).

LEVITICUS

Rules Regarding Sacrifices.

Offerings (First Version). A burnt offering of an unblemished male from one's cattle makes atonement for the offeror. Blood of the bull is thrown around and on the altar, cut in pieces in order, the legs and entrails washed and then laid on the altar, and the entirety burned. Similar rules follow for burnt offerings of sheep or goats, and birds. These burnt offerings create an odor pleasing to Yahweh (Leviticus 1:1-17). Flour offerings must be seasoned with salt (unleavened only and without honey). Hebrews must not let the salt of the covenant with their God be absent from cereal offerings. From all, the priests take a memorial portion for themselves, but the best is for Yahweh (Leviticus 2:1-16). Peace offerings may be male or females from the herd. The offeror lays his hands on the animal's head, kills the animal himself at the door of the tent of meeting, and Aaronic priests administer the burning. If a peace offering is sheep or goat, males or females without blemish must be killed by the offeror before the tent of meeting. All fat belongs to Yahweh. Hebrews may not eat fat or blood (Leviticus 3:1-17). Sin offering for the high priest's unwitting sins is a young bull without blemish. The priest burns the fat, kidneys, and a portion of the liver. The remainder shall be burned outside the tent of meeting where the ashes are discarded. If all Israel sins unwittingly, the same process suffices. If a ruler sins unwittingly, a male goat without blemish is brought to the place of burnt offerings, the ruler places his hands on the goat's head, and the animal is sacrificed and its fat burned. If common people sin unwittingly, a female goat or lamb suffices in the same manner. Unwitting sins may proceed from failure to offer testimony when qualified, touching unclean things, or uttering rash oaths. If too poor to afford a lamb, then the unwitting sinner may offer two turtle doves or pigeons, and if yet more poor, fine flour will suffice (Leviticus 4:1-5:13). Guilt offerings ensue for breach of faith. A ram without blemish and restitution to the person injured, plus twenty percent, atones. The same offering pertains to unwitting failure to follow laws (Leviticus 5:14-19). If one deceives a neighbor about money or property, or steals, or lies about found property, then one must make restitution plus twenty percent and offer a ram (Leviticus 6:1-7).

Offerings (Second Version). The fire of the altar must burn constantly, without lapse. The sacrifices burn all night long. A handful of cereal offerings is burned; the rest is for the males among Aaronic priests. High priests, upon appointment, shall offer fine flour, griddled; it shall be wholly burned. Sin offerings shall be killed before the Lord, then eaten by the priest offering it. The flesh is holy, and whatever touches it is holy [contagion theory of holiness]. Sin offerings differ from atonement offerings. All atonement offerings are burned in their entirety (Leviticus 6:8-30). Guilt offerings and sin offerings have the same rules. Peace offerings for thanksgiving, or just freewill sacrifices, shall be cakes of fine flour mixed with oil. It must all be eaten before the third day; any remainder must be burned. Eating peace offerings on the third day is an abomination. Flesh of peace offerings that touches unclean things may not be eaten. To do so cuts one off from the people (Leviticus 7:1-21). Israel may eat no fat or blood, on pain of exclusion from the people.

Peace Offerings (Third Version). From peace offerings, the priests take the breast and right thigh for themselves, which is their due. So much for the laws governing offerings (Leviticus 7:28-38).

Anointing Aaron and His Sons.

Consecrating Aaron. Moses gathers Israel at the tent of meeting. Moses washes Aaron and his sons with water. On Aaron, Moses puts the ritual garb. Then Moses anoints the tabernacle and its contents with oil, including Aaron. Moses clothes Aaron's sons. The priests lay their hands on the bull of sin offering. Moses kills it and burns the fat and kidneys. The remainder is burned outside the camp. Moses kills the ram of burnt offering, and burns it. Moses kills the ram of ordination. He puts some blood on the tip of Aaron and his sons' right ears. Then Moses burns the fat, kidneys, and right thigh, with a small portion of cereal offerings, after waving them before Yahweh. Moses sprinkles oil and blood on Aaron and his clothes, as well as his sons. Then Moses tells Aaron to boil the offerings and eat them, then burn the remainder. Aaron and his sons are commanded to sit at the door for seven days. On the eighth day, Moses tells Aaron to make sin offering of a bull calf and burnt offering of a ram, and other offerings. Moses addresses the people, saying that Yahweh will appear to them after these offerings. Aaron makes many sacrifices. Aaron blesses the people, then Moses and Aaron bless the people. Yahweh appears and burns the offerings and fat of the altar. Israel falls on their faces (Leviticus 8:1-9:24).

Rules for Priests.

Nadab and Abihu Die. Two priests, Nadab and Abihu, burn incense in a manner not prescribed. Yahweh incinerates them. Moses has relatives of Aaron carry away the charred corpses, and warns the family of Nadab and Abihu not to grieve. Israel may grieve, but not the family (Leviticus 10:1-7).

No Alcohol For Priests. Yahweh forbids Aaron to drink alcohol, and tells him to distinguish the holy from the common and to teach all Israel the difference (Leviticus 10:8-11).

Eating the Priest's Portion. Moses tells Aaron and his family to eat the cereal offering by the fire of Yahweh. Aaron's family can eat the breast wave offerings in any clean place (Leviticus 10:8-15).

Burning What Should Be Eaten. Aaron burns a sin offering, which should have been eaten [per Leviticus 6:24-30]. Moses castigates Aaron, who equivocates, mollifying Moses (Leviticus 10:16-20).

Ritual Purity Rules.

Pure and Impure Foods. Yahweh tells Israel that the people may eat animals with cloven hooves that chew cud. Take care not to eat camels, rock badgers, rabbits, or swine. Hebrews can eat all seafood with fins and scales; all other sea life is an abomination. Yahweh lists inedible birds and edible insects (Leviticus 11:1-23).

Uncleanness (First Version). Touching or carrying carcasses makes one unclean until sundown. Touching unclean animals makes one unclean. Animals with paws are unclean, as are swarming things (weasels, mice, lizards, geckos, crocodiles, lizards, chameleons). Items that touch the carcasses of unclean animals are unclean. If a pot or other food preparation tool touches an unclean animal, break it and do not use it. Touching unclean or dead unclean animals does not pollute springs or cisterns or dry sowing seed. For wet sowing seed, the result is opposite [note contagion theory of cleanness, with odd exceptions.] (Leviticus 11: 24-38).

Uncleanness (Second Version). Touching or eating the carcass of an edible animal makes one unclean until evening. Swarming things are an abomination, as are animals that go on their bellies, or have many feet. These animals make one unclean. Since Yahweh is Israel's god, Israel must keep itself holy and separate from crawling, swarming things. Israel must be holy as Yahweh is holy. These are the rules of edibility and uncleanness [note contagion theory of holiness] (Leviticus 11:39-45).

Female Uncleanness. Women who bear children are unclean for seven days, as at menstruation. Male children shall be circumcised on the eighth day. Then the woman who bore shall continue purification for thirty-three more days. If she bears a female child, she shall continue purification for sixty-six days. When purified, the mother shall take a lamb for burnt offering and a bird for sin offering to the priest. If poor, two birds suffice. Then she shall be clean (Leviticus 12:1-8).

Leprosy Uncleanness. If a man has skin blemishes and it becomes leprosy, a priest shall examine him to confirm the diagnosis. If uncertain, the person shall be quarantined for seven days and reexamined. If the disease has not spread, then the person shall be quarantined another seven days. If the disease has not spread, then the person shall be declared clean. If the disease spreads, the victim is unclean. If leprosy turns all of a man white, he is clean. But if raw flesh appears, he is unclean. If one has a boil, he is treated as a potential leper, subject to quarantine. If a burn on the skin shows some white, the priest shall treat the person as a potential leper, subject to quarantine. If one has thin yellow hair on head or beard with itchy spots, he is a potential leper, subject to quarantine. Dull white spots on the skin are not leprosy, but tetter [skin diseases such as ringworm, herpes, eczema]. Bald and partially bald men are clean, but if such a person has a reddish-white diseased scalp, he is a leper. Lepers must wear torn clothing, and not cut their hair. They announce their disease, crying "Unclean, unclean." Lepers live outside the camp. Garments may have leprosy as well, showing as green or red in the fabric. Such garments shall be burned. If the priest is uncertain, the garment is subject to rounds of quarantine, as are potential lepers. If leprous, the garment shall be burned. Clean lepers, after priestly examination, make elaborate sacrifices. If too poor for such expense, then less expensive sacrifices are employed. When the people take possession of Canaan, and a house has a disease, a priest shall inspect the house, and if uncertain, the priest shall quarantine the house, as with potential lepers. If it is leprous, the infected parts shall be removed and replaced. If the disease breaks out again, the house shall be destroyed and exported to an unclean place. If declared clean, the householder shall make elaborate sacrifices for the house using bird blood, and he shall release a living bird into the open field to make atonement for the house (Leviticus 13:1-14:57).

Discharge Uncleanness. If a man has bodily discharge, he and whatever he touches are unclean. When the discharge dissipates, he must wait seven days, and then follow a sacrificial regime (Leviticus 15:1-15).

Semen Uncleanness. If a man ejaculates, the semen is unclean, as are the man himself and his sexual partner (Leviticus 15:16-18).

Menstrual Uncleanness. If a woman menstruates, she and all she or her blood touches are unclean. If the discharge continues past normal menstruation, the woman shall remain unclean. When the discharge is ended, the woman must sacrifice two birds (Leviticus 15:19-30).

Defiling the Tabernacle. Unclean persons or objects may defile the tabernacle, and so must be separated from the people (Leviticus 15:31-33).

Day of Atonement. The author recounts that two of Aaron's sons died in Yahweh's presence. [Compare Leviticus 10:1-3.] Once annually, Aaron shall make a sin and burnt offering for himself and for the tabernacle, then take two goats. One is sacrificed for the sins of the people, the other goat, after Aaron lays his hands on its head and confesses the sins of Israel, is sent into the wilderness to Azazel [an evil spirit or demon]. Then Aaron shall burn the sacrificed animals. Moses does as commanded (Leviticus 16:1-34).

Yahweh's Ordinances.

Priest Rules (First Version). Yahweh tells Moses to instruct Aaron and his sons. One who kills an ox or goat incurs bloodguilt for shedding blood, unless he offers it as a sacrifice at the tabernacle. Such a person shall be cut off. This is to prevent the people from sacrificing to satyrs. No sacrifices shall be tolerated, except those to Yahweh. Blood is for atonement; blood is the life of the flesh. Any person who eats blood shall be cut off. If one eats what dies naturally or is killed by animals, that person shall be unclean until evening if he washes his body (Leviticus 17:1-16).

Forbidden Sexual and Sacrifice Habits of Neighboring Peoples (First Version). Yahweh is Israel's god. Israel shall not follow the rules given in Egypt or in Canaan, but rather Yahweh's rules. No person shall have sex with his father, mother, father's wife, sister, step-sister, niece, step-niece, paternal or maternal aunts, daughter-in-law, or sister-in-law. A man shall not have sex with a mother and her daughter, or that woman's grandchild. A man shall not wed a woman's sister, while the woman lives. No one may have sex during menstruation. One may not have sex with a neighbor's wife. No man shall burn his children as sacrifices to Molech. No male may have sex with a male, nor with beasts. No female may lie with beasts. These are the practices of the people of Canaan. Yahweh makes Canaan vomit out its inhabitants because of their practices. If Israel does as did the inhabitants of Canaan, then the land may vomit out Israel as well [Note this interpretative gloss concerning the Babylonian Exile.] (Leviticus 18:1-30).

DECALOGUE (LEVITICAL VERSION). [Compare Exodus 20:1-17, Leviticus 19:3-18, and Deuteronomy 5:6-21.] Israel must be holy as Yahweh is holy (Leviticus 19:1-2). Revere parents, mind the Sabbaths, make no idols or molten gods. Make peace offerings properly and eat them timely, on pain of exclusion from the people. Do not strip your fields or vineyards at harvest, but leave gleanings for the poor and travelers. Do not steal. Do not defraud. Do not lie. Do not use Yahweh's name to prop up lies. Do not oppress neighbors. Do not steal from neighbors. Pay wages owed promptly. Be kind to the deaf and blind. Judge fairly, without bowing to the rich or favoring the poor. Do not slander people. Do not condemn your neighbors, especially in serious matters. Do not hate your neighbors. Reason with them when you have disputes. Do not take vengeance against Hebrews. Love your neighbor as you love yourself [Note Jesus's use of the Levitical Decalogue and the Shema (Deuteronomy 6:4-10) and Deuteronomy 11:13 several hundred years later at Mark 12:29-31, Matthew 22:34-40, Luke 10:25-28.] (Leviticus 19:3-18).

Further Rules for the People. Do not let cattle breed with other animals. Do not plant two kinds of seed in a field. Do not wear clothing made of two different materials. If a man has sex with a betrothed slave, he shall bring a ram as a guilt offering to the tabernacle. When planting fruit trees, eat no fruit from the new trees until the fourth year. Do not eat flesh with blood in it. Do not foretell the future or cast spells. Do not round the hair at your temples or trim your beard. No ritual cutting. No tattoos. Do not let your daughter become a prostitute. Keep the Sabbaths. Respect the tabernacle. Do not seek people who speak with the dead or do magic. Honor old people. Take no advantage of foreigners; treat them as natives, who are due love like that you have for yourself. Remember, you were once foreigners in Egypt. Do not defraud customers. Make your balances just (Leviticus 19:1-18).

Forbidden Sexual and Sacrifice Habits of Neighboring Peoples (Second Version). Yahweh commands that any Hebrew or his visitor sacrificing a child to Molech shall be stoned to death. Hebrews who comfort such a man shall themselves be cut off. Employ no mediums or wizards, on pain of exclusion. Hebrews must be set apart for Yahweh by observing Yahweh's statutes. Do not curse your parents on pain of death. Fornicators shall be stoned to death, as shall the man who has sex with his father's wife. The death penalty also applies to sex with a man's daughter-in-law (which is incest), sex with males, sex with mothers and their daughters, sex with animals (death for all, including the animal). Sex with these persons results in exclusion from the people: sisters, step-sisters, menstruating women, aunts, near kin, uncle's wives. Men who have sex with a brother's wife shall be childless. [Compare Genesis 38:8-10.] Do not follow the customs of the people Yahweh drives out before Israel. Israel must be holy as Yahweh is holy. Stone wizards and mediums to death (Leviticus 19:19-20:27).

Priest Rules (Second Version). Yahweh instructs Moses to teach the priests. Priests must not have contact with the dead, except for near kin. Priests must not cut their hair or beards or make ritual cuts in their skin. Priests shall not marry prostitutes or divorced women. If a daughter of a priest becomes a prostitute, she must be burned. The high priest must bind his hair, avoid all dead bodies, even his own parents, and never leave the sanctuary [Note that this would not be possible were the tabernacle the sanctuary to which the text refers.] The high priest's wife must be a virgin. No blemished priest, such as the blind or lame, men with injured feet or hands, hunchbacks, dwarves, or men with poor eyesight, itching diseases, or crushed testicles, may serve. Such a person may remain a priest, but may not approach the inner sanctuary or altar. Priests must stay away from the people's sacrifices if the priests are not themselves ritually pure. The ritual cleanness rules are reiterated; no contact with bodily fluid discharge, dead flesh, semen, creeping things, animals that die naturally or by predation. [Compare Leviticus 11:1-45.] Foreigners shall not eat sacrifices, but members of a priest's household may eat. Daughters married to outsiders may not eat of sacrifices, unless widowed or divorced. If one eats unwittingly of sacrifices, he must add twenty percent and give it to Yahweh. (Leviticus 20:28-22:16).

Offerings (Third Version). Burnt offerings from Hebrews or foreigners shall be without blemish. No blind, disabled, mutilated, or sick animals with sores shall be accepted. Bulls and lambs with long or short parts may be offered, but only for freewill offerings, never as votive offerings. Animals with crushed testicles or tears or cuts shall not be offered in the land, especially if purchased from foreigners. No newborn animals shall be sacrificed until eight days old. No mother and her newborn offspring shall be sacrificed on the same day. Thanksgiving sacrifices must be eaten the same day. These are Yahweh's commandments (Leviticus 22:17-31).

Ritual Feasts. Keep the Sabbath every seventh day, free from work. These are ritual feasts: passover, unleavened bread, first fruits of harvest (weeks) (when you harvest, do not strip the fields, but leave gleanings for the poor and stranger) [Compare Leviticus 19:9-10], trumpets, day of atonement (on which no work may be done), and booths (Leviticus 23:1-44).

Tabernacle Lamp. Pure olive oil shall be burned in a gold censer perpetually before the inner sanctuary. Each Sabbath, twelve flour cakes must be offered on the pure gold table (Leviticus 24:1-9).

Blasphemy. A Hebrew woman's son by an Egyptian father blasphemes the Name (Yahweh). Yahweh commands that the man be stoned by the gathered people, as shall any person who blasphemes the Name. The people stone the blasphemer to death (Leviticus 24:10-16, 23).

Yahweh's Ordinances. [Compare Exodus 21:1-23:19.] Murderers shall be executed. One who kills an animal shall compensate its owner or suffer commensurate loss. If one injures another, the injury shall be reproduced in the perpetrator ("fracture for fracture, eye for eye, tooth for tooth"). All laws apply to the foreigner and native alike (Leviticus 24:17-22).

Land Sabbath. Keep the Sabbath in Canaan. Leave fields and vineyards fallow each seventh year; do not harvest even what grows without tending. The "Sabbath of the land" shall feed you. *Jubilee.* Each fiftieth year is sacred. All Hebrews return to their familial lands and families. Nothing shall be sown or reaped. All may eat of the fields without tending (Leviticus 25:1-7).

Jubilee Reversions. All sold land reverts to sellers in Jubilee year. In land sales, prices are prorated by years-remaining to Jubilee. Do not worry about eating during land Sabbath years. Yahweh will make the land produce more before the Sabbath year. Land shall not be sold in perpetuity, for Israel wanders with Yahweh. Families should redeem their members' parcels, but if they cannot, all should revert in Jubilee years. Redemption applies only for one year, and Jubilee does not apply to houses in walled cities. Levites (priests) may redeem at any time, regardless of other rules, and Jubilee always applies to Levitical families, even their houses in walled cities. Levitical fields may not be sold. [Compare Numbers 18:8-20.] If a brother becomes poor, he may live with your family. Do not lend at interest, nor sell him food. No Hebrew shall make a slave of another Hebrew, but shall treat him as hired help until Jubilee. Do not treat your employees harshly. Hebrews may hold slaves from among non-Hebrews. A Hebrew who sells himself into slavery to a non-Hebrew shall be redeemed by his family (Leviticus 25:8-55).

Obedience and Disobedience. If Israel worships other gods, Israel disrespects Yahweh. If Israel obeys Yahweh, then Yahweh will insure Israel's prosperity and peace. Israel will be unstoppable militarily, and have a growing population. Yahweh will dwell with the people and not hate them. Remember, Yahweh freed Israel from Egypt (Leviticus 26:1-13).

If Israel disobeys Yahweh, Yahweh will bring sickness and military defeat, give outsiders rule over Israel, break Israel's pride, and cause Israel's labors to be fruitless. Wild animals will kill your children and cattle. Israel shall eat her children, and her idols and hillside altars shall be destroyed. Yahweh shall destroy Israel's cities, and blow Israel's incense from his nostrils. Yahweh will devastate Canaan, and Israel will be scattered to enemy lands. Israel shall pine away because of her sins (Leviticus 26:14-39).

If Israel confesses her faithlessness and disobedience, which is Israel's uncircumcised heart, then Yahweh will forgive and remember his covenant with Abraham, Isaac, and Jacob. Even in foreign lands, Yahweh does not forget Israel or utterly destroy the people (Leviticus 26:40-46).

Value of Vows. Values for persons are set. When a man makes an offering, no substitutions are permitted. Dedications of houses may be redeemed, at a premium. Redemptions of dedications of land shall be computed in relation to the time remaining to Jubilee. No firstborn animals can be dedicated; all belong to Yahweh already. Things or animals or persons devoted to Yahweh cannot be redeemed; all are most holy. Men devoted to Yahweh must be killed [Does Leviticus 27:29 contemplate human sacrifice?] (Leviticus 27:1-29).

Tithe. The tithe (ten percent) of the land and fruit trees belongs to Yahweh. This property can be redeemed from Yahweh's claim upon it for a twenty percent premium. These are Yahweh's commandments (Leviticus 27:1-34).

NUMBERS

Sinai Census and Mustering.

Yahweh commands Moses to count Israel's men by families and tribes for a military draft. Moses numbers the fighting men in Sinai by tribe, some 603,550 men. Priests are not numbered, for they are charged with care of the tabernacle (Numbers 1:1-54). The fighting men of Israel muster around the tent of meeting, three tribes on each side (Numbers 2:1-34).

Priest Rules.

Call of the Levites. Aaron and his sons shall be priests of Israel. Sons Nadab and Abihu died when they offered unholy fire before Yahweh [compare Leviticus 10:1-7]. Yahweh tells Moses to bring the tribe of Levi near with Aaron. The Levites shall be priests for Israel and perform duties at the tabernacle under Aaron's supervision. Yahweh says he has taken the Levites instead of Israel's first born sons and beasts [compare Exodus 12:1-13:16].

Levitical Census. Yahweh tells Moses to number the Levites by families: Gershon, Kohath, and Merari. The Levites numbered 22,000 (Numbers 3:1-39).

First Born Census. Yahweh commands a census of Israel's first born sons, who were 22,273 in number. Yahweh takes the Levites in their stead. For the 273 exceeding the 22,000, each must pay five shekels per head, which sum shall be given to Aaron and his sons (Numbers 3:40-51).

Tabernacle Transportation Duties of Levite Families. The Kohath Levites are to disassemble the tabernacle and carry the inner sanctuary property when Israel moves. Eleazar is to take charge of the oil for the tabernacle lamp, and supervise the tabernacle and its contents. Yahweh commands that the Kohathites are to be protected from dying in their service of the tabernacle. The Gershon Levites shall disassemble the curtains of the tabernacle and carry them. The Merari Levites shall disassemble and carry the frame of the tabernacle. The Koathites were 2,750 in number. The Gershonites were 2,630 in number. The Merarites were 3,200 in number. In total, the number of men thirty to fifty, who could do the work of the tabernacle, were 8,580 (Numbers 4:1-49).

Yahweh's Ordinances.

Excluding Lepers. All lepers and persons with skin discharges and those who have had contact with dead bodies shall be put out of the camp (Numbers 5:1-4).

Civil Wrongs. When a person sins against Yahweh, he shall confess and make restitution plus twenty percent to his victim. If no kinsman survives to receive the restitution, then the restitution shall be paid to the priests (Numbers 5:5-10).

Jealousy and Fornicating Wives. If a man is jealous believing, rightly or wrongly, that his wife has fornicated, he shall offer a cereal offering for jealousy. The accused woman shall come to the priests, who shall put dust in water, put her hands in the water, make the woman swear an oath, write the oath and wash the letters into the water, and then make her drink the water. If she lies and has fornicated, the water of bitterness will cause her thigh to wither and body to swell. If she did not fornicate, she shall escape pain and bear children (Numbers 5:11-31).

Nazirite Vows. Nazirite vows require the person to separate for Yahweh, avoiding alcohol and grapes. No hair cutting or going near dead bodies (even close family members). If a person dies suddenly beside a Nazirite, the Nazirite must shave his head, and make appropriate sacrifices, which are specified. Upon completion of the term of the Nazirite's vow, he shall make sacrifices and shave his head at the door of the tent of meeting and burn the hair in the fire of the sacrifices. Then the Nazirite may drink wine (Numbers 6:1-23).

Establishing Tabernacle Worship.
[Compare Exodus 35:4–40:38].

Aaron's Blessing for the People. The [famous] Aaronic blessing is stated (Numbers 6:24-27).

Dedication of the Tabernacle. When the tabernacle is finished, the tribes make offerings to dedicate it. Each tribe makes its offering on one specific day, Judah being first, for twelve days. When the dedication is complete, Moses enters the inner sanctuary, and Yahweh speaks from above the mercy seat on the ark (Numbers 7:1-89).

Setting Up the Tabernacle. Yahweh instructs Aaron to set up the lamps. Yahweh instructs Aaron to cleanse the Levites and offer the Levites as a wave offering to Yahweh, sacrificing one bull as a sin offering and another as a burnt offering to make atonement for their sins. Yahweh takes the Levites in the place of the first-born of Israel. Levites are to serve from twenty-five years of age until fifty years of age. [Compare the thirty to fifty year service requirement of Numbers 4.] (Numbers 8:1-26).

Passover.
Uncleanness During Passover. Yahweh commands Israel to observe Passover. Some men were unclean from touching bodies and the priests would not let them participate in Passover. Yahweh tells even the unclean or those traveling in foreign lands to keep the Passover. If a Hebrew fails to keep Passover, he shall be cut off. Even willing foreigners should observe Passover (Numbers 9:1-14).

Israel Moves.
Divine Presence at the Tabernacle. Yahweh covers the tabernacle in cloud by day and fire by night. When the cloud and fire move, Israel sets out (Numbers 9:15-23).

Trumpets. Yahweh tells Moses to make two silver trumpets to summon the people and to alert them to break camp and to announce that Israel comes to an enemy to war. The trumpets are also blown on feast days (Numbers 10:1-10).

To Paran. Yahweh's cloud moves and Israel follows it north to the wilderness of Paran. Moses's brother-in-law wants to return to Midian, but Moses encourages him to stay. Israel travels three days north, following Yahweh's cloud. Moses prays for Israel's enemies to be scattered, and for Yahweh to persevere with Israel (Numbers 10:11-36).

Israel's Rebellions.

Meat for Israel. Israel grumbles about life's difficulties and Yahweh angers, burning some outlying portions of the camp. Moses intercedes and Yahweh relents. Israel complains about the boredom of the daily manna, demanding meat and vegetables. Yahweh angers greatly, and Moses is unhappy with Yahweh's fickleness. Moses complains that Yahweh should remember his promise; if Yahweh will not relent, Moses asks that Yahweh kill him. Yahweh commands Moses to assemble seventy men who are elders, upon whom Yahweh will put some of Moses' spirit. [Compare Exodus 18:13-26.] Yahweh promises that on the morrow, Israel will eat meat for a month until meat becomes irksome. Moses asks how Yahweh intends to provide so much meat. Yahweh tells Moses to watch and see. Yahweh puts spirit in seventy elders by speaking with them. These elders prophesy, but only this one time. Two of the seventy prophesy among the people. Joshua, son of Nun, asks Moses to forbid it, fearing for Moses' authority. Moses chastises Joshua, saying he wishes all the people were prophets with Yahweh's spirit. Yahweh sends a wind off the sea, and quails in great numbers descend on the camp. Yahweh angers and sends a plague upon the people (Numbers 11:1-35).

In-House Rebellion. Miriam and Aaron dispute Moses' authority because Moses married outside Israel. Moses is the most shy man on the earth. Yahweh confronts Miriam and Aaron, saying he speaks with prophets in dark speech, but with Moses mouth to mouth. Yahweh afflicts Miriam with leprosy. Moses intercedes on Miriam's behalf, but Yahweh insists she be quarantined outside the camp for seven days. Then Miriam returns (Numbers 12:1-16).

Rebellion at the Report of Spies. Moses sends spies into Canaan to gain intelligence about their strength and the quality of their land and crops. One spy goes from each tribe. The spies, after forty days, return with fruit, and report that the land is rich, but the people well-fortified. The spies are divided about whether Israel can conquer the land. Caleb believes they can prevail. The majority report represents the people of Canaan as evil giants. The people complain about Moses that Yahweh brought them out into the wilderness only to die in the end. They choose a captain to lead them back to Egypt. Caleb and Joshua contradict the spies' majority report, telling the people that the land is good and the inhabitants will fall before Yahweh. The people, however, move to stone Joshua and Caleb. Yahweh intervenes to kill the faithless people and make of Moses a great nation. Moses objects that the Egyptians will deride Yahweh if he kills the people. Moses asks Yahweh to forgive in steadfast love. Yahweh relents of his intent to destroy Israel, but refuses to let those who rebel enter the promised land. Israel shall wander in the Sinai another forty years, so this generation dies out. Yahweh instructs Moses to return to the wilderness near the Red Sea. Yahweh kills by plague the spies who spoke against Israel's conquest of the land. Only Joshua and Caleb remain (Numbers 13:1-14:38).

Rebellion at Punishment of Wandering. The people take it upon themselves, without Yahweh or Moses, to attack the Amalekites and Canaanites. Israel is routed (Numbers 14:39-45).

Interlude Pertaining to Offering Laws. Free will and feast offerings are specified. Vow and peace offerings are specified (Numbers 15:1-10). Yahweh's law shall pertain to all in the land, including the strangers and travelers. One law for all (Numbers 15:11-16). Offerings for eating meals are specified. Unwitting errors in following these sacrificial laws, either by the people or by individuals, are atoned by sacrifices, which are specified. But for the person who sins willfully, no remediation is possible; he shall be cut off from the people (Numbers 15:17-31).

Ignoring the Sabbath. A man gathers sticks on the Sabbath. Yahweh commands that the sinner be stoned, which the congregation does (Numbers 15:32-36).

Garment Corner Tassels. Yahweh commands that Israel wear tassels with blue cords on the corners of their garments to help them remember Yahweh's commandments (Numbers 15:37-40).

Korah's Rebellion. 250 leaders, lead by Korah the Levite, challenge Moses and Aaron about their presumption of leadership, since all Israel is holy. Many among the rebels are not of the priestly tribe of Levi. Moses puts a challenge. Let Yahweh choose. All the rebels shall burn incense to Yahweh in the morning. Moses negotiates with various leaders, to no avail. They allege Moses brought them into the wilderness to kill them and has not made good his promise of a land of milk and honey. Aaron and all the 250 bring their incense censers to the tabernacle. Yahweh decides to destroy the entire people. Moses intercedes, asking Yahweh why he will condemn all for the sins of the few. Yahweh relents. Moses warns the people away from the rebel leaders. Yahweh splits the ground beneath the rebel leaders and their families, who all go to Sheol alive. The remainder of the 250, Yahweh burns to death. Moses gathers the censers of the rebels, beats them into plates, and covers the altar with them, as a reminder to the people of the cost of rebellion. The next morning, the people complain that Moses killed Hebrews. Yahweh moves to wipe out the people by plague. Moses intercedes as the plague commences. Aaron takes incense into the midst of the people and stands between the well and the sick. The plague stops, but only after 14,700 died (Numbers 16:1-50).

Aaron's Rod. Yahweh tells Moses to gather a rod from each tribe and put them in the tabernacle. In the morning, Aaron's rod has blossomed and borne almonds. Aaron's rod becomes part of the tabernacle paraphernalia. The Hebrews murmur, fearing Yahweh (Numbers 17:1-13).

Priest Rules.
[Compare Leviticus 7:28-36.]

Aaron's Charge. Yahweh tells Aaron that he and his tribe bear the sins of Israel by being priests. Only Aaron may enter the inner sanctuary. Any others shall die (Numbers 18:1-7).

Levitical Share (First Version). Yahweh gives Aaron and the Levites whatever is not burned in sacrificial ceremonies. All the firstborn, which belong to Yahweh wholly, shall be redeemed for a fixed fee, and the Levites shall possess those monetary redemptions. The Levites shall have no lands, but only the service of Yahweh, as their inheritance [compare Leviticus 25:32-33] (Numbers 18:8-20).

Levitical Share (Second Version). [Compare Leviticus 27:30-33.] The Levites shall receive a tithe from the people which shall be their inheritance. From this tithe, the priests must tithe, a tenth of the tenth, to Yahweh as an offering, always and only the best part of what the Levites receive (Numbers 18:21-32).

Yahweh's Ordinances.
Water for Impurity. Yahweh commands a priest to burn a red heifer outside the camp. The heifer's ashes shall be gathered and retained outside the camp. When mixed with water, these become the water for impurity for removing sin (Numbers 19:1-10).

Contact with the Dead. When a man touches a dead body, he becomes unclean and must be washed with water for impurity, then remain outside the camp for seven days, lest he pollute the tabernacle. If one enters a tent where a dead person lies, he becomes unclean. The water for impurity must cleanse him and the tent and its furnishings. If one touches a dead person in the open or a grave, he becomes unclean and must wash in the water for impurity. If a person declines to wash in the water for impurity after contacting dead flesh, he shall be cut off from the people (Numbers 19:11-21).

Spread of Uncleanness. What an unclean person touches becomes unclean [note contagion theory of holiness] (Numbers 19:22).

Events in Sinai.

Miriam's Death. Israel moves to the wilderness of Zin (southeast of Dead Sea). Miriam dies and is buried there (Numbers 20:1).

Water from Rock. Israel lacks water, complaining to Moses about lack of food as well. Yahweh tells Moses to strike a rock twice with his rod. The water serves Israel's needs, and their cattle too. The waters are called Meribah (Numbers 20:2-13) [Compare Exodus 17:2-7].

Moses and Aaron Punished. Yahweh tells Moses and Aaron that they shall not lead the people into Canaan (Numbers 20:12).

No Safe Passage Through Edom. Moses seeks safe passage through Edom, but is denied. The king of Edom brings out a large army, and Israel withdraws (Numbers 20:14-21).

Aaron Dies. Yahweh decides that Aaron shall die for his part in Israel's faithlessness at Meribah. Moses takes Aaron up on Mount Hor, near Edom, strips the high priest garments from him and puts them on his son Eleazar, and Aaron dies. Israel mourns for thirty days (Numbers 20:22-29).

Beginning of the Conquest of Canaan.

Battle with Arad. In the Negeb [southern Palestine, southwest of Dead Sea], the king of Arad fights Israel and takes captives. Israel turns to Yahweh, who gives Arad to Israel. Israel destroys Arad's cities (Numbers 21:1-3).

Fiery Serpents. The people seek to travel around Edom, but grow impatient. They complain of lack of food and water. Yahweh sends fiery serpents to bite the people. Many die. Moses intercedes, and makes a bronze serpent. Everyone bitten by serpents who sees the bronze serpent lives (Numbers 21:4-9).

Traveling North. Israel travels north on the east side of Edom and Moab [Moab lies on the eastern shore of the Dead Sea and Edom immediately south of Moab]. The writer cites to the Book of the Wars of the Lord, and a song of the people (Numbers 21:10-20).

War with the Amorites and Neighbors. Israel seeks safe passage through Amor. King Sihon declines, and brings an army against Israel. Israel prevails and settles in the cities of Amor. The writer quotes a ballad sung of the Amorite's earlier victory over Moab. Spies reconnoiter Jazer, which Israel invades and ejects the Amorites there. Then Israel kills all the people of Bashan and takes their lands (Numbers 21:21-35).

Balaam's Ass. Israel camps east of Moab. Balak, king of Moab, fears, and sends for the wizard Balaam to curse Israel. Yahweh intervenes and tells Balaam to remain in his home, for Yahweh blesses Israel. Balak sends more princes. Yahweh speaks again to Balaam, letting him go, but only to do Yahweh's bidding. Then Yahweh angers because Balaam is going to the Moabites. An angel blocks his way, as Balaam rides on his ass. Balaam beats the ass in an attempt to get it to go around the fearsome angel. Yahweh speaks from the ass's mouth, asking why Balaam is beating the ass. Balaam answers. Yahweh reveals himself to Balaam in the angel. Yahweh permits Balaam to continue, but warns Balaam to do only what Yahweh commands. Balak sacrifices. Balaam asks for seven altars with seven bulls and seven rams to be provided. Balaam sacrifices, and Yahweh meets him on a low hill. Yahweh sends Balaam to bless Israel before Balak. Balak objects, and takes Balaam to another hill, offers another round of seven sacrifices. Yahweh comes to Balaam again, sending him back to sing a song to Balak extolling the power of Yahweh and prowess of Israel, who shall prevail. Balak urges Balaam to neither curse nor bless Israel. Balaam refuses. Yahweh has spoken. Balak is unsatisfied. He takes Balaam to a third hilltop, sacrifices on another seven altars. The spirit of god comes upon Balak, who again blesses Israel. Balak releases Balaam, disappointed. Balaam speaks one last time, telling him that a man from Jacob's tribe shall rule and crush Moab, Edom, and Amalek. Balaam and Balak go to their homes (Numbers 22:1-24:25).

Israel's Baal Apostasy. Being close to Moab, Israel begins sacrificing to Baal. [Balaam, of Numbers 22, is blamed for this event at Numbers 31:16.] Yahweh angers, ordering Moses to hang all of Israel's chiefs and slay all those who have worshipped Baal. 24,000 people are executed. One Hebrew, Zimri, marries a Midianite woman, Cozbi, and brings her to the camp. Phinehas drives a spear through both of them. Yahweh's plague is stopped, and Yahweh praises Phinehas. Yahweh sends Israelites to harass Midian, because they tempted Israel with Baal and with Cozbi (Numbers 25:1-18).

Moab Census of the People. [Compare Numbers 1:1-54.] Moses numbers the people by tribe. Their aggregate population numbers 601,730 (Numbers 26:1-51). Yahweh instructs that the land of Canaan is to be divided by lot, but larger tribes will get larger portions. The Levites are numbered at 23,000. At this time, none remain among the people of those who were numbered during the census taken in the Sinai, except Caleb and Joshua.

Daughters of Zelophehad Plead. The five daughters of Zelophehad, whose father died in the wilderness for his sins, seek a share of land. Yahweh agrees with these daughters, and orders a non-patrilineal inheritance scheme that passes land down the bloodline, even through daughters when no son exists (Numbers 27:1-11) [Note Numbers 36:1-12, in which the men of Manasseh complain about Yahweh's decision regarding the daughters of Zelophehad].

Moses' Death Foretold. Yahweh tells Moses to view Canaan from the mountain of Abarim, for he will die before Israel enters the land, as did Aaron (Numbers 27:12-14).

Joshua to Succeed Moses. Moses asks Yahweh to select his successor, so Israel shall not be as "sheep without a shepherd." Yahweh chooses Joshua, and tells Moses to pass his power to Joshua before all Israel (Numbers 27:12-23).

Ritual Rules.

Offerings at Ritual Feasts. [Compare Leviticus 23:1-44.] Yahweh commands Israel to make its food offerings, which are a pleasant smell to Yahweh, at the appropriate times. Two lambs must be burned daily, morning and evening, with a cereal offering and alcohol. On Sabbaths, offer two lambs. At the first of each month, greater sacrifices (all specified) are required. At Passover, the sacrifices are specified. At first fruits, the sacrifices are specified. At trumpets, there shall be no work; the sacrifices are specified for each of the three convocations, and the eight days following the mid-month convocation. These sacrifices are in addition to the usual freewill, burnt, cereal, drink, and peace offerings (Numbers 28:1-29:40).

Vows. Vows of men shall be honored. Vows of women shall be honored if their fathers approve or fail to object. If a woman's father disapproves her vow, the vow shall not be honored. If a woman is married, her husband must approve her vows or fail to object for them to be honored. If divorced or widowed, a woman's vows shall be honored (Numbers 30:1-16).

War with Midian.

Call to War. Yahweh sends 12,000 men of Israel to war with Midian. Israel killed all the males of Midian, including Balaam. Israel took the women and children captive, took the possessions as booty, and burned their towns to the ground. Moses angers, because the men have not killed all the male children and wives. Only the young virgins can become booty. The warriors must encamp outside for seven days to purify themselves, because they have touched dead bodies (Numbers 31:1-20).

Dividing Midianite Booty. Eleazar the high priest commands that from the Midianite possessions, only those which remain after being burned and being washed in the water of impurity can be retained. Moses instructs that the soldiers keep one half of the booty, and the other half must be distributed generally among the people. From the soldiers' share of booty, two tenths of one percent of all the booty belongs to Yahweh and must be given to Eleazar the high priest. From the people's share of booty, two percent shall belong to the Levites at the tabernacle. The spoils from the Midian campaign are enumerated for the soldiers' and people's shares: sheep, cattle, asses, virgins. The Israeli commanders count their soldiers. Not one Israeli has died in the battle. The soldiers give all the gold and jewelry to Yahweh to atone for themselves. This too is enumerated (Numbers 31:21-54).

Lands East of Jordan River. The tribes of Reuben and Gad seek to possess the conquered lands east of the Jordan. Moses complains to them that their desire will discourage Israel from its battles. Yahweh may dispossess them as did Yahweh with those who sinned in Sinai. Reuben and Gad promise that every fighting man will go up with Israel to fight until all have received lands in Canaan. Gad and Reuben promise before Yahweh and the assembled congregation to do as they have promised. And these tribes, including Manasseh, take possession of these lands and built cities (Numbers 32:1-42).

Stages of Travel.

Starting Places. The starting places for the sojourn of Israel in coming to Canaan are named, along with core events in the travel (Numbers 33:1-49).

Rules for Invasion.

Scorched Earth Policy. Yahweh commands that Israel must drive out all inhabitants of Canaan, and destroy their stone and molten gods and their high places. The people shall inherit by lot, small lands to small tribes, large lands to large tribes. Yahweh warns about leaving any of the natives in the land, for they will spell trouble down the road (Numbers 33:50-56).

The Extent and Division of the Land. The boundaries of the Israeli conquests are detailed, south, west, north and east. Moses authorizes Eleazar and Joshua to divide the land among the remaining tribes of Israel, with the help of one man from each tribe, who is named (Numbers 34:1-29).

Levitical Cities of Refuge (First Version). The people are to give the Levites cities and pasture lands surrounding those cities. The size of the pastures is specified. Six of these forty-eight cities shall be refuges where manslayers may flee. The Levitical cities shall be apportioned fairly among the tribes according to the size of their lands [Compare Numbers 18:8-20.] (Numbers 35:1-8).

Levitical Cities of Refuge (Second Version). Yahweh commands Moses to tell the people to select six cities as cities of refuge for manslayers (people who kill humans without intent to do so), where they may live without fear of avenging relatives. Murderers slay with intent, using iron or wood or stone tools. Murderers shall be executed by the person who avenges on the part of the dead person's family. Those who kill by any means to vent hatred, or by ambush are murderers. Execute them. If a person kills without hatred or ambush, by negligence without seeking harm to the victim, then the people may send the slayer to the city of refuge, and so long as the slayer stays in that city, the avenger shall not attack. The slayer must remain in the city of refuge as long as the high priest lives. If the slayer is found outside the city of refuge, the avenger may kill him without guilt. Murderers shall be executed, but only on the testimony of more than one witness. No ransom is acceptable; murderers must be executed. The blood of murder victims pollutes the land. It can be cleaned only by the shed blood of the murderer himself. To do less defiles the land (Numbers 35:9-34).

Marriage Rules for Inheriting Daughters. The heads of families in Manasseh's tribe complain about the decision that daughters of Zelophehad may inherit where no son intervenes. This scheme will transfer tribal land from one tribe to another as the daughters marry. Moses agrees, and orders that inheriting daughters shall marry only within their tribe. A tribe's land must remain with the tribe forever. The daughters of Zelophehad comply, marrying from among Manasseh's men. Thus Yahweh commands the people through Moses on the plains of Moab (Numbers 36: 1-13).

DEUTERONOMY

[Note that Deuteronomy is a long sermon on Yahweh's law. The purpose of Deuteronomy is to explain the law (Deuteronomy 1:5), which implies an unstated reservation about the renditions contained in previous four books of the Torah. Priests in Babylonian captivity rhapsodize Yahweh and the saving effect of precise obedience to the rules of the one god.]

Moses Explains the Law.

Recounting Israel's History from mid-Sinai to the Plains of Moab. From the plains of Moab, where the people are ready to invade Canaan, Moses explains the law: Yahweh sent the people from Mount Horeb, where Yahweh delivered the law, toward Canaan. All the land from Horeb to the Euphrates was promised to Israel. Moses created an administration, with judges and subjudges. Moses commanded the judges to decide impartially, and to bring hard cases to Moses. The people left Mount Horeb for Canaan. Moses sent in spies, who discouraged the people from invading. Yahweh forbade this generation from entering the land, and wandering commenced. Only Caleb and Joshua shall remain when the people enter the land. Joshua shall be apprenticed to Moses, and shall lead after Moses. The people took it upon themselves to fight the Amorites, who crushed Israel. Israel licked her wounds at Kadesh for a long while. Israel traveled though the land of Esau's descendants without incident. When all the rebellious generation had perished, Moses moved the people toward Canaan by way of Moab, through which they passed peacefully [Compare Numbers 20:14-21:20.] Yahweh sent Israel against Sihon the Amorite, and Israel utterly destroyed him, killing every man, woman, and child, and burning every city. Only the cattle were taken and city booty. Og, the king of Bashan, fought Israel, and they did to him as they had to Sihon, taking sixty cities. Moses gave the trans-Jordanian lands to Reuben, Dan, and the half-tribe of Manasseh, upon solemn promise that these tribes would fight until all Canaan was taken for Israel. Yahweh forbade Moses from entering the land, because of the cowering of the people in Sinai after the report of the spies. Moses saw Canaan from Mount Pisgah. Yahweh promoted Joshua as Moses's successor (Deuteronomy 1:1-3:29).

Prologue to the Law. [Note this section contains the rationale for the Torah, especially Deuteronomy. The people have been defeated and deported and scattered in disarray. If only they will cleave to Yahweh, they will be restored from Babylon.] Moses commands the people to heed the law, neither taking from nor adding to it, so they may survive conquest of Canaan. Moses reminds the people of the decimation at Peor when they worshipped Baal. Keep the ordinances, for Yahweh is near to Israel. Be diligent, and teach them to your children, how Yahweh delivered the law to Moses at Horeb, writing the ten words on stone tablets. Make no images of God to worship; Yahweh has no form. Do not worship heavenly objects. Sun, moon, and stars are for all people, but Yahweh has chosen Israel specifically. Yahweh angered with Moses because of the sin of the people, and will not let Moses into Canaan. Do not forget Yahweh's covenant by making little gods. Yahweh is jealous. If you provoke Yahweh to anger, you will disappear from Canaan and be destroyed. Yahweh will scatter you among other peoples and kill many of you. You will worship gods of wood and stone. But from that distant place, you will turn again to Yahweh, if you seek him with all your soul, and obey Yahweh again. For Yahweh will forgive and remember his covenant with the patriarchs. No god is like Yahweh, traveling with the people, rescuing them from within the Egyptian nation. You must know that there is no god like Yahweh; there is, in fact, no other god. [Note these first statements of intellectually-consistent monotheism.] Yahweh disciplined Israel to bring them out of Egypt and drive the inhabitants of Canaan out before Israel. [Note the lapse of story-telling perspective here. The conquest of the land is completed, though the narrative stands with Moses speaking pre-conquest from the plains of Moab.] Yahweh rules heaven and earth; there are no other gods. Israel shall obey him (Deuteronomy 4:1-40).

Cities of Refuge. Moses designates three trans-Jordanian cities as cities of refuge for manslayers (Deuteronomy 4:41-43).

DECALOGUE (DEUTERONOMIC VERSION). [Compare Exodus 20:1-17, Leviticus 19:3-18, and Deuteronomy 5:6-21.] These are the laws that Moses delivers in the trans-Jordan land of the Amorites (Deuteronomy 4:44-49). Yahweh made a covenant with Israel at Mount Horeb, which pertains to the people assembled today as much as to Israel at Sinai. Yahweh speaks directly to the congregation of Israel, with Moses mediating. Yahweh commands: worship no other gods, make no objects to worship because Yahweh is jealous and shows you steadfast love (chesed), do not hide your lies by using Yahweh's name, keep the Sabbath holy by not working, respect your parents, never murder, never steal, never tell falsehoods about your neighbors that get them in trouble with authorities, never pine after your neighbor's life or possessions. Yahweh wrote these rules on stone tables for you and gave them to Moses. All Israel feared, for they had seen Yahweh. Yahweh approves Israel's fear; that is the right attitude to have. Israel will live, if they will obey (Deuteronomy 5:1-33). Those who obey Yahweh's law prosper in the land of Canaan, live long, and bear many children (Deuteronomy 6:1-3).

Shema (First Version.) Listen, people. Yahweh is your god; he is the only god that exists. Love Yahweh completely. Take his commandments to heart. Teach them to your children. Talk about them with friends wherever you go. Wear them in phylacteries. Write them on your doorposts (Deuteronomy 6:4-9). [Note Jesus' use of the Levitical Decalogue and the Shema (Deuteronomy 6:4-9) and Deuteronomy 11:13 several hundred years later at Mark 12:29-31, Matthew 22:34-40, Luke 10:25-28.]

Warnings. Beware that when you take the land and its riches, you do not become complacent toward Yahweh. Fear him. Yahweh is jealous and might kill you for worshipping false gods. Keep the laws. Instruct your sons about the people's history with Yahweh. Diligent obedience becomes righteousness before Yahweh. Make no easy agreements with the people of Canaan. Show them no mercy. Do not marry their daughters or let your daughters marry their sons. Such marriages will erode your children's worship of Yahweh. Destroy the worship locales and liturgical props of the Canaanite peoples (Deuteronomy 6:10-7:5).

Election. Yahweh has chosen Israel from among all other peoples for no particular reason. Yahweh loves Israel and keeps his promises to your fathers. Yahweh is god, faithful and showing steadfast love to those of his people who obey and love him in return. But those who reject Yahweh, he will destroy. So, take care to obey. The blessings of the covenant belong to those who obey: fecundity, prosperity, health, and conquest without pity. When you tremble before enemies, remember what Yahweh did to Pharaoh. Yahweh will send hornets upon your enemies. Israel's Canaanite enemies will be slowly cleared from before the people [*contra* the representations of the book of Joshua], if only the Israelis will drive the natives out utterly, and hate their gods, even the gold and silver that clads their idols. Canaanite idols are a snare for the Hebrews. (Deuteronomy 7:6-26).

Discipline. Yahweh humbled Israel in the Sinai. A man lives not by food, but by the word of Yahweh. Yahweh provides for Israel. In the desert, Israel's clothing never wore out and their feet never swelled. For Yahweh disciplines Israel, as a father his son. Yahweh takes Israel to a rich land where the people will have resources and eat well. Yahweh is concerned that Israel will forget him when they are comfortable. Yahweh believes the people will say, when they prosper, that their own powers made them rich. Yahweh makes people rich to prove his faith to his covenant. When people get haughty, then they worship false gods. Then Israel will perish, just like the Canaanites (Deuteronomy 8:1-20). Yahweh is driving wicked peoples out of Canaan before Israel. Yahweh does not defend Israel because of Israel's good behavior, but because of the evil of the natives, and to confirm his promises to Abraham, Isaac, and Jacob. Israel is stubborn. Remember that the people angered Yahweh at Horeb when they made a molten calf. Moses broke the tables on which Yahweh had written his commandments. Moses ground down the idol, and threw it in the nearby stream. Moses prayed for Israel, because Yahweh wished to destroy Israel. Then Yahweh made new tables of the law for Moses. [The authors interpolate future material about Aaron's death.] Then as Israel traveled Aaron died, and Eleazar became high priest. [Note the difference in this event from its telling at Number 20:22-29.] Moses prevails in his intercession and cools Yahweh's anger. Yahweh reaffirms his covenant (Deuteronomy 9:1-10:11).

Obedience. Yahweh requires Israel to fear him and serve him willingly and obey. Yahweh chose Israel for no particular reason. Cease stubbornness. Yahweh is just. Praise him (Deuteronomy 10:12-22). Do this because of what Yahweh did for your people. He defeated Pharaoh. He destroyed Dathan and Abiram. [Co-conspirators in Korah's rebellion; see Numbers 16:31-33.] If Israel keeps Yahweh's commandments, the people shall take Canaan from the natives. There, Yahweh will make Israel prosper, unless the people serve the local gods. If they do so, Yahweh will be angry and cause Israel to perish from the land. So, heed Yahweh's laws.

Shema (Second Version). [See Deuteronomy 6:4-9.] Heed Yahweh's commandments in your heart and soul. Put them in phylacteries. Teach them to your children. Talk about them with friends. Write them on your doorposts. Then you will prosper in Canaan and Yahweh will drive out the natives before you (Deuteronomy 11:18-25).

Blessings and Curses. Yahweh promises blessings for the obedient and curses for the wayward, both of which are set on Mt. Gerizim and Mt. Ebal [adjacent to one another in central Palestine]. [See Joshua 8:30-35 and Deuteronomy 27:12-14.]

The Laws Explicated. Moses details the laws Israel must obey. *Idols.* Destroy all local altars and places of worship. *Temple.* Seek the place Yahweh designates for his temple sacrifices. Obey; do not let every man do what seems to him right. Sacrifice at the chosen place, not every place that seems adequate to a person. (You may eat flesh in any town.) Do not eat blood or tithed foods. Rejoice in Yahweh, and take care of the Levites. (If the temple is too far from you to slaughter there, you may eat flesh at your homes, but not the blood; that must be poured on the ground for it is the life of the animal. The sacrifices must, however, be taken to the temple site.) [Note the repetition below at Deuteronomy 15:19-23.] Do not imitate the worship of the natives; they even burn sons and daughters to their gods. Do as I command without alteration. *Prophets.* Yahweh will occasionally test you with false prophets who tempt you with other gods. Kill them. *Apostasy.* If a family member tempts you to false worship, kill that person by stoning. If a city turns to foreign gods, kill all the inhabitants with their cattle, gather the spoils into the city center and burn the entire town. *Pagan Rituals.* Do not perform ritual cuts or head shaving. You belong to Yahweh. *Food Rules.* Eat permitted animals (these are listed). Eat no forbidden thing (these are listed). Eat no carrion. Do not boil a kid in its mother's milk. *Sacrifices.* Tithe from your grain, wine, oil, and sacrifice your firstborn livestock. If the sacrificial location (temple) is too far, sell the animals for money, take the money to the temple, and there buy equivalents. *Levites.* Take care of the Levites financially. The tithe of every third year is devoted to the local Levites. *Sabbath Years.* Every seventh year, debts are forgiven to Hebrews, Don't worry; no one will be poor, if you obey Yahweh. Israel will lend to foreigners, but never borrow. *Charity.* If you meet a poor Hebrew, loan or give freely and without concern about repayment. The poor will always be with you, so help them [see Matthew 26:11 for Jesus use of this passage]. *Manumission.* Hebrew slaves are released after six years of service. When you release the slave, provide that person what they need to get started again, for you were slaves in Egypt. Slaves who decline manumission shall become permanent members of the household. *Blemished Firstborns.* (Sacrifice your livestock firstborns at Yahweh's sacrifice place. Offer nothing blemished.

Eat the blemished animals in your towns. Eat no blood.) [Note repetition of Deuteronomy 12:21-26.] *Feasts.* Keep the Passover remembrance. The sacrifices must be at the temple location. Observe the feast of Weeks and the feast of Booths at harvest time. All males must attend the temple site three times yearly, during these festivals. Bring a sacrifice at those times, each according to his prosperity. *Judges.* Appoint judges in every town who refuse bribes. Always follow justice and nothing else. *Pagan Rituals.* Plant no holy trees to Yahweh and set up no idolatrous pillars. *Blemished Sacrifices.* Sacrifice no blemished livestock. *Stoning.* A man or woman who worships any god other than Yahweh shall be stoned at the city gates, if convicted after diligent inquiry and the testimony of two or three witnesses. The witnesses must participate in the execution. If cases are difficult, they must be taken to the temple priesthood for decision. Anyone who fails to do as the priests have ordered shall be killed. [Note the rising authority of the priests in Deuteronomy.] *Kings.* Israel may choose a king from among the Hebrews. Kings shall not gather many horses or return to Egypt to get horses. Kings shall not have many wives, lest they distract him from Yahweh. Kings shall not make themselves rich. The Israeli king shall have a copy of the Mosaic law from the Levites, which he shall read constantly so he does not grow arrogant or prideful. [Note the lightly veiled criticism of Solomon here.] *Levitical Share.* Levites shall have no land; their share is Yahweh and a portion of the people's sacrifices. [Note that somehow a Levite may still sell his patrimony (Deuteronomy 18:8).] *Pagan Rituals.* Sacrifice no children as offerings, and drive out people practicing magical arts. *Prophets.* Yahweh will send a prophet whom you should heed. [Note Paul's use of this passage as a harbinger of Jesus' ministry at Acts 3:22-23.] Yahweh's prophets make predictions that prove true. False prophets must be killed. *Cities of Refuge.* Dedicate three cities as manslayer refuges. If all the land of Canaan becomes Israel's, then add three more cities of refuge. If intentional murderers enter cities of refuge, the elders shall turn such persons over to avengers. Do not move land markers. Two or three witnesses are required for all convictions of crime. False witnesses shall receive the penalty they sought for their opponent by their lies. Show no pity: eye for eye, tooth for tooth, hand for hand, foot for foot. [Compare Exodus 21:23-24 and Leviticus 24:19-20.] *Taking Lands.* When Israel fights the Canaanites, be confident. Yahweh fights with you. If the fighters have distractions at home, or undue fear, let them return home to deal with these matters, lest they breed cowardice in the army. When taking distant cities outside Canaan, if the residents surrender, enslave them. If they resist, kill all the men and take the women, children, and cattle as spoils. Enjoy them. When taking Canaanite cities, utterly destroy them. Do not destroy fruit trees, but only non-fruit trees, for your seigeworks. *Unexplained Deaths.* When a person dies, and none knows the cause, the elders of the nearest city shall break the neck of a young heifer and all of the city shall wash their hands over it, disclaiming knowledge, so that blood guilt shall not lie on the city. *Enemy Wives.* If a Hebrew wishes a captive as spouse, she shall shave her head, trim her nails, and grieve her parents for one month before the Hebrew weds her. If the man declines to marry, he shall release and not sell the woman. *Inverting Birth Order.* Sons of wives, one preferred above the other, shall not be inverted in inheritance order on that account. The son first born shall receive his usual double portion. *Stoning Disobedient Sons.* Sons who ignore parental counsel and become drunkards and gluttons shall be denounced publicly and stoned by the people. *Corpse of the Executed.* The corpse of an executed person shall not hang on a tree overnight, but shall be buried the same day. *Returning Lost Property.* If farm animals get lost, return them to their owners. Do the same with garments and any lost thing. *Help.* If someone's ass or ox falls, help lift the animal. *Cross-Dressing.* Men and women shall not wear one another's clothes. *Eating Birds.* Do not eat young and mother; release the mother. *Roofing Dangers.* Protect people from falling from roofs under construction. *Mixing Things.* Do now sow two kinds of vines or plow with an ox and an ass together or wear wool and linen clothing together. *Tassles.* Make tassels for the four corners of coats. *Wife's Virginity.* If a man claims his bride is not a virgin, he shall so state publicly and divorce her. If her father produces evidence of her virginity, then the lying husband shall be whipped and fined, and he shall never divorce the woman. If she is not a virgin, she shall be stoned. *Fornication.* Fornicators shall be executed. *Rape Rules.* If a man has sex with another man's fiancée in a city, then both shall be stoned, because the woman did not call for help. If the rape occurs in open country, only the man shall be stoned. If a man rapes an unbetrothed woman, then he shall marry her and never divorce. *Marrying Step-Mothers.* No man may marry his father's wife. *Sex Injuries.* No man with crushed testicles or severed penis is a member of the people. *Bastards.* No bastard shall be a member of the people, or his descendants for ten generations. *Ammonites and Moabites.* Neither Ammonites nor Moabites may be part of the people for ten generations, and Hebrews shall never help them prosper. *Edomites and Egyptians.* Edomites and Egyptians may join the assembly after the third generation. *Evil During Campaigns.* Do no evil during war. *Nocturnal Emission.* If a man has nocturnal emission, leave the camp, wash, and return at day's end. *Defecation.* When one defecates, do so in the common location, dig a hole, and bury your feces. *Escaped Slaves.* If an escaped slave comes to you, he may live with you. *Ritual Prostitutes.* There shall be no ritual prostitutes in Israel, nor shall money from such trade pay any religious vow. *Usury.* No one shall lend at interest to a Hebrew. One may do so with foreigners. *Vow-Keeping.* If one vows, one must perform. *Others' Crops.* In a neighbor's vineyard or grainfield, one may eat one's fill, but gather none for later. *Ex-Wives.* If a man divorces and the woman remarries, if that second husband dies or divorces the woman, the first ex-spouse shall not remarry her. *Newly-Wed Haitus.* A man newly married shall not be called to fight or do business for one year. *Millstones.* No one can take a millstone in pledge, for that would be taking life in pledge. *Slavers.* If a Hebrew enslaves a Hebrew, he shall be executed. *Leprosy.* Take care to do as God commands the Levites. *Loan Pledges.* If you loan to someone and take security in some possession of his, do not pressure him for the pledge, and if he is poor, return the pledge at night so he can sleep in his cloak. *Wages.* Pay day laborers on the day of labor. *Vendetta.* No man shall be killed for the crimes or sins of his children or parents. Each man shall be judged on his own behavior. [But see Exodus 34:7.] *Justice.* No one shall deny justice to foreigners or orphans. Take no widow's garment in pledge. *Gleaning.* When harvesting, leave some of the crop; do not strip the field. Leave some fruit and grain for travelers, widows, and orphans. *Punishment.* A judge may demand forty lashes of the guilty, but no more. *Oxen Muzzles.* Do not muzzle an ox when it treads grain. *Brothers' Widows.* A brother must wed his brother's widow. Their first son shall take the deceased brother's name. If the surviving brother declines this duty, the widow may publicly denounce him, take his sandal, and spit in his face. *Grabbing Testicles.* If men fight, and one's wife seizes the testicles of her husband's opponent, cut off her hand. *Trade Ethics.* No man shall have two sets of weights in his bag. Give a just measure for every man. *Amalekites.* Destroy even the memory of Amalekites. *Initial Fruits.* When you get your first harvest from conquered land, sacrifice some to Yahweh. The liturgy of first fruits is described. *Third-Year Tithes.* Give the tithe of the third year to Levites, foreigners, orphans and widows. (Deuteronomy 12:1-26:15).

Mosaic Covenant.

[Note the deviation from the Abrahamic covenant, and the absence of the land from the Mosaic covenant formulation. Compare Genesis 12:1, Genesis 28:13-15, Exodus 6:2-4, Exodus 34:6-9, Leviticus 11:44-45, Leviticus 18:1-5, Leviticus 22:31-33, Leviticus 26:3-45, Deuteronomy 4:1-2, Deuteronomy 5:2-5, and Deuteronomy 10:12-22, to gain a sense of the decreasing role of land in the covenant and the increasing role of law and obedience.]

Yahweh commands you to obey his laws. If you do so, Yahweh will be your god, and will exalt Israel in the eyes of the other nations (Deuteronomy 26:16-19).

Entering the Land.

Plastered Pillars. Yahweh commands that when the people cross the Jordan River, they will set up large stones on Mount Ebal, plaster them, and write Yahweh's laws upon them. Build an altar of unhewn stones and make burnt offerings to Yahweh, rejoicing. Moses tells the people that they have today become Yahweh's people, so obey (Deuteronomy 27:1-10).

Antiphonal Curses and Blessings. Six tribes assemble at Mount Ebal for curses. Six tribes assemble at Mount Gerizim for blessings. [These two mountains lie adjacent to one another in cis-Jordan Palestine midway up the Jordan River between the Dead Sea and the Sea of Galilee.] The Levites announce that a man is cursed if he: makes idols, dishonors parents, removes neighbor's landmarks, misleads blind people, distorts justice for foreigners, orphans, and widows, has sex with his father's wife, has sex with beasts, has sex with his sister, has sex with his mother-in-law, secretly murders, murders for hire, or disobeys Yahweh's laws. All the people agreed (Deuteronomy 27:11-26). The Levites announce that a man is blessed if he obeys Yahweh's commandments. The blessed man will be blessed wherever he lives, and he will be fruitful and prosperous. His enemies will fall. He will be the Lord's and all peoples will see his abundance. He will have rain. He will lend to outsiders. Everything will get better and better for him (Deuteronomy 28:1-14). If one disobeys Yahweh, a long list of horrors will ensue. These horrors include deportation to a distant land. His sons and daughters shall be led away into captivity. A foreign enemy shall breach all Israel's walled cities, and Hebrews shall eat Hebrews. In the end, Israel shall be scattered across the earth. Hebrews shall offer themselves as slaves, but no one will buy them (Deuteronomy 28:15-68).

Covenant in Edom. Yahweh makes an additional covenant with Israel as they are poised in Edom to enter Canaan. Moses recites Israel's historical liturgy. This covenant is with the patriarchs, the people today, and future Hebrews. If Israel tolerates any man who is secretly stubborn, refusing to follow Yahweh's laws from his heart, all Israel may suffer the curses listed. The land will be incinerated, like Sodom and Gomorrah. Even secrets belong to Yahweh [Note the emergence of psychological integrity as a criterion of obedience, not mere conformity. This emphasis is consonant with the prophetic message.] (Deuteronomy 29:1-29).

Promise to Restore. After Israel has been beaten and dispersed, if Israel turns to Yahweh heart and soul, Yahweh will restore Israel, gathering Israel from where Yahweh scattered them. Yahweh will circumcise your hearts and those of your children, and you shall love Yahweh. The curses shall fall upon Israel's foes, and Israel shall prosper. Obedience is within Israel's grasp. It is not too hard. Israel will dwell in the land promised to the patriarchs only if the people obey. So, choose life (Deuteronomy 30:1-20).

Moses' Death. Moses says Yahweh has forbidden him to enter Canaan with the people. Moses encourages the people. Yahweh commissions Joshua to lead. Moses writes down all of the law, gives it to the Levites, and tells them to read the law to the people every seventh year at the feast of booths. Yahweh appears to Joshua. Yahweh tells Moses that the people will whore with other gods in Canaan. Yahweh has Moses write a song against the people from Yahweh. Moses puts the book of the law beside the ark of the covenant in the inner sanctuary. Moses summons the people, and speaks the song of Yahweh to them: "Yahweh is great and his work perfect. Israel deals corruptly with Yahweh and is cut off. Yahweh chose Israel through Jacob. But Israel grew complacent and scoffed at Yahweh by idolatry. Yahweh grew jealous and heaped evils upon Israel. Yahweh scattered Israel out of the land. But Yahweh will yet save his people. He alone is god. None can stand against Yahweh." Yahweh sends Moses up Mount Nebo, from which Moses sees Canaan. Moses blesses Israel: Yahweh brought the people out of Sinai into the land. Moses encourages and advises all Israel by individual tribes. Moses extols Yahweh. Moses dies in Moab on Mount Nebo and is buried in the valley at age 120. Israel weeps for thirty days. Then Israel follows Joshua (Deuteronomy 31:1-34:9)

Eulogy for Moses. No prophet has risen in Israel like Moses, who did many wonders (Deuteronomy 34:10-12).

CHAPTER 9
LOCKE

LADY JUSTICE, JUSTICIA, GOES TO HER EIGHTH PSYCHIATRIC APPOINTMENT. *Justicia opens the heavy oak door to find a finely-dressed Englishman with a gaunt triangular face. Prominent, thoughtful eyes peer from below a high forehead and neck-length white hair. The gentleman smiles warmly. Justicia removes her sword and sets her scales and blindfold on the end of her divan. She settles her toga on her sturdy marble thighs. Justicia had no time to change to jeans and sweatshirt this harried afternoon. The black box of conscience jostles a bit of its own accord on the coffee table.*

LOCKE: My name is John Locke. I am denominated your counselor this session, though I fail to see how *Two Treatises of Government* and *An Essay Concerning Human Understanding* qualify me for this task. My education makes of me a philosopher. I am no priest.

JUSTICIA: I know your work, Sir. I am American these days. You influenced Jefferson and others.

LOCKE: Your constitution drafters wracked my ideas. Sickly spawn oozes from their distortions.

JUSTICIA: You surprise me. Thanks at least in part to you, we remain free and loud. I have come this afternoon from protests. A menagerie of semi-employed citizens in tents makes shrill demands for income redistribution and environmental reform. A rabble of opponents, having tea it seems, rankle just as loudly about spiraling government debt and taxation and loss of liberties. My ears are ringing. America splits down her middle: urbanites against rural folk, evangelicals against secularists. Who is right? How can I decide? You have pondered my file. I am confused.

LOCKE: Indeed. You seem to believe you possess the luxury of time to deliberate. Would that be correct?

JUSTICIA: Well... I cannot decide rashly. I must find some measure of certainty before I....

LOCKE: You can be replaced, dear creature. The American people have inherent liberty to throw off your yoke. Rightful government proceeds from the people; it is their natural and inalienable right. The people therefore possess a natural right to rebellion. They form government; they can substitute another as easily. You must hear and respond. Now! Not when you feel comfortable doing so. My entire theory aims to produce government responsive to its people.

The black box of conscience springs open, revealing Plato. The ugly, little man in his dirty toga stands a full five inches. "Ever, John, you spout democratic obscenities. Socrates taught me, as I reported to you in my *Republic,* the true structure for government. Philosopher-kings must rule. They alone harbor the requisite wisdom. Justice legitimates the commands of carefully-groomed rulers. The people, as you rightly note, are blank slates. But the Good imprints itself upon the rabble's mind dimly. Only a philosopher-king achieves clarity. Lacking regal acumen, governments fester like brimming spittoons." *John smiles wanly at the contentious Greek. Plato sits and the black box closes itself.*

LOCKE: Plato may be right, Justicia. I taught that human brains become beacons of light if benefited by careful education. But see what has come of America! Trash in, trash out. Minds shaped by Viagra and Twitter.

JUSTICIA: We Americans are certainly suffering some behavioral dysfunctions. Congress cannot seem to find its way. Some lost souls, guns in hand, come wholly unhinged. Too many Americans revel in vapid materialism. Still, most Americans are productive, caring people. And the world is really a very much better place than it was in your day, John Locke.

LOCKE: That is perhaps so. We suffered the Great Fire and the Great Plague of London. And we gave ourselves to colonial frenzy. Nevertheless, the United States Constitution surrenders every American's independence to representative government. So, "representatives" travel to swampy Washington D.C., where they rule like French despots. It is scant improvement when a people overthrows one fractured king in favor of 535. Plutocracy is nothing more than tyranny in a party mood.

JUSTICIA: What would you have me do, John? Is there a way out of this forest of confusion?

> **JUSTICE IS:**
>
> **POPULISM
> WITH
> SAFEGUARDS.**

LOCKE: Certainly, Justicia. Do less. Government, including the courts, must abandon its sentiment to do everything for everybody. Limitations, my dear. Circumspection born of observation of the human condition. Frame laws to protect property and liberty. Make utterly certain that education works. Crush crime and foreign invasions. Step aside and let the planet's future emerge.

JUSTICIA: You sound like Robert Nozick. Nozick undoubtedly cherished dog-eared copies of your works.

LOCKE: Robert and I are intellectual kin. Our philosophical family enjoys little applause in America, I fear.

JUSTICIA: It is worse than that, John. America has forgotten you and Nozick. When I learned that John Locke was today's visiting psychiatrist, I thought I would be chatting with the bald guy from *Lost*.

LOCKE: What? Who…?

Before Justicia can explain, Locke vanishes. The limestone lady gathers her things and trudges back to the courts.

Locke, *The Second Treatise of Government*. Norwalk, Connecticut: The Easton Press, 1991.

John Locke (1632-1704), an English philosopher, influenced Rousseau, Voltaire, social contract theory, and the American revolutionaries, as well as Kant, Hume, and Nozick. Locke argues against absolute monarchy, contrary to Hobbes. Political legitimacy derives from consent of the governed, and church and state must be separated. Locke's political works had little influence during his lifetime. Locke never married and had no children. The Second Treatise of Government was published anonymously in 1689.

Book II.

Chapter 1. 1. Adam has much less authority over his descendants than the church pretends, and none of it descends to Adam's offspring. No nation knows which of man's several nations came first in time. Government does not fall to the violent, but is otherwise constituted. 2. Political power differs from that of parents, slave owners, spouses, and employers. 3. Political power makes laws and punishments to defend the borders and enact public good.

Chapter 1.   *Of the State of Nature.* 4. Humans are naturally free to choose and dispose as they please, within nature's bounds, without the permission of any person. Men are naturally equal. None has more claim to rule than another. 5. Men are naturally given to love one another, which creates reciprocal duties. 6. Mankind, naturally, is subject to natural laws and each to his own reason, which dictate that none should injure another in life, health, liberty, or property. 7. Every man may punish others who transgress natural laws. 8. Yet such punishment has bounds of proportion. 9. Were there no natural right to punish transgression, no king could punish a foreigner. 10. Victims have a right to reparations. 11. People yield their rights to punish others to a magistrate, though they retain their right to seek reparations personally. Every man may kill a murderer, as one slaughters a tiger. 12. In nature, one may punish, even to the extent of death, to give pause to offenders and deter like-minded others. Locke declines to specify particular laws of nature at length. 13. Government exists to remedy men's partiality and excesses in punishing. But kings are men. No king may wield untempered power, or exact punishments in his wrath. 14. Not every agreement between men ends the state of nature. One ends the natural state by agreeing with others to make of themselves one community. 15. No lone man can provide all he needs for a life of dignity. So, we join forces in political societies.

Chapter 2.   *Of the State of War.* 16. To declare a well-settled intention to kill another is a state of war. One may kill another who wars with him. 17. To seek absolute power over another is a state of war. Hence, slavery is war. 18. One who uses some force to injure another may be killed, though the criminal intended no murder, for one never knows what lengths a criminal may reach. 19. Where government fails to prevent harm, one's own right to war with a criminal intent upon harm opens the door to individual punishment, including death. 20. Where a civil judge exists, war ceases. Lacking a judge, one acts according to conscience, and answers to God.

Chapter 3.   *Of Slavery.* 22. Men under government are free except to the extent a legislature makes rules applicable to all members of that society. 23. No man can agree to be enslaved. 24. Where men make agreements, there is no slavery, for dominion over a man is not absolute.

Chapter 4.   *Of Property.* 25. Nature gave to men in common a right to subsistence (food and drink). 26. Common things become property when appropriated to one person's use. 27. A man's person is his property, as well as his labor. When a man adds his labor to something common, it becomes his property, at least so long as sufficient goods remain for others to appropriate. 28. When one picks an apple in the woods, it becomes his. 29. Labor takes a thing from common use to private use. 30. Even in civilization, the commencement of property remains the same. 31. We can take from nature no more than what we may reasonably use. 32. One acquires land similarly, by using it to advantage. 33. So long as sufficient remains for all others, none injures others by taking possession of a thing. 34. God gave all good things to man to be used, not to lie fallow. 35. In civilized areas, some land is held open by agreement. This is not a commons, open to aliens to take. 36. No man can consume so much or make property his own to a sufficient degree as to injure another by leaving nothing so good for others as what he has procured for himself. 37. Money changed valuations, and men hoarded more than their needs required. Before money, waste offended others, for a man had no right to what he could not use. 38. In early times, men wandered with their flocks. But towns and cities followed. 39. Use gave men right to property, both land and conveniences. 40. Ninety-nine percent of the utility of any thing is owed to the labor invested in it. 41. The American nations have an abundance of resources, but, for lack of labored improvement of those resources, live worse than a common laborer in England. 42. Most of what we enjoy has benefitted by a great deal of labor improvement. 43. Even the value of land derives mostly from the labor expended in making it fruitful. A great array of labor-improved materials and tools are required to produce even one loaf of bread. 44. So the spring of property lies in man: his labor. 45. Where money arises, however, men gather more than can be used. Land becomes scarce, though still unimproved. 46. He who hoards things he cannot use spoils them and robs others. The wrong in property consists not in owning much, but rather in wasting any. 47. Money, you see, never rots. Money preserves unused value. 48. Without money, none hoards. 49. In primitive societies, there is no money. 50. Men agree to use and value money. Money enables some to gather more than they can use. 51. Before money, no one wasted labor on something that would spoil. So none invaded what was common in a manner that excluded others. That would be dishonest.

Chapter 5.   *Of Paternal Powers*. 52. Paternal power should be parental power, since women have a just claim as much as men. 53. Paternal power is likened to regal power. If women had shared paternal powers, that theory would have failed. 54. Locke argues for human equality, though men are patently unequal. None should be under another's authority, being naturally free. 55. Children lack equality, for a time. When they mature, they become free. 56. Every parent is obliged to keep their children safe, to feed and educate them. 57. Adam lived under reason, but not his children, who were born differently from Adam. Liberty requires law, under which one is free from depredations of others. 58. Parents guide children during their immaturity. When grown, children become free. 59. If a father dies, the law provides a guardian for children until they become reasonable. 60. If maturity never arrives, the child, though a man, is never free. 61. So, children are born free and rational, though they have the use of neither at that time. 62. Governments recognize that children are not yet able to act freely. 63. Reason binds a man's freedom, guiding him. 64. Paternal power, which mothers also exercise, is not absolute, but extends only to acts necessary to protect and nurture children. 65. Paternal power derives from the nourishment and education of children, and passes to whomever provides such care. When a child reaches discretion, paternal power terminates, a father having no more authority over his adult child than over strangers. 66. God requires parents to protect children, but requires children to honor parents. No father has absolute power over adult children. 67. Nothing can dissolve the obligation of parents to care for children and children to honor parents. 68. The biblical admonition for children to obey parents aims at young children, not adults. 69. The duty to obey, but not the duty to honor, ends at adulthood. 70. Some may owe obligations to another that can never be repaid. It is so with parents. Such unpayable obligations do not, however, grant any authority to parents over adult children. 71. Political power does not derive from paternal powers. The two are of different species. 72. Fathers have powers to give their estates to children. 73. Children may choose countries in which to dwell. But if they want inheritance, they take it in their father's country, and must keep the father happy enough with them. 74. A father might, if isolated with his family, naturally continue dominion of a political sort over his adult children. 75. This might be quite natural. 76. Monarchies may have arisen by such events.

Chapter 6.   *Of Political or Civil Society.*   77. Humans are naturally social. 78. The society of marital partners aims at procreation, but also support, sharing, and affection. 79. Breeding partners, even among animals, stay together so long as the needs of offspring demand. 80. Humans remain together so long because their young are far from mature when their brothers and sisters are born. The family's needs are great and ongoing. God gave humans the ability to plan, to mate for long periods, to be industrious, to preserve children safe in families. 81. Nothing, however, requires the mating to be permanent. 82. When spouses disagree, decision falls to the husband, since he is stronger and abler. But the wife retains her powers over her husband, and he retains his powers over her. They may separate. 83. So, paternal power over a spouse is far from absolute. Spouses have only such powers as are necessary for bearing and nurturing children. 84. Parental power differs strongly from political power. 85. Employment affords temporary and limited powers to the employer. Slaves (captured in a just war), having lost all property, are no part of society, since society exists to preserve property. 86. All parents lack power of legislation and death over their children, servants, and slaves. 87. Men, naturally free to judge and execute offensive others, surrender this right to the community, which thereafter judges and executes on their behalf. Where men have one law and judicial system, those share civil society. 88. So, the commonwealth has powers to make laws and inflict punishments for the preservation of property. 89. When men give up their executive power to the public, those men leave the state of nature and become a body politic or join an already existing civil society. 90. Absolute monarchy is no government at all, since the prince remains in the state of nature. 91. Wherever there is no judge between men, they are in the state of nature. As to an absolute monarch, no one judges. 92. Monarchs offer no guidance, but rather silence their critics with swords or pious justifications. 93. Defenders of absolute monarchy argue that whatever the king does, it is right, because he is powerful. 94. If citizens feel that some man may do whatever he pleases, they conclude they remain in a state of nature. None are secure until all submit to a legislature of elected citizens.

Chapter 7.   *Of the Beginning of Political Societies.*   95. Free men may join together in civil society, their majority governing all. 96. Majorities must act for the whole, since, absent such agreement, the body politic would disintegrate. 97. If one who dissents from a majority declines to acquiesce, he is under no more obligation than he was in the state of nature. 98. If dissenters can elect not to follow majorities, then at each dissent, the political society dissolves. 99. All lawful government commences with the consent of a group of men to be subject to the majority among them. 100. First, some object that no government was actually created in this manner. Second, some object that men are born into governments and lack liberty to commence new ones. 101. In prehistory, when men found one another, they immediately joined together. Government predates human records. 102. What evidence exists indicates that free men united and chose governments together voluntarily. 103. Those who contend that governments evolved from pre-existing paternal authority may be right, but this fact will not support the absolute monarchy for which they contend. 104. So, all governments commence from consent, except where they begin in conquest. 105. Locke concedes that most governments began in paternal rule. Upon succession, however, people want the best man, not merely the paternal heir. 106. Most monarchies are, then, ultimately elective. 107. Paternal monarchies must seem usual to people who have lived under paternal monarchy. The great threat lay in external aggression, so people wanted a brave and wise man to rule. 108. Such kings were potent in war, but easy during peace. 109. This pattern exists in the biblical history of Israel, from Jephtha to David. 110. Early governments held great power, for the dangers were great. 111. This golden age, before evil infected leaders' minds, lacked overreaching, luxuries, and thirst for power. When power-hungry men ruled and claimed divine right to do so, common people sought a way to restrain governments. 112. Thus, though governments commenced with strongmen, these governments were still governments of consent of the people. 113. To the second objection, about the lack of freedom for most to erect new governments, Locke argues that many monarchies exist, and so there exists some such freedom. 114. Men do not consider the governments into which they are born an imposition. 115. No, men readily withdraw and move off to another place and set up governments there. That is how the world's nations got started. 116. No man, by promising himself to a government, obligates his progeny to share his oath. 117. But those sons who dissent cannot expect to inherit a father's wealth, since they have abandoned the society that produced it. 118. Governments agree. A child is under his father, until majority, when he chooses his country. 119. Men give such consent either expressly or tacitly. To take benefit of a country is to tacitly consent to its government, as does a traveler. 120. If one inherits or purchases land, one takes the government of that land in the acquisition. 121. Every man is free to start his own country in some empty place. But if once he gives consent to some society, he departs the state of nature and enters that society for so long as that society exists. 122. Resident aliens, though they live a lifetime in a country, do not become members except by their express choice to do so.

Chapter 8.   *Of the Ends of Political Society and Government.* 123. Men abandon their natural freedoms for society to make their property (life, health, liberty, and estates) more secure. 124. Governments exist to protect property. Natural men know natural law, but are not likely to impose it upon themselves. 125. Nature lacks a judge to impose law. 126. Men in nature often lack power to execute natural laws. 127. So, men quickly flee to societies of laws for their well-being. 128. Desperate and corrupt men make natural community unappealing. One gives up freedoms to be protected from them. 129. One gives up self-regulation for common laws. 130. One also relinquishes power to punish to the collective. 131. Governments must exercise their power impartially, without corruption, at home and abroad, to the ends of peace, safety, and well-being of the people.

Chapter 9.   *Of the Forms of a Commonwealth.* 132. The people hold power, but may devolve it to executives and legislatures. If one, monarchy. If a few, oligarchy. If many, democracy. Mixed governments exist. 133. "Commonwealth" means no particular form of government, but rather any independent community.

Chapter 10.   *Of the Extent of Legislative Power.* 134. Supreme power lies with the legislature, which makes laws. 135. Legislative power is limited to doing public good. The law of nature still binds, being the will of God. 136. Legislatures rule by standing laws, not arbitrary decrees, and appeal to known, impartial judges. 137. No absolute power exists in legislatures, because men have no absolute powers even over their own persons, being reasonable creatures. Granting such powers would make the condition of citizens worse than natural insecurity. 138. Governments lack power to take property arbitrarily. 139. No legislature or prince may take what it pleases, for this would be to rob all of all property. 140. Taxes are payment of one's share of collective expenses. 141. No legislative power is delegable to others. 142. To rule by law is to have one rule that governs rich and poor, as well as the famous and commoner. Law must aim at common good. No tax is valid without the people's consent. No lawmaking power can be delegated to others than the legislators chosen by the people.

Chapter 11.   *Of the Legislative, Executive, and Federative Power of the Commonwealth.* 143. The legislature should not be always in session, nor hold executive power to execute the laws, so that legislators are themselves subject to those laws they make. 144. The executive should exist always to enforce laws. 145. When foreign agents injure one, all the people respond in their government. 146. Such is the power of war, peace, alliances, and exchanges with those outside the commonwealth. 147. This external power (which Locke calls "federative") is *ad hoc*, action chosen by prudent leaders. 148. Most often, the executive and federative powers should be held by one person or group.

Chapter 12.   *Of the Subordination of the Powers of the Commonwealth.* 149. The people of a commonwealth retain power to dissolve or change their legislature. 150. When not removed from power, the legislature is supreme, governing all. 151. The executive shares a derivative supremacy, but loses all claim to obedience whenever the executive acts to benefit himself against the people. Then he loses all power. 152. Always, the executive remains subordinate to the legislative, and may be removed by the legislative. 153. Legislatures may meet occasionally, but executives must function constantly. Legislatures may punish the executive for mal-administration. 154. The executive may convoke the legislature, unless the constitution provides for their regular meeting. 155. If the executive hinders the legislative, the people may remove the executive by force. 156. Legislative conventions must differ in their length, for the needs of the people differ over time. The executive, if it convenes the legislative, does so as a trust, not in superiority. 157. The legislative districts will need to be changed as populations shift. 158. The legislative should do the redistricting.

Chapter 13.   *Of Prerogative.* 159. Executives may act, where (and until) the legislative guides. A prince may relieve unanticipated harshness in the application of law, or act in emergencies. 160. Prerogative is the executive's power to act for public good without legislation, or even against legislation. 161. The issue is this: does a prerogative act help or hurt the people? 162. Prerogative may be distorted by weak princes, mistake, flattery, and so forth. 163. A community may limit the executive prerogative without injuring the executive, for societies get to determine their own goods. 164. The people grant good princes prerogative, for the people's benefit and confidence in the king's commitment to their good. 165. So, the best kings have the widest latitude in prerogative. 166. Good kings are followed by lesser kings, who use prerogative wrongly, for the benefit of themselves or friends. 167. Kings summon parliaments, and it is right for them to do so. 168. When the executive and legislative conflict, one appeals to Heaven. For no law of man decides between these two.

Chapter 14.   *Of Paternal, Political, and Despotical Power considered together.* 169. Locke has previously considered these powers, but takes them together now. 170. Parental power is that granted to parents to work the good of their children. 171. Political power is that which men grant to governments for the good of society. 172. Despotical power is an unnatural grasping that leaves one with absolute power over others. No man can grant such powers. Despotical powers are just the war of individuals, one against the others, raging unabated. 173. Nature gives paternal power; agreement gives political power; forfeiture gives despotical power. 174. Paternal pertains to minor children; political to men of property; despotical to men stripped of property (as with war prisoners).

Chapter 15.   *Of Conquest.* 175. No true government begins in military conquest. 176. Unjust conquerors claim no allegiance from those subjected. 177. Even in just war, a conqueror gains no power over those who fought with the conqueror. 178. The unjust warrior gains no power over non-combatants or even over combatants' possessions. 179. No people give their government power to wage unjust war. So, conquerors gain no just power over non-participants. 180. Those whom a just conqueror overpowers, he rules as a despot. He may rule, or even kill, them. But he gains no claim to their property. 181. Unjust force makes war. 182. Conquest entitles a man to kill his opponent, who commenced war, but not to take his property, except in reparations, and even that subject to the needs of wives and children. 183. The conqueror may take reparation, but not to the extent he robs wives and children of their subsistence. The needs of families take precedence over reparation. 184. Among princes, no damage done to one another justifies the winner taking the lands of the defeated. 185. So, conquering princes have no right to rule defeated lands. Those defeated groups may form a new government. 186. No coerced promise binds anyone. 187. Conquered peoples have no duty to conquerors. 188. Suppose all the men of a country opposed the conqueror. 189. This does not make their minor children prey. Over the children, a despot has no claim. 190. Every person born has personal freedom, of which only he can dispose, and the right to inherit his father's possessions. 191. Even being born in a place does not subject a man to the government of that place, which only his choice can do. If he does not acquiesce, neither shall he inherit under the laws of his birthplace. 192. No conquered people need obey an usurper, unless he puts forth a government to their liking. 193. In a just war, the conqueror may grant property to the conquered citizens, which then is theirs, and cannot be taken. 194. To violate property that has been rightly received voids all contracts everywhere. 195. Locke declines to say if princes must obey the laws, like every other person. They must, however, certainly obey God's and nature's laws. Princes and their pretensions are nothing as compared to God. 196. Locke summarizes his core points. Every conquered people has the right to rebel when they find the moment and courage to do so.

Chapter 16.   *Of Usurpation.* 197. There are no just usurpations. The usurper changes persons, not governments. 198. The persons granted power, and the method by which those are chosen, are as much a part of government as the form of government itself. A usurper violates the method of choosing governors. None owe him obedience.

Chapter 17.   *Of Tyranny.* 199. The tyrant does what no person can do rightly, using public power for personal purposes. 200. King James said as much in 1603 and 1609. 201. Any form of government that uses its power arbitrarily is tyrannical. 202. When law ends, tyranny begins, if it takes from one what is rightly his. 203. Some object that if every person decides whether a prince's acts are just, there will be anarchy. 204. Force is warranted only to oppose unjust force. 205. First, where kings are sacred, one may nevertheless oppose his inferior officers. 206. Second, no minister has authority to act in a manner not authorized by law. 207. Third, tyrants are worse than robbers, for they have sought trust, and now breach it. Yet, one may not kill the king, as one might a robber. For one has time to appeal to law for redress. 208. Fourth, even where the government acts wrongly, unless such acts be wide-spread, none will follow injured parties into armed rebellion. 209. But if governmental law-lessness extends widely, then the rulers stand in peril. 210. Where government persists in wrong acts, one may overthrow the prince like a foolish sea captain.

Chapter 18.   *Of the Dissolution of Governments.* 211. When a society dissolves, the premise of government falls with it. Usually this happens by war, which tears a society to shreds and is too folly-ridden to require further comment. 212. Governments may also be dissolved by a society. A society may change its legislative form, which is the first principle of creating a commonwealth. 213. Consider a monarchical parliamentary system. 214. When the king overrules the legislature, the government is dissolved. 215. The king may prevent the legislature from meeting. So the government is dissolved. 216. When someone other than the people changes the way legislators are chosen, the government is dissolved. 217. Surrendering to a foreign power also dissolves government. 218. The princes get blamed often, for they alone have sufficient power to alter the legislative. 219. Governments also dissolve when the executive fails to execute the laws. 220. When a government has been dissolved, the society may choose a new approach to making and enforcing laws. Men need to recognize oncoming tyranny, and avoid it. 221. Governments dissolve when the legislature or executive acts con-trary to its trust. When government agents unlawfully invade the people's property, the gov-ernment dissolves. 222. Men form governments and empower executives to protect their prop-erty, not savage it. They choose legislators, reasonably after debate, to save them and their well-being. This the people can do only after weighing reason on both sides of questions de-bated. 223. Some object that founding government in the people's opinion will make govern-ments fragile. Locke argues otherwise. People cling to their governments, even their corrupt governments. They are loathe to change. 224. The people will not welcome rebellion. If they are miserable, they will seek relief. 225. People do not rebel lightly. They endure foibles. 226. Giving people power to change their government prevents rebellions. It is governors who ignore law that are the true rebels, not the people that depose them. 227. Those who pervert a legislature are rebels. When rebellion occurs, a state of nature ensues, where force is exercised without consent of the people. 228. When violence occurs, it is the fault of him who invades a neighbor's property. 229. Government exists for human well-being. 230. People will not overthrow government, except when bad acts torment them generally. Those men who wrongly unsettle just governments are pests of mankind. Treat them harshly. 231. Some deny that citizens may resist authorities acting unfaithfully. They are wrong. 232. Locke cites Barclay in Latin about rebellion. 233. Locke translates Barclay's position: A people may defend itself against an unjust king. They may defend only, not attack their prince. 234. So, even Barclay allows people to resist their intolerable kings. 235. Barclay is unintelligible when he argues that one must resist with reverence and retribute without punishment. Locke argues that an unjust king has forsaken his office, and is nothing more than an unjust man in a state of nature with every other man. He can expect abuse. Barclay admits that kings may unking themselves. 236. Barclay's Latin text continues. 237. Locke translates Barclay again: None may attack a king while he remains king. But kings become no kings when they attempt to overturn a government. 238. Kings also cease to be kings when they voluntarily submit to another king. 239. Locke argues that whenever a king exceeds his authority, he ceases to be a king and may be resisted. Locke cites other defenders of monarchical power who agree. 240. The people determine whether a king acts according to his trust. Who else might judge? 241. Apart from divine acts, every man judges for himself of his king. 242. In great controversies, the people should be judge. 243. A people grants power to legislatures, which power cannot be retrieved so long as the government acts within its trust. If a government has a time limit, the people may form such new government as they deem best.

CHAPTER 10
MARX

LADY JUSTICE, JUSTICIA, GOES TO HER NINTH PSYCHIATRIC APPOINTMENT. *Justicia removes her blindfold and bumps open the door with her shoulder, to avoid scraping its fine surface with her sword's scabbard or her scales of equity. A face framed in an integrated bush of graying black hair, moustache, and beard sits atop a stocky frame. Justicia settles herself, and scratches a bit of limestone scale from her right elbow. Marx, the German Ashkenazi Jew, smiles broadly. The black box of conscience hunkers on the coffee table, boding a pregnant intrusion.*

MARX: I cannot stop smiling. Your beauty so reminds me of Jenny, my departed wife—the love of my life.

JUSTICIA: I am glad for our resemblance. You still grieve. Has she been gone long?

MARX: Time is a bit confused in this psychoanalysis. My time was the nineteenth century. Before I lost her, we lost four of our seven children. She parented. I wrote and I agitated. I got us expelled from country after country. Times were hard for the Marx tribe.... But let's talk about your family, Justicia.

JUSTICIA: There's a topic.... My father was Chaos, and my mother Power. I am born of their union. Every member of papa's family was an anarchist and never deigned to cooperate. Every member of mama's tribe marched lockstep to grandfather's whim. My parents charged me, from my earliest days, to structure human society with a balance none among their own families had ever managed. I was their hope. And I am a huge disappointment.

MARX: I doubt that. Parents seldom feel that way about their children. Your task, as a demi-god, brims with complexity. So, what of your siblings? They must be a handful at Thanksgiving dinners.

JUSTICIA: That they are. Goodness, of course, prospers. He is the heir apparent. My sister, Truth, has, frankly, suffered a nervous breakdown. One just cannot count on her these days. My younger siblings, Kindness, Beauty, Rationality, and Community struggle through these difficult times. But let's talk of my confusions. You know, some deem you, Karl, to be the most influential thinker of the last two centuries. Do you have ideas you believe I should mull? Your dialectical materialism wowed global politics for a century, and still....

MARX: Pahhh! I aimed not to talk about the world, but to make it a better place. That, I see, has gone poorly....

The black box of conscience bursts open. Chairman Mao Zedong rises to his full six inches. "You err, Comrade. In my hands, and those of our brethren Stalin, Lenin, Pol Pot, and the many champions of peoples oppressed by capitalist pigs, your glorious insight governed half the planet. We inspired billions and silenced dissenters. We realized the dictatorship of the proletariat. You dreamed. We implemented. You have our gratitude." *A tear rolls down Marx's cheek and into his bramble of beard. Marx shuts the black box of conscience firmly, shaking his head despondently.*

MARX: I advocated short-term violence. I embraced socialism as an interim stage, foisted by revolution, leading, so I dreamed, to a classless and stateless society of utopian sharing. Unintentionally, I threw open the doors of government to homicidal sociopaths. Chairman Mao squeaks as my conscience because he remains the most vicious of mankind's murderous maniacs. Seventy million died in that idiot's Cultural Revolution. I designed the bullets. Mao and his ilk pulled the trigger.

JUSTICIA: The road to communist utopia held more switchbacks than you imagined?

MARX: Many more. I found capitalist abuses damnable, but I missed so much. When I discarded the foibles of capitalism, I also tossed the baby of global trade. It is now obvious that expansive trade creates a positive-sum game in which every nation prays fervently for the prosperity of every other, despite the pains of recessions and class oppressions. The impulse to war has plummeted. What's more, I tossed out god as an opiate stupefying the masses. The divine stands more firmly rooted in human affections than I ever imagined. I overstepped in projecting my atheism upon the human canvas.

> **JUSTICE IS:**
>
> UTOPIAN
> WEALTH
> SHARING

JUSTICIA: Still, a world without class distinctions or states.... A world where people give their skills freely and take only the measure they lack. That all sounds so right to me.

MARX: Toward the end of my life, I devoted less energy to revolutionary rhetoric and more to ethical argument. In the *Gotha Program*, I urged communists and people of good faith everywhere to live by this principle: "From each according to his ability, to each according to his need." My ideology is little more than pedestrian family structure telescoped to include all people. In families, children and elders and the disabled work little, but consume much. Healthy adults produce and share with kin less able. We all believe that arrangement quite natural and desirable. So, too society.

JUSTICIA: So communism is just family values writ large? The global homestead?

MARX: I think that captures my gist, Justicia. Too bad my speculations did not come to fruit as I had imagined.

JUSTICIA: That may be the understatement of the last half-millennium.....

Marx raises his eyebrows, and shrugs his shoulders. A frown teases his lips. He vanishes.

Justicia chews the inside of her marble cheek, deliberating her several psychiatric conversations. She can feel insights tickling marble folds of her stony cerebrum.

Marx, Karl. *The Communist Manifesto.* **Translated by Samuel Moore. Edited by Fredric L. Bender. New York: W. W. Norton & Company, 1988.**

Karl Marx (1818-1883) worked as a German philosopher and social revolutionary. Marx, who has been deemed by some as one of the great economists of history, worked closely with his friend Friedrich Engels in producing The Communist Manifesto and Capital, his major works. Engels, during the many lean times the communist agitators experienced, supported Marx and his wife and seven children with profits from the Engels family business. With Emile Durkheim and Max Weber, Marx is regarded as a founder of social science. In the name of Marxist revolution, Stalin, Trotsky, Lenin, and Mao fomented communist revolutions which proved to be among the most murderous of history.

Preface to the German Edition of 1872. The Communist League commissioned this work in secret in 1847. The Manifesto is as true today as the day it was written. Experience with communist revolutions (February Revolution and Paris Commune) has demonstrated that workers cannot simply co-opt existing state governments and run them.

Preface to the Russian Edition of 1882. So much has changed since the Manifesto was published. America becomes a giant economically. Russia has taken the forefront in communist agitation.

Preface to the German Edition of 1883. Marx has died and been buried in London. His thought perseveres. Economics determines the character of an epoch. Since primitive tribal society crumbled, class struggles have defined western Europe. Communism will define the next epoch. This is Marx's thought.

Preface to the English Edition of 1888. Communists have been beleaguered all over the continent. The Communist League disbanded. The Manifesto seemed destined for obscurity. Yet, the Manifesto's principles worked behind the scenes, winning adherents silently. Intellectual and social history derives from economic structure. History holds class struggle between exploiters (bourgeoisie) and exploited (proletariat).

Preface to the German Edition of 1890. Engels recounts the recent history of translations of the Manifesto. Working men, especially in America and Europe, continue uniting, working for improved labor conditions.

Preface to the Polish Edition of 1892. As industrialism spreads, so too does Marxism. As Poland has turned to manufacturing, so its workers demand copies of the Manifesto.

Preface to the Italian Edition of 1893. A country must be free of foreign domination to become a communist nation. So, all wars of independence augur well for Marxists. Italy was the first capitalist nation. Perhaps from its ancient lands will come the first communist society.

MANIFESTO OF THE COMMUNIST PARTY

Communism threatens Europe. Establishment leaders make common cause to address the inroads of communism. By so doing, they admit that communism is potent. It is high time communists declared their views to the world. This work is an internationally authorized summary of the communist worldview.

I.   Bourgeois and Proletarians.

All history is a tale of economic struggles between classes. The bourgeoisie controls land and production, while oppressing and prospering. The proletariat labors, while being oppressed and suffering. With industrialization and new trade routes, markets grew and the medieval status quo crumbled. The industrial bourgeoisie emerged in the long course of these changes. The bourgeoisie controls the state executive, which serves monied interests. The bourgeoisie dismantled feudalism in favor of raw profit exchanges. Its only value is unimpeded exchange of goods manufactured by pitiless exploitation. Money has rendered everything a marketable entity: religion, law, family, poetry. The market has accomplished wonders by monetizing mankind. Each time the bourgeoisie modernizes its factories, all of society is upended. All tends to make of the planet a single marketplace, and so makes all nations interdependent. So, the entire globe, in order to survive, becomes bourgeois. Rural populations abandon the inanity of farming, and all grow dependent upon cities. Power, and government, centralizes. The bourgeoisie has done more in 100 years than have all previous generations. Just as bourgeois society grew from the soil of feudalism, so now communism sprouts from capitalism. Periodic depressions savage workers, which depressions result from overproduction of goods. Markets collapse, and new social structures threaten to emerge. The bourgeoisie compel mass suffering in the masses and open new markets as remedies for depressions, only to set the stage for a yet more expansive depression in the future. The workers rebel at these depredations. They market themselves like commodities, and are tied to machines. Wages fall as machines supplant human skills. As labor loses its personal character, the labor of women draws equal to that of men, and all are fungible. Slowly, even the middle class sinks into the proletariat, because even these lack the huge resources to compete with modern industry. The proletariat goes through stages. First, workers fight individual capitalists. Later, they organize themselves as unions, and riots break out. The bourgeoisie are themselves embattled with landed aristocracies and other capitalists, and so they educate and enlist the workers to help, making the workers able to rebel. Some few of the bourgeoisie understand the historical current, and go over to the proletariat. For it is the proletariat that brings revolution. The lower middle class seeks to roll history back, and so is reactionary. Unlike other classes, the proletariat lacks property to defend, a nation, or other values. He lives to destroy the old order of private property. Unlike previous class transitions, the proletariat are a majority seeking its own benefit. All will change. So, the relation of bourgeoisie and proletariat is a simmering civil war that will issue in outright violent revolution.

History is everywhere the tale of oppressors oppressing and the oppressed resisting. The bourgeoisie has lost its claim to legitimacy because it crushes the workers, leaving them paupers and in need of assistance just to survive. Capitalists need capital, which they get from the sweat of laborers. Laborers compete, and eventually form unions. And these labor unions undermine the bourgeoisie control of production and capital. Proletarian victory is inevitable.

II.   Proletarians and Communists.

Communists focus attention of workers on international aspects of all workers everywhere. Communists want what all workers want: to unite workers and seize power from capitalists. Private property is the root cause, and so must be forbidden, because it underpins all capitalists do. What is at issue here is not worker's tools and hovels, but industrial capital. Capital emerges only by social action, and therefore belongs to the collective. As to wages, capitalists set those so workers support themselves, but never have excess by which to improve their lot. Capitalists steal all the excess. In a communist society, all excess would improve the life of workers. To seize capital is to overthrow the capitalists.

Objectors complain that collectivizing property diminishes individuality and freedom. Communists respond that what is lost is bourgeois society only. Objectors predict that workers owning capital will breed laziness. Has it done so for the capitalists, who never work? Objectors predict the collapse of artistic culture. Only bourgeois culture will collapse. All bourgeois ideas reflect capitalist production: law, culture, freedom, individuality, family, education, marriage, nations. All are the thoughts of that bourgeois life to be eradicated. It is so in every epoch. Rulers claim their views divine, and impose them over the majority. Workers have no nations. Their families and children have been turned into tools of capital. Global trade renders nations less and less relevant. The rule of workers will do so even more quickly. When class antagonisms decline, so too will international tensions.

Religious and philosophical criticisms of communism lack merit. Rulers impose their ideas on subjects. Ideas emerge from economic relations. Since communism strikes at the heart of private property, it portends a huge change in thought patterns.

The proletariat will take over State mechanisms at the polls, then seize private property for the State, and, bit by bit, eliminate the social order of the past. This process will most often include: 1) public ownership of all land, 2) high income taxes, 3) confiscatory inheritance taxation, 4) seizure of all property of state enemies, 5) centralized banking and credit, 6) nationalizing transportation and communications, 7) rapid industrial expansion, 8) forcing all people to work, especially as farmers, 9) redistribution of population out of cities and into the countryside, and 10) free universal education and abolition of child labor. When all power lies with the proletariat, the state will cease functioning politically (for political power is the oppression of one class by another). The freedoms of one will be the freedoms of all.

III. Socialist and Communist Literature.

1. **Reactionary Socialism.**
    A. **Feudal Socialism**. English and French aristocrats railed against the upstart middle class by facetiously complaining of the bourgeoisie's abuse of their workers. The "feudal socialism" of endangered gentry complained that shopkeepers radicalized workers. The church joined these feudal socialists, since Christian piety weds neatly with aristocratic rhetoric.
    B. **Petty-Bourgeois Socialism**. The petty-bourgeoisie hover between workers and capitalists, aspiring to wealth, but often suffering defeat and becoming proletarian. Such socialism offers helpful critique of capitalism, but in the end seeks restoration of the old, now passing, values.
    C. **German, or "True," Socialism**. German socialists created an arid idealism from the French Revolution's ideas. In so doing, they rendered the French ideas impotent. German socialism became the silly mouthpiece of the petty bourgeoisie. It wrongly condemned the heedless destructiveness of communism.

2. **Conservative, or Bourgeois, Socialism**. The conservative socialist reforms capitalist society, shaving off its sharp corners, to make it more palatable to workers. Conservative socialism seeks administrative improvements, not revolutionary upheaval of the economic mode of production.

3. **Critical-Utopian Socialism and Communism**. Early communist theorists could not adequately formulate a theory because the proletariat was in its infancy. The workers exist in their minds only as a beleaguered group, not as an inexorable social force. These utopians think themselves above class struggles. Their schemes propose to benefit all, even the wealthy. And they seek the approbation of rulers, since their proposals portend no injury to them. These dreamers imagine that little experiments and peaceful persuasion will win the day. Still, though dreamers, they

are communists. They attack every foundation of society and make many worthy reform proposals. Because they miss the role of the workers in revolution, they end up dampening class struggle, and waste their time with little experimental communities. In the end, they serve the capitalists with their mystical view of the power of their social thinking and their pacifistic opposition to meaningful conflict.

IV. Position of the Communists in Relation to the Various Existing Opposition Parties.

Communists support Chartists and Agrarian Reformers, social-democrats and radicals everywhere. Wherever action overthrows existing institutions, Communists provide support, redirecting enthusiasm to the question of property. Communists unite all parties seeking change. Communists coerce others to create a society they approve. The capitalists should quake. Workers have nothing, and so stand to lose nothing, but their miseries. If they will unite internationally, workers shall control the world.

CHAPTER 11
NAOMI

LADY JUSTICE, JUSTICIA, GOES TO HER TENTH AND FINAL PSYCHIATRIC APPOINT-
MENT. *Justicia finds the door ajar. A young girl, possibly seven years old, sits in the
psychiatrist's armchair, her black leather shoes swinging four inches off the floor.
The juvenile's white linen bonnet and black ankle-length long-sleeved dress with its
blue apron identify her as Lancaster Pennsylvania Amish. A small blood stain damp-
ens the front left of her starched bonnet. The black box of conscience rests quietly
beside the child. Justicia smiles. Justicia lays to one side her sword, scales, and
blindfold, and settles herself on the divan. The woman's eyes meet the girl's. Both
relax.*

NAOMI: My name is Naomi--Naomi Rose Ebersol. What's yours?

JUSTICIA: I am Justicia. I work in the courts and around town. Are you my
psychiatrist for the day?

NAOMI: I do not know what that is. I am supposed to talk to you. Do you want
to talk?

JUSTICIA: That would be very pleasant, I am sure. My email said you are from
West Nickel Mines School.

NAOMI: Uh-huh. I got hurt. In October 2006. A man hurt my head.

JUSTICIA: Someone hurt your head? Can you tell me about that?

NAOMI: A bad man came to the school just after morning recess. He blocked
the front door with his pickup. He had a gun. The bad man forced the boys to haul
in lumber, guns, chains, and toilet paper from his truck. I was crying, and a pregnant
lady comforted me. He made us girls line up against the classroom chalk board. He
made all the boys and babies and adults leave. He kept ten of us girls. He tied our
feet together. We heard the police come in a few minutes. They had loudspeakers.
We girls knew what was happening. Marian and Barbie asked to be shot first, if the
bad man would let the rest of us go. The bad man shot them, and then most of the
rest of us. All in the head. He shot some of us over and over. Blood was everywhere.
Five of us died. Five survived. Some of the girls who lived are not healthy still. The
bad man was Charles Roberts IV. He died too. When he saw the police would get
him, he shot himself. When Mr. Roberts was hurting me and my friends, I wanted to
hurt him back. I wanted to....

*The black box of conscience slides open. No little person stands, but a voice
wafts over Naomi and Justicia.* "Naomi, this is your muttie. Amish do not talk, or
even think, in this way. Mr. Roberts did a very bad thing. God will speak with him;
God is just. Our task is to fix what can be fixed, and to forgive the bad man. You
remember, we have talked about this at meeting and at bedside prayers." *Naomi nods.
A little tear wets her cheek.* "Yes, mama. I remember. I am sorry." *Muttie soothes,*
"Do not worry, Naomi. You are a little girl. You are just learning." *Justicia hears
kissing sounds from the box. The lid of the black box of conscience shuts silently.*

JUSTICIA: Was that your mother?

NAOMI: Yes. Muttie and the Amish ladies and all of the Amish people forgave
Mr. Roberts right away. They comforted the Roberts family--the bad man's wife and

three children and relatives. They collected money for them. Many attended the bad man's funeral. The Amish surrounded the families of us girls, the dead and the living, and paid our medical expenses. That cost a lot of money because God does not want us to have health insurance, momma says. They helped Muttie--all the mutties and papas really—to get better. All our families miss us terribly. And everyone else misses us too. My people tore down our school house. They built a new one in a different place. When the pregnant lady's baby girl was born, she remembered me and named that little one Naomi Rose after me. That made me happy.

JUSTICIA: Why did the bad man attack you, Naomi? Do you know?

NAOMI: He was sick. He left suicide notes. The notes said Mr. Roberts molested children. Mr. Roberts named children he molested. But when the police checked with those people, there was nothing. Mr. Roberts wanted to hurt girls, and thought he had hurt them. But he was wrong. His baby who came too early died her first day. Mr. Roberts got mad at God. Maybe that is a reason he came to our school. He did not touch us in private places. But he hurt us. Mr. Roberts was broken in the head, momma says.

JUSTICIA: You are a very brave little girl. Thank you for telling me your story. My job is to help people decide what to do when people hurt one another. That's what justice is about. Do you have advice for me?

NAOMI: They told me you would ask that. So I have thought about it a lot.

JUSTICIA: Go ahead, then, Naomi. How should I change?

> **JUSTICE IS:**
>
> RESTORING
> FRACTURED
> COMMUNITIES.

NAOMI: The Amish think you are confused. You try to fix the past. The past cannot be fixed. You can change the future, but not the past. Make the future better. And you spend too much time deciding about money. Money does not make hurts better. Money distracts everyone from what is wrong. People's hugs get broken. Momma says that love mends broken hugs. Not feeling love. I do not have lovey feelings about Mr. Roberts. Neither do any of the Amish. I mean love as doing stuff. You have to work to forgive bad people, work on yourself—just like momma said. People who suffer need help. They need real hugging and weed-the-garden kind of help. Put away your sword, Lady Justice. Leave your blindfold at home. Fix your scales. Momma says that justice should restore people's community, not hurt bad people. I like what my muttie says. Do you?

JUSTICIA: I do, Naomi. Of all my psychiatrists, your insights cut deepest. If I heed you, everything will change. I am thinking about the things all the people who sat in your chair have said to me. Thank you, Naomi.

Naomi smiles, a dazzling toothy beatitude. That grace lingers, as she vanishes. A Cheshire cat moment....

SAYINGS FROM THE AMISH TRADITION[3]

- "Death isn't the greatest loss in life. It's what dies inside of us while we live."
- "Forgiveness withheld: drinking poison and waiting for the offender to die."
- "Forgiveness is not a matter of what we remember, but how we remember."
- "Tomorrow's world will be shaped by what we teach our children today."
- "A man should not grieve overmuch, for that is a complaint against God."
- "We value the light more fully after we've come through the darkness."
- "He who strikes the first blow confesses that he has run out of ideas."
- "Love's power to forgive is stronger than hate's power to get even."
- "You can preach a better sermon with your life than with your lips."
- "We can stop forgiving others when Christ stops forgiving us."
- "We should not put a question mark where God puts a period."
- "Forgiveness can straighten what failures have made crooked."
- "It is better to hold out a helping hand than to point a finger."
- "Revenge appears to be love, as a wrong dressed up in right."
- "Deal with the faults of others as gently as your own."
- "Forgiveness means giving up your right to revenge."
- "The longer you carry a grudge, the heavier it gets."
- "Kindness, when given away, keeps coming back."
- "Forgive us our debts, as we forgive our debtors."
- "Survival lies in reaching out, not striking back."
- "The smallest vengeance poisons the soul."
- "The acid of hate destroys the container."
- "Do unto others as if you were the other."
- "Forgiveness is not a one-time event."
- "Good deeds have echoes."

---

[3] These Amish proverbs derive from three books on Amish communities: Fisher, *The Heart of the Amish*; Fisher, *Amish Peace*, and Kraybill *et al.*, *Amish Grace*.

CHAPTER 12
NUMEN

LADY JUSTICE, JUSTICIA, IS SUMMONED TO HER PSYCHIATRIC DIVAN. *Justicia lays aside her blindfold, sword, and scales. No psychiatric stand-in awaits her. Alone, but not quite alone, Justicia sits. She folds her marble hands in her limestone lap. She smooths her stony toga. The black box of conscience on the coffee table slides toward Justicia. A depression in the seat cushion of the psychiatrist's armchair shifts. Justicia perceives a presence, but sees and hears nothing. Suddenly, a gravelly voice interrupts Justicia's reverie.*

NUMEN: Tell me, Justicia. How do you imagine god?

JUSTICIA: God is a social construct that augments cohesion in human groups. I am not religious.

NUMEN: You blather what god is and state your orientation. I asked, How do you imagine god?

JUSTICIA: You mean, like a photo....? Well, I suppose god looks like Charlton Heston in my mind.

Air swirls, rustling. Charlton Heston sits in the psychiatrist's armchair, beaming his patented smile.

NUMEN: I bring a gift for you. And I come to hear the fruit of this psychiatric regime I orchestrated.

JUSTICIA: Are you....god?

NUMEN: I am me. People name me. Those names always mislead. Humans know nothing of me. They see my acts, but I elude them. Human confabulations about gods amuse. The very best humor is theological.... Enough of me. Tell me how goes this introspective and conversational process for you, O demi-god of justice.

JUSTICIA: Well, I have loved the talks. I was repulsed, chided, fascinated, and challenged.

NUMEN: Decisions. I need decisions from you, Justicia. You require a quick review.

The room enlarges and darkens. A stage appears, and a band. Her several psychiatrists march in from stage left. The band strikes up a breezy tune. The drafted shrinks begin an intricate tap dance, shoulder to shoulder. Except for the capuchin. The monkey skitters across the stage before the queued tappers. The assembly breaks into song: "To heal confusions and make them few, We sing our thoughts in brief for you!" Sequentially, each master steps forward, falls to one knee, and belts out a three-word lyric summary for Justicia.

Capuchin: Deep mammalian feeling.
Rawls: Micromanaging societal malformations.
Nozick: Markets amidst freedoms.
Nietzsche: Eagles eating lambs.
Jesus: Heartfelt divine intervention.
Confucius: Gentlemen ruling benevolently.
Moses: Commandments and sanctions.
Locke: Populism with safeguards.
Marx: Utopian wealth-sharing.
Amish Naomi: Restoring fractured communities.

   With a flourish, the band crescendos. The tapping psychiatrists pratfall in unison, then crawl to exit stage right. Naomi peeks around the curtain to curtsy. The capuchin, a bit lost, twirls, and climbs into the rigging overhead. Justicia laughs and applauds. Charlton smiles. He then turns his head toward Justicia, and raises an eyebrow.

   JUSTICIA: Okay, okay…. Changes. I have to change myself to be rid of divided loyalties. Those make me confused. I have to deviate from my English and Roman heritages more readily. In particular, I must change my values. *Money*: I am going to make justice less about money and more about social capital. I will start caring about people's relationships more than their pocketbooks. *Access*: I am going to make court process transparent, simple, and cheap, and dismantle the attorney legal monopoly. Courts will decentralize and open lay dispute resolution centers in each neighborhood. People will need lawyers for wisdom, but not to navigate a labyrinthine bramble. Lawyers will make less money, but be more valued. *Poverty*: I am going to open courts to the issues poor people face. The rich have resources to protect themselves. The poor have only me. *Bad actors*: I am going to restrain sociopathic bad actors without participating in victims' thirst for vengeance. I am discarding my sword of vengeance. I am taking off my blindfold and learning to recognize sociopaths when I see them. I see that most corporations are sociopathic; they lack consciences, being monomaniacal profit-takers. I am going to prevent corporations from using money to tip my scales of equity in their favor. *Judges*: I am going to push judges to make their rulings wise, regardless of precedent. I will tamp down "appeal aversion." Judges will let *normal* people bring cases that change society incrementally; judges will issue orders that effect those changes. *Lawyers*: I am going to encourage lawyers to be good people *before* they are advocates. I am going to punish lawyers who do evil, inside courtrooms or outside them. *Public*: I am going to teach conflict resolution skills in elementary schools. I am going to require serious peacemaking efforts from disputants before they gain access to courts. I am going to empower disenfranchised peacemakers--religious leaders, grandmothers, and shop supervisors. Courts will be much less busy, and produce much better results. *Peace:* I am going to make the prime purpose of courts the restoration of cohesive community

> **JUSTICE IS:**
>
> RESTORING
> AMITY.

among disputants, not the allocation of scarce resources. The core mission of courts will be amity, not enmity. Amity, even before equity.

NUMEN: That's a good start, Justicia. Change yourself. You make society work. I built you for friendship. Do not forsake that vision. I installed you in every human heart for a purpose: workable relationships. Now, your gift.

JUSTICIA: You are too good to me. My heart feels full. What is it?

NUMEN: A metaphor.

The black box of conscience begins to grow. Numen and Justicia catapult through the atmosphere and into lunar orbit. The black box of conscience expands until the earth hangs within the box. The earth glows. The halo of stars gleams warmly, as though showering silent applause.

NUMEN: When all human efforts are
                    Amicable acts of conscience,
                          The earth will not be perfect,
                                But mankind shall be well,
                                      And the deluge of justice
                                            Shall quench every thirst.

The capuchin chittered. Joy or derision?
None could tell.

EPILOGUE

ELIXIR FOR WHAT AILS JUSTICIA

Washington lawyers avoid substantive talk of justice. The topic is dangerous. It quakes our fragile civility. When we must, we indulge the word gently, never probing. Justice is, after all, a sticky metaphysical residue of medieval glue. Like an ugly mole sprouting troublesome hairs in the middle of one's back, justice is best left undiscussed. To broach justice portends frantic idealogues pontificating, lacerating one another's jugulars. That, of course, will not do. So, we duck and run. Then there is money. No money changes hands for examinations of justice. Clients seek results, not philosophical subtlety. My phone would never stop jangling if invoices contained time entries like "Debated feminist jurisprudence with opposing counsel," or "Talked over implications of Rawls's 'original position' with the court in chambers."

Our reticence is small surprise. Justice confuses lawyers. Courts seek justice. When trial judges decide, that is justice. When judge's decisions are reversed, that is justice. When supreme courts reinstate overturned verdicts, that is justice as well. Civil advocates seek justice by defeating opponents who themselves seek justice. Prosecutors lock up felons to enact justice. Criminal defenders frustrate prosecutors to get justice. When attorneys mumble about justice, we merely give voice to the clarity about justice which our circumstance has taught us.

It is not only we who are confused. Voices are many, their common ground meager and swampy. History offers polyglot cacophony. Ancient Judaism defined justice as obedience to the laws of Yahweh. "Justice, and only justice, you shall follow."[4] Thrasymachus insists justice is what advantages the stronger; Glaucon argues that justice is mere convention, the shape of agreements people make to avoid mutual harm.[5] Aristotle finds justice in treating equals equally, and treating unequals in proportion to their differentiation.[6] Aristotle tolerated slavery with no great qualms. Jesus said that justice is forgiveness; the Father provides rain for the just and unjust alike.[7] Marcus Aurelius, the Stoic Roman emperor, claimed, "[A]ll that befalls befalleth justly. Keep close watch and thou wilt find this true, I do not say, as a matter of sequence merely but as a matter of justice also."[8] Mohammed found justice in defending submission to Allah (*jihad*).[9] Confucius said, "Do not impose on others what you yourself do not desire."[10] Buddha might have suggested that justice is a

---

[4] *Torah, Deuteronomy* 16:18-20.

[5] Plato, *The Republic*, 336a-376e, pages 13-49.

[6] Aristotle, *Nichomachean Ethics*, 1159b-1160a, 153-155.

[7] *New Testament, Matthew* 5:45.

[8] Aurelius, *Meditations*, Book IV, Section 10, page 75.

[9] Mohammed, *Quran*, Sura 4:76.

[10] Confucius, *Analects*, Section XII.2, page 112.

confusion derived from believing that the world of appearances matters: "Gone greed, gone guile, gone thirst, gone grudge, And winnowed all delusions, faults, Wantless in all the world become. Fare lonely as rhinoceros."[11] Calvin found justice in obedience to an irresistible Divine Will, which, nevertheless, failed to prevent him from burning Michael Servetus, a suspected papist, at the stake.[12] Kant incongruously baptized the Golden Rule in the holy waters of metaphysics, and derived his paradigm of justice, the categorical imperative, one expression of which is that every person, including oneself, be treated as an end, never only as a means.[13] For Marx, justice lay in the revolution of commoners, a stark inversion of economic aristocracy.[14] Nietzsche asserted that justice cascades when a lawyer gets his guilty client adjudged innocent by painting the terrible beauty of the felon's deed winningly.[15] Pol Pot rained justice when a million Kampuchean skulls clogged rice paddies, his enemies vanquished. Ludwig Wittgenstein, colloquially paraphrased, might have said that justice is a sound we make with our mouths when banding together to stomp the hell out of someone.[16] Benjamin Cardozo recognized some of our confusions: "Perhaps we shall even find at times that when talking about justice, the quality we have in mind is charity, and this though the one quality is often contrasted with the other."[17]

Roscoe Pound came close to a definition:

> Justice, which is the end of law, is the ideal compromise between the activities of each and the activities of all in a crowded world. The law seeks to harmonize these activities and to adjust the relations of every man with his fellows so as to accord with the moral sense of the community. When the community is at one in its ideas of justice, this is possible. When the community is divided and diversified, and groups and classes and interests, understanding each other none too well, have conflicting ideas of justice, the task is extremely difficult.[18]

[11] Conze, *Buddhist Scriptures, The Rhinoceros*, 81.

[12] Calvin, *Institutes*.

[13] Kant, *Fundamental Principles of the Metaphysics of Morals*, 186.

[14] Marx, *The Communist Manifesto*.

[15] Nietzsche, *Beyond Good and Evil*, extrapolation from Epigram 110.

[16] Wittgenstein, *Philosophical Investigations*.

[17] Cardozo, *The Growth of the Law*, 87.

[18] Pound, "The Causes of Popular Dissatisfaction with the Administration of Justice," *American Bar Association Report*, Part I, 395-417, 1906.

H. L. A. Hart observed that justice is a zero-sum game; we work justice in one circumstance only by creating injustice in another.[19] Perhaps most cynical is Clarence Darrow: "There is no such thing as justice—in or out of court."[20]

Small wonder we are confused.

So, what of justice? Is it just a dream, a pleasant hallucination, vacant of content? Lacking clarity, one finds justice-talk being used to paper over substantive disputes. "Justice" in our mealy mouths obfuscates, smooths, puts a band-aid on ragged antagonisms toward divergent views of society.

We can unpack justice. It comes with ready-to-use instructions that read, "Some disassembly required." First, justice presupposes human conflict. Those who blunder along tranquilly need no justice. Second, justice commits each person to the proposition that some outcomes to conflict are preferable to others. Third, effectuating justice demands wisdom. Some humans recognize preferable outcomes when they see them. Others do not. So, not every person is positioned to recognize justice. Last, justice implies adaptation. Justice is embedded in specific acts in a detail-laden context. So, justice moves and develops. What was just yesterday may no longer be just tomorrow. We adjust our view of justice to its changes, or we lapse into fossilized pedantry.

Justice implies conversation, a perpetually smoldering discussion of rudiments. This talk tackles tough questions. What is a human? What shapes are natural for human communities? What relationships are desirable between persons? Which are horrid? How should communities relate to members, and members to communities? When should we intervene, insist, inject, and when acquiesce, attenuate, accept? What actions do we value sufficiently to insist upon them? How should we relate to fellow members who dissent? What costs are too high a price to pay for equity in our togetherness? What process of determination of disputed claims is adequate, and to whom should that process be available? How may we, as communities, remediate historical inequities? Which differences in societal outcomes merit revision of our collective norms? What are the limits of such adjustments? Are there matters which, despite our earnest efforts, cannot be remediated? Which are those? The inquiries mount, driving our dialogue toward the roots of morality, law, and collective obligation.

Justice talk may prove uncomfortable, like shrunken underwear, chafing sensitive bits. Exchanges may erupt into invective. The threat convinces some to cower. One can float ideas that sound stupid the instant they are spoken. Justice talk melts the line between rationality and feeling, leaving us vulnerable and exposed. But the exchange, charitably conducted, bears wonder in its wake. "[F]or you must understand that in no other kind of discussion can one bring out so clearly what Nature's gifts to man are, what a wealth of most excellent possessions the human mind enjoys, what the purpose is, to strive after and accomplish which we have been born and placed in this work, what it is that unites men, and what natural fellowship there is

---

[19] Hart, *The Concept of Law*, 162-163.

[20] Widely attributed to Darrow. Yet, I am unable to identify the provenance of this aphorism.

among them. For it is only after all these things have been made clear that the origins of Law and Justice can be discovered."[21]

We neglect justice talk at a price. When we fail to speak with one another about core values, justice fragments. Cherished diversity shrinks to inescapable insularity. The just become balkanized. We trip over feminist justice, black justice, AARP justice, NRA justice, and, if the wave of mass shootings is any indication, terrorist justice. We may allow our minds to evade the fact that we live together and need one another. The richness of life consists in identity, collectively conceived and jointly lived. Where we speak nothing of justice, we see myopically, through a lens of politicized demagoguery. We talk at, but not with, one another, like blaring bullhorns—I very loud; you quite drowned out. Difference makes us anorexic aliens, rather than children of common parents feasting at a laden family table.

Can we speak of justice? Can we utter our values, and listen while others speak theirs? We can. One might use this little book as fodder for first stabs at such exchanges.

We abandon deep questions of justice at our peril. Academicians and metaphysicians cannot rescue us, if we fail to help ourselves. We lawyers can ill-afford impoverished minds. Many have suffered law schools. Our well-being depends on those (and others) thinking justly. Cicero warns: "[T]he origin of Justice is to be found in Law, and Law is a natural force; it is the mind and reason of the intelligent man, the standard by which Justice and Injustice are measured."[22] The conversation evaded, we splash into a wallow of ill-deliberate bickering. Justice avoided becomes justice denied.

Failing to analyze Justicia: that is plainly insane.

---

[21] Cicero, *De Legibus*, I.v.16.

[22] Cicero, *De Legibus*, I.vi.19.

TRAIN TO HIROSHIMA

Oh, Miyajima.
We found your train.
Your torii gate so tall,
Temples of glory, cool forests,
Tame deer, Buddhas, male and female,
Forsaking evil, bronze and stone.
Shrine Island, thalassic gem,
We praise you.

Your floating gate repaired,
Snatched from salt, dry rot.
Your paths, well-weeded,
Gondola lubed, floors swept,
Gardens planted, trash plucked.
Island denizens labor,
Painting, sanding, buffing,
Burnishing beauty-spot glory.

WONDROUS PLACES
ARE BORN OF
ATTENTIVE
CARE.

Peace ever borders horror.
Near Miyajima, scorched cities,
Bomb shame, grounds zero.
The weak brag their might. Oh My.
Plant amity, prune hatred,
Scrub away gore, bitterness,
Be never again shoved aboard
The train to Hiroshima.

広島

APPENDIX A

CENSORSHIP BY SNOHOMISH COUNTY BAR ASSOCIATION

Snohomish County Bar News (SCBA) published the first five of these justice essays in the months of April (*Analyzing Justicia*), May (*Capuchin*), June (*Rawls*), July/August (*Nozick*), and September (*Nietzsche*). I submitted my October 2012 essay (*Jesus*), and received the following email from the administrator of the SCBA News: "We will not be able to run this essay, sorry. Keep them coming though!" I replied, inquiring about this decision. The administrator called me on the telephone. She said that the SCBA Editor and SCBA president thought the essay might offend someone, which they are loathe to do. I objected to the administrator that their action is religious censorship. Each of my essays certainly offends some and edifies others. I told the administrator that we need deeper dialogue about more important issues, not pablum of inoffensive mush. I asked if I sent an essay expressing my displeasure, would she publish that. She did not respond. I promptly sent the following to SCBA News for publication:

> A note to readers of Brad Lancaster's essay series on justice, *Analyzing Justicia*:
>
> SCBA News declines to publish my essay on Justicia's encounter with Jesus. The editor of SCBA News and the president of the Snohomish County Bar have concern that my essay might offend the religious sensitivities of some. I understand these leaders' concerns, and believe they are correct. Each of my essays offends some persons, heartens others, and is ignored by most.
>
> I view the SCBA News decision to reject my essay on Jesus' view of justice as religious censorship. The point of having an association is to associate. I am being denied that freedom. If you read my essays, you too are being denied the freedom to think about justice with me. With the editors, I share the desire to avoid senselessly offending others. Here, however, that concern has metastasized into a regime in which speech that might prove offensive is preemptively gagged.   An un-American odor swirls around this rule. Under such an editorial razor, what survives is pablum. If you object to SCBA's decision, please express yourself to the association.
>
> For my part, I decline to write for organizations that seek to control the content of my essays. So, I bid those of you who have enjoyed or profited from my writings farewell. Those who object to my views can sigh in relief. I welcome all comments and responses.
>
> BRAD LANCASTER

The October 2012 SCBA Bar News did not contain this essay. I ceased writing for SCBA News.

BIBLIOGRAPHY

Aurelius, Marcus. *Marcus Aurelius Antoninus, Emperor, To Himself.* (Also known as the *Meditations.*) Translated by C. R. Haines. Cambridge, Massachusetts: Harvard University Press (2003).

Bible. Revised Standard Version. Camden, New Jersey: Thomas Nelson & Sons, 1952.

Buddhist Scriptures. Selected and translated by Edward Conze. London: Penguin Books, 1959.

Calvin, John. *Institutes of the Christian Religion.* Translated by Henry Beveridge. Grand Rapids, Michigan: Wm. B. Eerdmans Publishing Company, 1993.

Cardozo, Benjamin. *The Growth of the Law.* New Haven, Connecticut: Yale University Press, 1924.

Cicero. *De Legibus.* Translated by Clinton Walker Keyes. Cambridge, Massachusetts: Harvard University Press, 1988.

Confucius. *Analects.* Translated by D. C. Lau. London: Penguin Books, 1979.

Fisher, Suzanne Woods. *Amish Peace: Simple Wisdom for a Complicate World.* Grand Rapids, Michigan: Revell, 2009.

Fisher, Suzanne Woods. *The Heart of the Amish: Life Lessons on Peacemaking and the Power of Forgiveness.* Grand Rapids, Michigan: Revell, 2015.

Gandhi, Mohandas K. *Non-Violent Resistance (Satyagraha).* Mineola, New York: Dover Publications, Inc., 2001.

Hart, H.L.A. *The Concept of Law.* Oxford: Oxford University Press: 1961.

Kant, Immanuel. *Fundamental Principles of the Metaphysics of Morals.* Translated by Thomas K. Abbott. In *Basic Writings of Kant,* Allen W. Wood, ed. New York: The Modern Library, 2001.

Kraybill, Donald B, Steven M. Nolt and David L Weaver-Zercher. *Amish Grace: How Forgiveness Transcended Tragedy.* San Francisco, California: Jossey-Bass, 2007.

Lancaster, Brad. *Gethsemane Soliloquy: An Epitome of the Reliable Sayings of Jesus.* Shoreline, Washington: St. George's Hill Press, 2017.

Locke, John. *Two Treatises of Government.* Norwalk, Connecticut: The Easton Press, 1991.

Mao Zedong. *Quotations from Chairman Mao Tsetung,* which work is also known as the *"Little Red Book."* Translator unknown. Peking: Foreign Languages Press, 1972.

Marx, Karl. *The Communist Manifesto.* Edited by Frederick L. Bender. New York: W. W. Norton & Company, 1988.

Mozi. Translated by Burton Watson. New York: Columbia University Press, 2003.

Nietzsche, Friedrich. *Beyond Good and Evil, (Jenseits von Gut und Bose).* Translated by Walter Kaufmann. New York: Modern Library, 1992.

Nietzsche, Friedrich. *Beyond Good and Evil (Zur Genealogie der Moral).* Translated by Douglas Smith. Oxford: Oxford University Press, 1996.

Nozick, Robert. *Anarchy, State, and Utopia.* New York: Basic Books, Inc., Publishers,1974.

Plato. *The Republic.* Translated by Tom Griffith. Edited by G. R.F. Ferrari. Cambridge: Cambridge University Press, 2000.

Pound, Roscoe, "The Causes of Popular Dissatisfaction with the Administration of Justice," *American Bar Association Report*, Part I, 395-417, 1906.

Qutb, Seyyid. *Milestones*. Translator unknown. Damascus, Syria: Dar al-Ilm, publication date unstated.

Rawls, John. *Justice as Fairness: A Restatement*. Cambridge, Massachusetts: Harvard University Press, 2001.

Wittgenstein, Ludwig. *Philosophical Investigations*. Translated by G. E. M. Anscombe. Malden, Massachusetts: Blackwell Publishing Ltd., 2001.

APPRECIATIONS

I have written portions of this book in Seal Rock, Oregon, vacationing with my spouse, Kim, and miniature pinscher puppy, Ruby. The Pacific pummels rock to wide sands. Herons pluck dinner from tidal pools. Ravens scavenge. Red-tail hawks scout. Seals duck. Whales spout. Kim learns law, as a Rule 6 intern (attorney by apprenticeship), despite not knowing, with any certainty, what justice may be. A brave woman. A daunting task. And a loving editor. Ruby would appear to have no aptitude for law whatsoever, and takes no interest in what I write. Reprehensible little dog. Tom Andrews has contributed to this short book. Tom relishes dialogue about justice, and many topics. He enriches the lives of many, mine included. My primary context for talk of justice is Saturday mornings, nine to noon, around a six-foot cross-section of a cedar trunk, legs fitted, to become the table at which the members of Witless Protection Program share many words. For our togetherness, and for each member individually, I am grateful. We are students of the authors of books we read. I thank those mostly dead scribblers of philosophical ethics and political theory for devoting so much of their lives to speaking in a way that permits me, who never met them, who cannot share their various centuries and provinces, to sit at their feet. I also appreciate you, my reader, who steals time from pressing matters to consider what I have to say of justice. I hope you laughed on occasion.

SAINT GEORGE'S HILL PRESS

On St. George's Hill (southwest of London), in 1648, poor people, under the influence of Gerrard Winstanley, tilled and built shacks on public land to feed themselves, when food prices soared during the English Civil War. They called themselves True Levellers, and sought reduction of the financial chasm between the poor and the wealthy. The king sent a representative, who found the group doing no appreciable harm. A local lord felt otherwise, and commissioned thugs to assault the True Levellers. Some were beaten. Their common meal house was burned. Leaders were tried; the judge refused to let them speak in their defense. The True Levellers, dubbed Diggers by opponents, abandoned their plots for less hostile locations. In the twenty-first century, St. George's Hill is home to an exclusive gated and closely-guarded community, consisting in 450 mansions with tennis club and golf course amenities. St. George's Hill claims to be the premier private residential estate in Europe, close to London and Britain's most desirable private preparatory schools. The median price of a residence on St. George's Hill exceeds £3,000,000. St. George's Hill, then, is the dirt upon which clash desperate diggers and entrenched elites, a metaphor barely metaphorical.

www.ingramcontent.com/pod-product-compliance
Lightning Source LLC
LaVergne TN
LVHW021509080426
835509LV00018B/2447